Key Concepts in
Urban Studies

The SAGE Key Concepts series provide students with accessible and authoritative knowledge of the essential topics in a variety of disciplines. Cross-referenced throughout, the format encourages critical evaluation through understanding. Written by experienced and respected academics, the books are indispensable study aids and guides to comprehension.

M. GOTTDIENER

and

LESLIE BUDD

Key Concepts in
Urban Studies

 SAGE Publications
London ● Thousand Oaks ● New Delhi

© M. Gottdiener and Leslie Budd 2005

First published 2005
Reprinted 2005 (twice)

 SAGE Publications Ltd
1 Oliver's Yard
55 City Road
London EC1Y 1SP

SAGE Publications Inc
2455 Teller Road
Thousand Oaks, California 91320

SAGE Publications India Pvt Ltd
B-42 Panchsheel Enclave
Post Box 4109
New Delhi 110 017

British Library Cataloguing in Publication data

A catalogue record for this book is
available from the British Library

ISBN 0 7619 4097 9
ISBN 0 7619 4098 7

Library of Congress control number available

Typeset by M Rules
Printed in Great Britain by The Cromwell Press Ltd, Trowbridge, Wiltshire

introduction

When Chris Rojek, of SAGE Publications UK, approved this book, we were impressed with his desire to support a 'Key Concepts' series, but we also expected a fairly straightforward experience as authors. This was not to be the case.

Starting out as a simple guide for undergraduates, this book became much more. As we examined concepts, it was evident that urban studies had been victimized by several decades of sloppy writing and loose thinking. A great confusion and misunderstanding crept into published work on the urban condition at the same time as significant advances were made. Assembling these basic concepts in urban studies and writing about them in a clear and concise manner proved a difficult task.

In what follows we have tried to identify sources of confusion in the usage of terms as well as discuss in as precise language as possible the advances that have been made by the discipline. In the end, we hope our efforts are of some value in returning key concepts to urban studies in a language free of ambiguity and fuzzy thinking. Our enterprise is a true collaboration between Budd (UK) and Gottdiener (US). Knowing that the field of urban studies depends on comparative knowledge, we have tried to cover UK and US cases, as well as provide information on research pertinent to locations across the globe.

This book is not meant to be read starting with the first entry, *The Chicago School*, and proceeding to its last page. It is a reference work that we hope will supplement other books used in courses or projects on urbanism. Consequently, it can be picked up and opened to any topic depending on need. As the authors however, we would like to suggest that the entries below might be used in another way that would lend themselves more directly to teaching courses in urban studies. Wherever appropriate, we have cross-referenced access to similar topics. There is also a cumulative way of assembling separate entries into discussions that might transpire throughout a course in urban studies, geography, planning or sociology. For this latter purpose, we humbly offer the following suggestions which, at the minimum, attest to the flexible way the entries below can be used:

URBAN SOCIOLOGY AND URBAN STUDIES

The City, Models of Urban Growth, Counties, The Multi-centered Metropolitan Region, The Chicago School, Urbanization and Urbanism, Socio-spatial Approach, Community, Neighborhood, Postmodernism and Modern Urbanism, De- and Re-territorialization, Feminine Space, Masculine Space, Immigration and Migration, Nightlife and Urban Nightscapes, Pedestrian and Automobile, Suburb and Suburbanization, Education and Reproduction of Labor, Environmental Concerns, Ghetto and Racial Segregation, Global Cities, Globalization, Homelessness, Housing, Inequality and Poverty, The Informal Economy, Overurbanization, Real Estate, Slums and Shanty Towns, Sprawl, Uneven Development, Urban Violence and Crime, Planning, Sustainable Urbanization, Urban Politics and Suburban Politics, Urban and Suburban Social Movements.

URBAN PLANNING

The City, Models of Urban Growth, Counties, The Multi-centered Metropolitan Region, Urbanization and Urbanism, Socio-spatial Approach, Community, Neighborhood, Postmodernism and Modern Urbanism, De- and Re-territorialization, Feminine Space, Masculine Space, Immigration and Migration, Nightlife and Urban Nightscapes, Pedestrian and Automobile, Suburb and Suburbanization, Ghetto and Racial Segregation, Global Cities, Globalization, Homelessness, Housing, Inequality and Poverty, The Informal Economy, Overurbanization, Slums and Shanty Towns, Uneven Development, Urban Politics and Suburban Politics, Urban and Suburban Social Movements, Sprawl, Environmental Concerns, New Urbanism, Planning, Real Estate, Sustainable Urbanization, Preservation, Gentrification.

URBAN GEOGRAPHY

The City, Models of Urban Growth, Counties, The Multi-centered Metropolitan Region, The Chicago School, Urbanization and Urbanism, The Socio-spatial Approach, Suburb and Suburbanization, Community, Neighborhood, New Urbanism, Postmodernism and Modern Urbanism, De- and Re-territorialization, Feminine Space, Masculine Space, Ghetto and Racial Segregation, Immigration and Migration, Global Cities, Globalization, Homelessness, Housing, Inequality and Poverty, The Informal Economy, Overurbanization, Real Estate, Slums and Shanty

Towns, Sprawl, Uneven Development, Urban Violence and Crime, Environmental Concerns, Planning.

To be sure, there is no definitive way of locking down the exact number of basic concepts that 'must' be included in this type of project, nor how to use this book in various courses across disciplines. We had a difficult time merely making entry choices.

In this regard, M. Gottdiener was helped greatly by the suggestions of a number of people: 'My thanks for guidance to Ray Hutchison, Chigon Kim, Joe Feagin, Michael Ryan, Kevin Fox Gotham, Talmadge Wright, John Eade, Jill R. Gottdiener, Richard Mancuso, Sueli Schiffer, Mervi Ilmonen, Heli Vaaranen, Noam Shoval, Gustavo Mesch, José Luis Beraud, Phil Gunn, Paavo Lehtuovari, Massimo Russo, Susana Finquelievitch, Christos Kousidonis, Thomas Maloutas, Jesús Leal, José Candelario, David Diaz, John Altevogt, Andrew Jacobs, Bob Catterall, Paul Chatterton, Virve Sarapik, Trin Ojari, Shira Habot, Dan Webb, Frank Ekhardt, and to several anonymous referees.'

Leslie Budd wishes to acknowledge a debt of gratitude to the following people: 'the late Len Stafford, the late Mike Cowan, the late Georgina Budd, and John Parr, who have all been important influences in my development. I would also like to thank Vanessa Davidson for her continuing love, personal and professional support over many years.'

vii

table of entries

urban studies

ix

key concepts

X

Key Concepts in
Urban Studies

— The Chicago School —

Academic studies of the city as a unique form of settlement space were rare until the 1800s when the German sociologist Max Weber wrote a sophisticated analysis tracing its history as a phenomenon of social organization (1966). Somewhat later, the Anglo-German, Friedrich Engels, also the lifelong friend of Karl Marx, wrote a critique of urban living under capitalism (1973). These efforts stood alone until the turn of the 20th Century. Just prior to World War I, the University of Chicago founded the very first department of sociology in the US under the leadership of W.I. Thomas and Albion Small, who had been a student of Weber. Their interests were in general aspects of sociology, but in 1913 they hired Robert Park who possessed a specific and strong interest in the urban condition. Park was a newspaper reporter who had acquired extensive experience in the southern US which conditioned him to the injustice of racial discrimination. He also had experience as an urban crime news reporter in Minneapolis, New York City and Detroit. When he was obtaining his doctorate in sociology, he spent some time at the University of Berlin, Germany, where he studied under Georg Simmel, the European sociologist most responsible for writing about urban life (see entry on *The City*). When the Chicago department hired another sociologist with an interest in the city, Ernest W. Burgess, the two set about to study Chicago as an urban laboratory. Together they founded the first 'school' of urban analysis, the Chicago School, and both they and their students published a prolific amount of research until the 1940s, including the first systematic field studies and ethnographies written by professional sociologists.

The members of the Chicago School were uniquely concerned about city life. They called their approach, *Human Ecology*, because they were influenced by Darwin to consider human social adjustments to the urban environment as similar to the way plant and animal species attuned themselves to their more natural space (for a critique, see Gottdiener, 1994; Gottdiener and Hutchison, 2000). In place of the emphasis on political economy characteristic of the *New Urban Sociology*, the Chicago School preferred a biologically based metaphor typifying human interaction (see entry on *Socio-spatial Approach*; also Gottdiener and Hutchison, 2000). Thus, they avoided the study of capitalism preferring instead to view economic competition as a manifestation of the general struggle for survival that unites all species on the planet. According to Park, the social organization of the city resulted from this struggle over scarce resources. It produced a complex division of labor because people would adjust to the biologically based competition for survival by finding specific ways they could compete based on their 'natural' abilities.

Other members of the Chicago School took a more spatially sensitive approach while retaining their emphasis on biological rather than political-economic forces operating in the environment. Roderick McKenzie emphasized the role of location and argued that establishing a physical position within the environment was most important in the struggle for survival. Individuals or groups that were successful took over the best locations within the city – the higher ground, the best business location, the preferred neighborhoods. Those that were not as successful in this spatial competition wound up in less attractive locations. Thus, the population sorted itself out within the environment as a consequence of this process. McKenzie studied the patterns that this spatial sorting produced for both social groups and businesses.

Ernest W. Burgess was also a member of the early Chicago School (see entry on *Models of Urban Growth*). For him the spatial competition created by the struggle for survival produced a land use pattern of concentric rings of settlement around a centralized business district.

Louis Wirth was also a member of the early school (see the entry on *The City*). The Chicago School researchers viewed city life principally in negative terms. They explained phenomena, such as crime and family break-up, in terms of social disorganization. For them the city broke down traditional primary relations and therefore contributed to various negative aspects of urban living. Later on this approach was criticized for its overly disparaging view of city life. Another criticism was that their work favored the biologically based approach to locational adjustment and ignored the factor of culture or the role that symbols played in determining spatial patterns within the city. In 1945 Walter Firey wrote a critique of Burgess' concentric zone model by showing how the land-use pattern of Boston was an expression of 'sentiments and symbols' in addition to the ecological competition over space. Despite these criticisms, the idea of ecology persisted as American urbanists preferred to ignore issues of class and race which the political economic approach demands (see entry on *Socio-spatial Approach*).

After World War II the ecological approach was revived, but it ignored the Chicago School's emphasis on spatial competition in favor of a form of technological determinism. The new perspective was called *Contemporary Human Ecology*. Urban land-use patterns and the distribution of population and activities were a product of communication and transportation technologies. As the technology of these means of interaction changed, human ecologists argued that so did the patterns of social organization. For example, it was claimed that, although the process of suburbanization had been present since the late 1800s in American cities, it did not become a mass phenomenon until after the automobile became a consumer good that many people could afford. Subsequent research reversed this claim and established the fact that 'while the street car, electric trains and automobile may be credited with lowering initial density levels in cities . . . they were not responsible for "emptying out"' urban areas on a mass scale.

Another argument by human ecologists in the 1970s claimed that while cities expanded in size their central business districts also had to grow in administrative functions. This was so, they argued, because the command and control activities of the urban area had to increase as the size of that region grew, just as a cell's nucleus expands when the cell develops. A similar argument was advanced in the 1990s when Saskia Sassen (1991) claimed that globalization had produced 'world cities' through the concentration of command and control activities. Upon closer examination, the human ecology argument was shown to be false (Gottdiener, 1994). Command and control functions in the form of corporate headquarters had been dispersing throughout multi-centered metropolitan regions as those agglomerations themselves expanded. In the 1960s, for example, New York City was home to over 120 national and international corporations. By the 1990s that figure had dropped to slightly less than 90, at the very same time that globalization advocates were calling New York a 'global city'. Later on Sassen's argument about the effects of command and control concentration was also proved false (see entry on *Inequality and Poverty*). There is no evidence that these activities require central city location, as the human ecology approach maintains. However, global financial activities possess components that still do prefer such inner business district locations (see entries on *The City; Globalization*).

There are many things wrong with the ecological perspective, both the old and contemporary schools, in addition to its false biologically-based conception. Ecologists avoid any mention of social groupings belonging to the analysis of late·capitalism, such as class and race. They see social interaction as a process of adaptation to an environment, in keeping with

3

their biological or ecological emphasis, rather than being produced by relations deriving from powerful factors in economic, political and cultural organization, as the socio-spatial perspective suggests. Although they emphasize location, they ignore aspects of the real estate industry (see entry on *Real Estate*) and its role in producing spatial patterns of development. Finally, human ecologists completely ignore the role of political institutions in channeling resources and in regulating competition over scarce resources in a market-based, capitalist economy. With regard to the latter, they focus on the demand-side view of markets which emphasizes individual decisions, rather than the supply-side that highlights the role of powerful actors in manipulating the market for desired ends.

REFERENCES

Engels, F. 1973. *The Condition of the Working Class in England*, Moscow: Progress Publishers.
Gottdiener, M. 1994. *The Social Production of Urban Space, 2nd Edition*. Austin, TX: University of Texas Press.
Gottdiener, M. and R. Hutchison, 2000. *The New Urban Sociology, 2nd Edition*, NY: McGraw-Hill.
Sassen, S. 1991. *The Global City*. Princeton, NJ: Princeton University Press.
Weber, Max, 1966. *The City*, NY: The Free Press.

The City

4

A city is a bounded space that is densely settled and has a relatively large, culturally heterogeneous population. According to the US census, which has a very loose definition, a city can be any urban place of 2,500 people or more that is incorporated as a municipality (see entries on *Counties; Urbanization and Urbanism* for more discussion).

Many places that are commonly referred to in the US, such as Los Angeles, Las Vegas or New York, are not really cities, but urbanized multi-centered metropolitan regions or MMRs (see entry on Multi-centered Metropolitan Region). The term 'city' is much overused and is often merely a shorthand designation for these massive areas of continuous urbanization. In Europe, the words 'megapolis' and 'metropolis' have been used interchangeably in the post-war period, describing cities as different as London and Paris. Now these terms have given way to 'city-region'. Partly this change reflects the bounded nature of metropolitan development because of planning restraints. That is, many city limits are artificially maintained by government regulations. For example, the Green Belt in London limits the outward growth of the metropolitan area. Green Belt policy that sustains a green ring round London may prevent regional sprawl, but it also contributes to the NIMBY (Not in My Back Yard) phenomenon. In this case, residents who have gained advantage of suburban development on greenfield sites subsequently seek to limit newcomers from acquiring these same benefits by opposing subsequent development, including new infrastructure. This policy of maintaining city boundaries through government restrictions also distorts land markets, which results in sustaining the wealth effects of housing for existing residents.

Cities are important principally because of their political clout. A US city, as an incorporated municipality, has the power to tax and the power to raise money via bonds and other financial instruments. Legally it can hire its own police force and provide for all social services to its residents. Cities have the power of self-governance and they have their own elected officials. As a consequence of the latter, city administrations have political power nationally. Mayors of cities have national political clout, much more so than their suburban counterparts, and this is why cities themselves are important.

In Europe, unlike the US, the formal municipal situation varies enormously depending on different systems of government and governance. In France, the big five cities, Paris, Lyon, Marseilles, Lille and Bordeaux exert enormous formal and informal power. In Germany, the City-Länder of Hamburg, Bremen and Berlin operate with a regional system of government that boosts their position relative to other cities. In the UK, London is the dominant city and its power and influence formally and informally outstrips other cities. The system of sub-national government also has tended to change frequently in the UK. Currently, there has been a shift back to notions of city-regions and ideas of regional balance in the UK.

The political power of cities is related to their position as sites of economic activity. Despite the apparent remorseless march of globalization and digitization, the activities of large transnational firms still crowd into some of the world's major cities. The benefits of co-location are expressed as agglomeration economies in the form of specialist labor markets, transport accessibility and access to shared lifestyle aspirations. The city of London retains its position as one of the world's leading financial centers as a result of these agglomeration benefits (Budd and Whimster, 1992).

Cities are also considered to be important because they are the site of 'urban culture'. In the past, this characteristic was easy to understand because of its contrast to the culture of the countryside, i.e., rural areas. However, decades of suburbanization and the ubiquitous influence of national media have considerably blurred this distinction so that it has limited value today. One feature of cities that is not characteristic of other areas is the presence of a viable street and pedestrian culture. The urbanist, Jane Jacobs (1961), claimed that the urban street is the fundamental aspect of city life (see entries on the *Neighborhood; New Urbanism*). Often this distinctive pedestrian feature is simulated by purposely constructed environments, such as mall arcades and city-themed amusement parks like Universal Studio's *CityWalk* (see entry on the *Pedestrian and Automobile*). In London, in the 1970s, the former fruit and vegetable market Covent Garden was transformed into an ersatz urban village, complete with *faux* Georgian arcades, as an exercise in simulation much like the one at Universal Studios in Los Angeles.

Since World War II, US cities have gone through enormous changes, industrial decline, crumbling homes and schools, overcrowded neighborhoods, rigid segregation and racial trauma, rising crime and violence, and an alarming drain of revenues have all contributed to creating a troubled urban landscape. For a brief time, in the 1960s and early 1970s, large-scale government interventions seemed to point the way to urban salvation. But, in the wake of massive urban renewal, expressway construction, and ambitious public housing projects, cities still seem worse off than ever.

In Europe, the impact of World War II has been profound, despite the destruction of much of the urban landscape. Re-building the sense of historical urban identity has been the key focus. Vienna, or the *City as Pleasure Principle*, and Paris, as the *Capital of Light*, because of music and art in the late 19th and early 20th centuries, still resonates today in the re-forming of the urban landscape (Hall, 1998).

LOUIS WIRTH AND THE CITY AS A WAY OF LIFE

Wirth defined the city as the combination of three key variables – size, density and heterogeneity or diversity of population. He proposed a theory that, the more intense were the three variables, the more urban the place would be. For example, the larger the population, the more formal, secondary and tertiary social relations would there be replacing the primary relations of a traditional community; the more anonymous would the crowds be. The greater density would accentuate the effects of anonymity and also produce a blasé attitude due to the need to turn out excessive stimulation. Greater density produces greater tolerance of strangers but also greater stress – both attributes of city living. Heterogeneity also creates tolerance because there are so many different people interacting.

Despite many years of research, there is no evidence to support Wirth's theory. Clearly, size, density and heterogeneity all define urban places, especially when these variables are large, but increasing any one of these or in combination does not necessarily produce more 'urban' effects. Some relatively smaller cities, like San Francisco, are highly urban and diverse, other larger ones, like Indianapolis or Nashville, are much less urban. Wirth's theory does not consider how different national cultures determine the path of urban development. In the UK, Glasgow could be considered the only true urban city, with high levels of centrally located flats (apartments) and residential services. In England, the nostalgia for a 'green and pleasant land', expressed strongly in Constable's painting, *The Hay Wain*, and in William Cobbett's book, *Rural Rides*, has until recently created an anti-urban culture and promoted the 'ideal' of suburbia. The dominance of owner-occupation in UK housing markets also tended to encourage suburbanization. Meanwhile, during the last ten years, there has been a counter tendency towards urbanization and an increase in city-dwelling in places like London and Paris. Population influx was occasioned by a combination of active cultural resources, new immigration, especially from Asia or North Africa, and real estate interests re-developing office buildings often overlooking watersides as up-market and gated apartments for the affluent.

One important contribution made by Wirth involves identification of different kinds of relationship. Any definition of the city must distinguish among *primary, secondary* and *tertiary social relationships*. Wirth accepted the view that rural, community areas were dominated by *primary*, that is, face to face and personal relationships. In contrast, cities were less personal and dominated by *secondary* and *tertiary* relations. *Secondary* relations are those based on infrequent but direct interpersonal contacts. They are specific to a given role or function, such as the relationship between a customer and a service worker. At the bank, for example, the tellers are courteous to customers, but a customer may not get the exact same teller every time. Hence this relationship is limited to the brief encounter based on an economic function. Such interaction, as is true of tertiary relations, is quite different and more impersonal than the primary relations people enjoy with friends, family and close community ties.

Tertiary relations are also characteristic of large urban environments. They are based on indirect relations and contacts, such as through the use of a telephone, or, through the most formal types of business relations. When individuals have business with a firm, they may speak to a person, but he/she is only a representative of the firm itself. This is a tertiary relationship when the interaction is strictly formal.

In Wirth's theory he believed that urban life was quite different from rural, community existence because of the dominance in the city of secondary and tertiary relations. He did not live long enough to witness the appearance of the new kind of internet relationships we have in society today. Cyber interaction involves non-face to face, disembodied relations that range from the very personal to the tertiary depending on individual circumstances. Thus, the internet constitutes a separate dimension of interaction that can either reinforce or transcend the culture of the impersonal urban life which Wirth believed characterized all cities.

LEWIS MUMFORD AND THE CITY AS THE SITE OF CIVILIZATION

The US urbanist, Lewis Mumford (1961) had a different view of urban life from that of Wirth. Mumfordian ideas stressed the interactive and social role cities fostered in behavior. He did not make the Wirthian distinction that cities nurtured impersonal relations. Instead he believed that important primary relations were established in cities that led to social innovations. For Mumford, urban life was creative and theatrical and the city was the site of civilization which, over the centuries, produced countless innovations. 'The city is a theater of social action,' he said. All urban functions were greatly intensified by having to take place on the stage set of city street life.

Mumford's view that dense social interaction was the very life blood of city living influenced an entire generation of urbanists. Jane Jacobs, for example, argued strongly for walkable cities and the important role of street culture, as did William H. Whyte (1988; see entries on *New Urbanism*; *Pedestrian and Automobile*). The French urbanist, Roland Barthes, viewed the compact life in the city center as a kind of eroticism where diversity prevailed and people could observe others from a safe distance (Gottdiener, 2001). This stimulated fantasies and excitement. The planners, Allan Jacobs and Donald Appleyard, resonated with these ideas as well by urging designers to emphasize street life (2003). Their work was extended in concept by the New Urbanists (see entry on page 96). Like Mumford and Whyte, the public places of the city were stages upon which residents could act out and interact to the benefit of urban culture.

In one sense Mumford and Wirth agreed. In the city, which was conceived by both of them as a limited space (for a critique see entry on *Multi-centered Metropolitan Region*), social relations were also organized into groups and social associations. There were families, neighborhoods, as well as voluntary and business associations. Many of these group associations produced fixed sites as they were housed in organized, physical structures, like homes, government bureaucracies and office buildings. According to Mumford:

> 'The essential physical means of a city's existence are the fixed site, the durable shelter, the permanent facilities for assembly, interchange and storage; the essential social means are the social division of labor, which serves not merely the economic life but the cultural processes . . . The city in its complete sense, then, is a geographic plexus, an economic organization, an institutional process, a theater of social action, and an aesthetic symbol of collective unity.' (2003: 94)

We see here a kind of old fashioned thinking that has turned into nostalgia by current writers. Mumford equates the city with civilization, which was once a very trenchant but now dated observation in the US. Once an important conception of the city when the only other alternatives were rural life or immature suburbs, Mumford's idea, as universal, is now archaic. Furthermore, his glorification of metropolitan culture was based on the limited evidence of early history, the history of ancient civilizations alone. But, all of the claims for the city's uniqueness in these terms are proved false by considering the same importance that suburban regions play in contemporary society (see entries on the *Suburb and Suburbanization*; *Multi-centered Metropolitan Region*). Furthermore, now much of this kind of theatrical social interaction takes place on the internet, in chat rooms, and in the new cell phone society, although the virtual stage can, by no means, replace interaction on the street or in the many centers of the 'multi-centered' and fully urbanized region (Gottdiener and Hutchison, 2000; Gottdiener, 2001).

Surprisingly, in contrast, Mumford's thesis of the city as the 'site of civilization' has been revived recently in Europe by the unified European Community. It has been running a yearly competition for a decade called The City of Culture, or Cultural Capitol, that has highlighted the centrality of European cities in regard to their nations' patrimony. Furthermore, current ideas about reviving cities place an increased emphasis on the creativity of the people that specifically live in dense urban areas. This idea was not only articulated first in the US by Richard Florida, but is becoming quite popular in Europe. Yet, whether urban development depends primarily on the creativity of the city population alone remains a thesis that still has to be proved, although no one can deny that artists, designers, computer innovators, and other creative people, such as those working in finance and trade, are critical to a nation's economy. These same people are usually found in cities, although mature suburbs in the US, such as Silicon Valley or the region centered around Seattle, also possess their fair share.

SOME RELEVANT ASPECTS OF CITY LIFE TODAY

Another unique aspect of cities, compared to suburban and rural areas, in addition to pedestrian culture and interaction, is the presence of night-time activities. The social aspects of this world were revealed when academics began to study contemporary subcultures and discovered a variety of socially marginalized groups that had colonized the night-time by creating personalized spaces of participation in the city. It was not street life per se, as in Mumford, Jacobs and Whyte, which created this dynamism, but the enacting of subcultural practices within the city, especially at night when the more conventional population was at home and asleep (Chatterton and Hollands, 2003). (See entry on *Nightlife and Urban Nightscapes*.)

Yet another unique aspect of cities resides in their architecture, especially the tall structures known as skyscrapers. The tall building was not a contribution of a particular place, but is viewed, rather, as an evolutionary innovation resulting from the unique city aspect of limited locationally valuable land. Now these structures are valued again for their cultural meaning and the sense of place they give cities. Signature architecture and the creation of hallmark urban landscapes are important elements in the marketing of place during the current phase of globalization. Combined into a tableau, the city 'skyline' is an important marker for place. When that skyline is instantly recognizable, such as the case of Paris, it creates an important tool for the valorization of location in a global economic system.

Housing also represents a difference between the city and suburbia. In the city, housing tends to be of high density. If single family homes are built, they are usually on small lots. Many structures are multi-family apartments, some of which are actually skyscraper in scale. Suburbs possess a contrasting land use with larger size plots and an emphasis on single family home construction that results in considerably less social density. Historically, it is within the city that new forms of housing have been innovated. The emergence of the tenement in the 1800s, for example, marked the transformation of cities into centers of manufacturing, with a working class of renters.

Today cities remain important as do their contributions to society. However, a true understanding of the city must involve its relationship with other areas of urbanized regions, such as suburbs and the networks of locations that are tied together through electronic means in the information economy. Consequently, the subject of urban studies is no longer confined to the study of the city alone. Other entries in this book deal with aspects that were once viewed more in isolation from each other than they are today. Now urban studies deals with many environmental forms and regional configurations.

REFERENCES

Chatterton, P. and R. Hollands, 2003. *Urban Nightscapes: Youth Subcultures, Pleasure Spaces and Corporate Power*. London: Routledge.

Gottdiener, M. and R. Hutchison, 2000. *The New Urban Sociology, 2nd Edition*. NY: McGraw-Hill.

Gottdiener, M. 2001. *Life in the Air: Surviving the New Culture of Air Travel*. Lanham, MD: Rowman and Littlefield.

Mumford, L. 1961. *The City in History*. NY: Harcourt Brace.

Mumford, L. 2003. 'What is a City?' in R. LeGates and F. Stout (eds) *The City Reader, 3rd Edition*. London: Routledge. pp. 93–6.

Jacobs, A. and D. Appleyard, 2003. 'Toward an Urban Design Manifesto' in R. LeGates and F. Stout (eds) *The City Reader, 3rd Edition*. London: Routledge. pp. 437–47.

Jacobs, Jane, 1961. *The Death and Life of Great American Cities*, NY: Modern Library Edition.

Whyte, W.H. 1988. *City: Rediscovering the Center*. Garden City, NY: Doubleday.

11

Community

A community is a group that perceives itself as having strong and lasting bonds, particularly when the group shares a geographic location. One measure of community is regular participation by individuals in its activities. Another is the strength of identification among members with the perceived social bond of the group. A third is the specific physical space and location that is commonly understood as the group's territory. This space provides its own set of material markers to which community members have strong emotional ties.

Often community is discussed in terms of its 'attachments' – the attachment of the individuals who are part of a community to each other and to the physical location; the feeling of belonging to a community. In this sense, the concept 'community' refers to a deep psychological and emotional relationship to a group and/or a particular space.

The concept of community is also used to define an organized unit of the society that performs certain functions. The so-called 'community' of school teachers would be one example. When this form of the concept is tied to a particular territory by forms of government we have the concept of community as a unit of city, suburban or rural life. The neighborhood sections of the city, for example, are often referred to as 'communities' whether they possess strong social ties and attachments or not. A Community Development Corporation, in the US, is a localized group situated in a particular section of a city and organized to promote economic and social development. While the term 'community policing' refers to programs in which the police work with community residents to address crime, in the UK, the concept and notion of community is varied. In 2003, the UK government launched the *Sustainable Communities Plan*. In respect of urban policy, the Plan stresses: building social capital; maximizing engagement in local decision-making; facilitating different types of service provision; and facilitating the building up of local economic activity and social enterprise. (Office of the Deputy Prime Minister, 2002). In France, the historical basis of community is the *commune*, of which there are about 360,000. Because of the small size of many of the communes they are administratively bundled into *collectivités locales*. Similarly, since the de-centralization project of the 1980s, certain towns and cities have been absorbed into *communités urbaines* (for example Lille-Roubaix-Tourcoing).

The concept of community owes much to the ideas of the European sociologist, Ferdinand Tonnies who wrote in the 1930s. His term for community was 'gemeinschaft' which is a close-knit spatial unit in which tradition, extended family and religion structure social life. This concept was opposed by the concept of 'gesellschaft' in which impersonal, secondary relations prevailed and which was governed by formal codes of conduct. Louis Wirth used these ideas to discuss the types of relationships characteristic of urban life (see entry *The City*). Today, Tonnies' concept of a traditional community is over used as applicable to modern societies while the term 'community' is itself so loosely used as to have little specific meaning. According to one observer, there are at least 100 different definitions (Berger, 1978: 8).

Some urbanists today understand that the closely-knit network of

12

friendship ties often referred to as 'community' no longer requires a specific spatial location. This concept of 'community without propinquity', as it is sometimes called, means that the way the term is loosely applied to particular sections of the city may be quite misleading in its social, if not political, implications. The concept of community as a far-flung sparsely-knit network of ties stretching beyond the boundaries of neighborhood or kinship solidarities may be more relevant to our society because many people have only the loosest link to their neighbors, yet retain strong family and/or friendship networks. For this expanded definition of community, its essence lies in its social rather than its spatial structure. Rather than being full members of one physical neighborhood, people in contemporary city and suburban environments enjoy limited memberships in multiple social networks extending throughout space. Furthermore, their ties to others are no less strong than that of the more traditional and spatially limited concept of community (see entries on *Neighborhood; New Urbanism*).

Perhaps the best example of how community has changed involves the advent of the internet and the many ways it is used to connect people on a regular basis across the globe. ICQ or ICT software and e-mail features allow families and friends to remain in constant contact through the virtual space of the internet. To speak of 'community' in some localized way, as many academics still do, in the face of these new 'space-less' manifestations of social networks may be somewhat absurd. Explorations of urban relations and internet flows have given rise to the concept of the 'cyber city' (see entry on *The City*). I believe this term is misleading, because its use of the term 'city' has no meaning in this context (see entry on the *Multi-centered Metropolitan Region*).

The political scientist, Robert D. Putnam, believes that community life has drastically declined in the US with corresponding disturbing implications: 'Whereas cities once held out the promise of a wider, higher form of human community, Putnam argues that contemporary urbanites now follow a path of less, not more, civic engagement and that our collective stock of "Social Capital" – the meaningful human contacts of all kinds that characterize true communities – is so dangerously eroded that it verges on depletion.' (LeGates and Stout, 2003: 105). Putnam uses the concept of 'bowling alone' as a metaphor for the decline of community participation in America. By his measure, the participation of individuals in local bowling leagues, and other localized group organizations, has drastically declined since the 1960s. This, according to Putnam, indicates a general decline in connection to neighborhoods and communities themselves.

13

For Putnam, the close ties that neighbors have with each other constitute a powerful social resource that he defines as 'social capital'. The more social capital a community possesses, the greater is their ability to preserve and strengthen their way of life in the city. Thus, for followers of Putnam, the decline of urban areas in the US can, in part, be reversed by strengthening local participation in local organizations.

Putnam's argument that people today have much less involvement in politics and local political clubs is extremely well taken. Yet, the concept of neighborhood 'social capital' is not dependent on the scope of local resident participation alone, as he suggests. In many cases, having a few politically influential residents in a given neighborhood is all that is needed for there to be a response by city government to community concerns. The power of communal associations may be overrated by Putnam.

Are civic associations and other community associations on the decline? Perhaps in many areas of the city, but there is an unevenness to this decline. Yet, the overall participation in politics has eroded. If this is what Putnam means by community social capital, then he is right. However, he is wrong if he necessarily believes that people are more isolated today than in previous periods of our history. They may not care much about politics, or even about the bowling leagues that Putnam loves so well, but they continue to have viable social networks and these are most often spread out in space.

Across the Atlantic, Putnam has become an important influence in the design of social policy, particularly under the present Prime Minister of the UK, Tony Blair. He shares Putnam's nostalgia for an imagined community, because of dystopian views of the decline of urban civic order. Similarly, the heir to the English throne perceives the lack of a community imperative in urban architecture as an important loss of social capital. In the British context this ideology shares the same nostalgic vision of a 'green and pleasant land' being imported in to urban space and culture, despite evidence to the contrary.

Cell phone use and internet e-mail are positive indicators of the persisting close ties among individuals in society, as are sustained social networks that exist without the need for proximity (Graham, 2004). Now, in fact, both e-mailing with computers and cell phone conversations, which seem to be ubiquitous these days, are even assisted by video connections between discussants. The importance of Putnam's community organizations, in short, may be exaggerated. To what extent do localized groups keep social capital alive, or are they simply limited to consumption practices and chit-chat? Finally, most cities today face a heavy legacy of de-industrialization and the flight of substantial economic resources. These are hardly problems that greater social capital of local neighborhoods can alleviate.

In critiques of contemporary living, such as Putnam's, there is a subtext – an implied assumption – that we need proximity and density for cities and suburbs to work. But this is a premise, derived from Louis Wirth, that is quite out of date in the information society. Furthermore, there is another and more important counter trend that is not discussed by Putnam. Since the late 1990s, many urban areas in the advanced economies of the world have joined the 'sustainable city' movement which requires a revival of civic associations and activism in order to promote environmentally sound growth. The cities of Portland and Chattanooga, in the US as well as some cities in Europe are examples of a turn around in both environmental quality and in civic life. In this movement, the issue is not a revival of the social basis of neighborhood participation, as it is in Putnam's conception, but the organization of all local residents into a strong force that can push for control of development in order to make their local space a better place to live. Such values are more important to society than the stress on neighboring chit-chat and common consumption practices that discussions of 'social capital' often entail. The entry on *Sustainable Urbanization* speaks to the issue of community revival in a new way.

REFERENCES

Berger, A. 1978. *The City: Urban Communities and their Problems*. Dubuque, Iowa: Wm. C. Brown and Co.

Graham, S. 2004. *The Cybercities Reader*. London: Routledge.

Office of the Deputy Prime Minister (2002) www.odpm.gov.uk accessed 10 May 2004.

Putnam, R. 2003. 'Bowling Alone: America's Declining Social Capital' in R. LeGates and F. Stout (eds) 2003. *The City Reader, 3rd Edition*. London: Routledge. pp. 105–13.

Counties, Places, MSAs and Other Census Definitions

(NOTE: the following consists of definitions alone. For a more analytical perspective on these spatial distinctions see the entry on the *Multi-centered Metropolitan Region*.)

IN THE UNITED STATES

Counties

Counties and their equivalents are the primary political and administrative divisions of states. These areas are called parishes in Louisiana. In Alaska, 27 boroughs and 'census areas' are treated as county equivalents for census purposes. Several cities – Baltimore, MD, St. Louis, MO, Carson City, NV and 40 cities in Virginia – are independent of any county organization and, because they constitute primary divisions of their states, are accorded the same treatment as counties in census tabulations. The District of Columbia, i.e., Washington, DC, has no primary divisions and the entire area is treated as a county.

Places

Incorporated Places – Legally defined, incorporated municipalities (cities, towns, villages and boroughs) with 2,500 or more inhabitants as of the 2000 US census. Hawaii does not have incorporated places that are recognized for census purposes, so data there are provided for census designated places (CDPs) with 2,500 or more inhabitants.

Selected Towns and Townships – Some county subdivisions, such as towns and townships, are not classified as incorporated places for census purposes. The six New England states, New York, Wisconsin, Michigan, Minnesota, New Jersey and Pennsylvania, have townships and the census counts them as such if they have a population of 10,000 or more as of the 2000 census.

All other areas, both unincorporated and those incorporated places with fewer than 2,500 inhabitants are lumped together by the census as 'Balance of County'.

Metropolitan Areas and Micropolitan Areas

Metropolitan Statistical Areas (MeSAs) – have at least one urbanized area of 50,000 or more population, plus adjacent territory that has a high degree of social and economic integration with the core as measured by commuting ties. There were 362 of these areas in the 2000 census.

Micropolitan Statistical Areas (MiSAs) – A new set of statistical areas that have at least one urban cluster of at least 10,000 but less than 50,000 population, plus adjacent territory that has a high degree of social and economic integration with the core as measured by commuting ties.

Metropolitan Divisions (MDs) – A Metropolitan Statistical Area containing a single core with a population of 2.5 million or more may be subdivided to form smaller groupings of counties referred to as Metropolitan Divisions.

Combined Statistical Areas (CSAs) – If specified criteria are met, adjacent Metropolitan and Micropolitan Satistical Areas, in various combinations, may become the components of a new set of areas called Combined Statistical Areas. For instance, a CSA may comprise two or more MeSAs, a MeSA and a MiSA, two or more MiSAs, or multiples of these. The areas that combine for census purposes, retain their own designations as Metro or Micro SAs within the larger CSA. Combinations for adjacent areas with an employment interchange of 25% or more are automatic. Combinations for adjacent areas with an employment interchange of at least 15% but less than 25% are based on local opinion as expressed through Congressional delegations.

Regions

Census regions are groupings of states that subdivide the US for the presentation of data. There are four regions: Northeast, Midwest, South and West.

Northeast: Maine, New Hampshire, Vermont, Massachusetts, Rhode Island, Connecticut, New York, New Jersey, Pennsylvania.

Midwest: Ohio, Indiana, Illinois, Michigan, Wisconisn, Minnesota, Iowa, Missouri, N. Dakota, S. Dakota, Nebraska, Kansas.

South: Delaware, Maryland, District of Columbia, Virginia, West Virginia,

17

N. Carolina, S. Carolina, Georgia, Florida, Kentucky, Tennessee, Alabama, Mississippi, Arkansas, Louisiana, Oklahoma, Texas.

West Region: California, Oregon, Washington, Montana, Idaho, Colorado, New Mexico, Arizona, Utah, Nevada, Wyoming, Alaska, Hawaii.

IN THE UNITED KINGDOM

In the UK, cities and towns are independent legal entities. The *county councils* are the administrative areas that cover the countryside and parts of suburbs. They were created in the 19th Century as a bulwark against the rising power of towns and cities and to forestall the development of regional functional administrations that had been proposed by the political philosopher, Jeremy Bentham.

Regional definitions have changed over time. Earlier the Standard Regions consisted of:

> South-East; South-West; East Anglia; East Midlands; West Midlands; North West; Yorkshire and Humberside; Northern; Wales and Scotland.

Now, the current regions are:

> London; South-East, Eastern; South-West; East Midlands; West Midlands; North-West; Yorkshire and Humberside; North-East.

In some instances, however, the boundaries are not the same. For example, the Eastern region includes the old Standard Regions of East Anglia, but also parts of the old South-East Standard Region.

IN FRANCE

There are 22 regions, which were purely administrative until elected assemblies were instituted in 1984, under the de-centralization legislation which also bestowed some limited tax raising powers and devolved certain governmental functions.

The regions are:

> Ile-de-France; Picardie; Haute-Normandie; Centre; Basse-Normandie; Lorraine; Alsace; France-Comté; Pays de la Loire; Bretagne; Poitou-Charentes; Aquitaine; Midi-Pyrénées; Limousin; Rhône-Alpes; Auvergne; Languedoc-Roussillon; Provence-Alpes-Côte d'Azur; Corse.

IN GERMANY

There are 16 regions plus East Berlin. The former are known as Länder and have considerable governmental powers within a federal constitution. The former West Germany had 11 Länder: Schleswig-Holstein; Hamburg; Bremen; Lower Saxony; Nord-Rhine Westphalia; Hesse; Rhineland-Palatinate; Saarland; Baden-Württemberg: Bavaria; West Berlin. They are joined in the re-united Germany by the Länder of the former German Democratic Republic: Thuringia; Saxony; Saxony-Anhalt; Brandenburg; Mecklenburg-Western Pomerania.

There is a current debate in the UK about the nature of regional identity and whether it is strong enough to provide a mandate for establishing regional assemblies and creating regional government in England. In contrast, regional government is more formalized and powerful in France and Germany and is most strongly expressed in the concept of *Europe of the Regions* promulgated by French former Foreign Minister and former president of the European Commission, Jacques Delors in 1996.

REFERENCES

US Bureau of the Census, *Guide to the 2002 Economic Census*, www.census.gov, accessed 25 June 2003.
INSEE. 2003. *Tableux de l'Economie Française*. Paris: INSEE.
Anderson, J.J. 1992 *The Territorial Imperative: Pluralism, Corporatism and Economic Crisis*. Cambridge: Cambridge University Press.

19

De-territorialization and Re-territorialization

Recently, urbanists have been concerned about large scale migrations of particular people as a result of war, famine, political oppression, religious intolerance and enduring poverty. This phenomenon is referred to as 'de-territorialization' and often the people themselves are known as 'refugees'. When such mass movements of people are accompanied by the persisting organization of daily life centered on cultural practices of the place of origin, urbanists refer to this phenomenon as 're-territorialization'. These twin aspects are important topics for an understanding of changes in the ethnic composition of urban places throughout the world since World War II because of the profound impact that modern political unrest, global economic changes and warfare have had on local peoples (Appadurai, 1996).

The processes of de- and re-territorialization can be illustrated by the effect of the holocaust on European Jewry. As a consequence of mass murders and mass dislocations of Jews within the nations of Europe attacked by the German Nazi regime, age old aspirations for a specific Jewish homeland in the ancient Holy Land, known as Zionism, were given world-wide credence and power resulting in the creation of a Jewish State, Israel, in 1948. The de-territorialization of radically diverse ethnic groups, all of whom were Jews, in both European and Middle Eastern countries, resulted in a subsequent re-territorialization or in-gathering within the State of Israel and a consequent, and qualitatively new, emergent culture once this process was institutionalized.

Unfortunately, many de-territorialized ethnic and religious groups have only experienced limited success in re-territorializing, if at all. Among these people, the Tibetans are one of the most long-suffering. After the Chinese invasion of Tibet in 1950 and consequent crackdown on Tibetan religion and culture, a steady stream of refugees escaped to other countries, principally India. Arriving in foreign locations, religious leaders have recreated centers of Tibetan culture on a limited basis, such as the community in Darjeeling. Tibetans, however, can be found in many countries around the globe. For the most part they remain de-territorialized because, having once possessed their own country, they now find themselves living elsewhere and without a state of their own. This makes their case more politically extreme, if not as harsh, as other refugee groups that have been de-territorialized in modern times but who have never possessed a state of their own, such as the Palestinians, Biafrans or Kurds. Nevertheless, the latter groups, as well as many others that have large populations in other lands, but which retain a certain level of ethnic identity, are examples of the displacement of people on a mass basis and on a world scale characteristic of 20th Century upheavals.

In other cases, refugees in large numbers can transform cities. This has been true of Miami, Florida after the Castro-led revolution in Cuba. An area once called 'Little Havana' became too small to contain all the Cubans fleeing their native land. In the process, the city of Miami, once a curious blend of white and black southerners mixed together with predominantly retired Jews from the north, became Hispanic (Portes and Stepick, 1993).

In the UK, migration from the former Commonwealth countries (the successor of the old colonial empire) has transformed British cities. The ebb and flow of finance and population between the colonial core and former dependent territories has been a feature of globalization since the 17th Century. Now London contains over 300 different languages. Some ethnic communities have moved from the urban core to the suburbs as they have economically flourished, just as they have in the US. In other cases, the de-territorialization of many ethnic groups, for example in the Balkans or in Afghanistan, has led to re-territorializing many parts of European cities. The failure of host cities to fully absorb these populations and their failure in sharing the socio-economic benefits of the larger society has made many of their young men susceptible to recruitment by criminal groups and even terrorist organizations. The culture of Paris, for example, has been altered forever by the influx of immigrants from former North African colonies.

The issues of de- and re-territorialization for people from Asia, Africa, the Middle East and Latin America are also linked to contemporary processes of immigration and globalization, colonialism and post-colonialism. See the entries on *Globalization* and *Immigration and Migration* for more information.

REFERENCES

Appadurai, A. 1996. *Modernity at Large: Cultural Dimensions of Globalization.* Minneapolis, MN: University of Minnesota Press.
Portes, A. and A. Stepick, 1993. *City on the Edge: The Transformation of Miami.* Berkeley, CA: University of California Press.

Education and
Reproduction of Labor

The crisis of public education and the urban crisis in many countries are related. The ability of American cities, for example, to reproduce a qualified labor force under present conditions of an information driven and global economy is limited, just as the inner city quality of life has also declined. Student performance as a whole declined over the last several decades, and in world comparisons US grade school students do poorly in science and maths. But throughout metropolitan regions, the quality of local schools is a function of where one lives. For the most part, the better schools are located in the wealthier areas and in the suburbs. Even inner-city school systems that historically have functioned at a relatively high level, despite the poverty of their pupils, have had to contend with both a prolonged fiscal crisis and recession, which have combined to cut into the quality of education (see entry on *Fiscal Crisis*). Today the pupils attending city public schools are predominantly poor minority group members with low educational attainment.

In most UK cities, there is now a positive correlation among quality of secondary school, student performance and house prices. Estate agents (realtors) advertise houses on the basis of being within the catchment area of local schools. Housing is an important source of wealth and potential future personal income in the UK as it is in the US. The interaction of housing and access to education reinforces inequality in cities. In many inner city areas, youth unemployment is in the order of 40%, particularly among ethnic groups. These figures attest to the relative failure of education in British cities and inner suburbs as a means of mobility. These particular problems compound a general one of literacy that puts the UK on a par with Kazakstan for the mathematical ability of 11–14 year olds, according to the Organization for Economic Co-operation and Development (OECD, 2003).

Similar failures mark the educational process in the US. In large city school districts across the country, fewer than half of the students who start high school will graduate in their senior year. In low-income school districts, a majority of teachers are teaching subjects for which they have not been trained or certified. Although all public high school teachers are supposed to be certified to teach, school districts make use of legal loopholes to allow temporary hiring of non-certified instructional staff. In some schools, nearly a quarter or more of instructors are not certified. When public school teachers in Texas, for example, took a required test of general knowledge expected for college graduates, more than one third earned a failing grade. And in Florida, where students who have graduated with degrees in education are required to take similar tests, more than half have flunked. In this way, the crisis of education continues at all levels, not just in the public schools but also in college where the students remain ill prepared.

Problems with schools are compounded by urban problems such as poverty and economic decline of inner cities. Schools are increasingly segregated in metropolitan areas because many white parents send their children to private or parochial schools. Another critical concern is that many children in the public school system are either immigrants or have parents who have immigrated to this country and possess facility in English as only a second language. In some urban districts immigrant children make up as much as half of all students and teachers have to contend with 30 or 40 different languages spoken by pupils under their care. The federal government mandates that school districts establish English as a Second Language (ESL) programs whenever there are significant numbers of students whose home language is not English. But, characteristically, the federal government also does not fund these programs. With a constant fiscal crisis operating in the background, there is really no local money for these programs and the problem of language difficulties persists. One finds a similar pattern in the cities of Europe. Economic segregation is reinforced by the lack of access to a level educational playing field that governments mistakenly deem separate from social policy.

In the past there has been a general failure of American society to fund education at the national level making the quality of public schooling a direct function of the level of wealth within any given community. It is for this reason that students in suburban school districts do much better than those in the city. This makes the suburbs more attractive to parents wishing the best schooling for their children. When they move out of the city for this reason, it adds further to the general decline of the urban school district thereby reinforcing a vicious cycle. Because of the close tie between the wealth of the local area and the quality of education, there is considerable inequity in the way children are trained for future careers. Now the reproduction of labor is highly dependent on the relative affluence of people in our society. Those that can afford to live in wealthier areas or can afford private education, send their children to schools that will prepare them for the better jobs. The replication of the Americanization of economic life, replete with all its inequalities, is to some extent being effected by globalization in large parts of Europe, with the exception of countries like the Nordic ones who still believe that a large provision of public resources for education is the basis of civil society. In the latter region, students consistently score the highest in standardized tests with the country of Finland currently the world leader in educational quality.

REFERENCES

OECD, 2003. www.oecd.org accessed 12 May 2004.

Environmental Concerns

Water, air, and noise pollution along with toxic waste from industry are environmental concerns. Sewage and garbage pollution from housing, a lack of open space and dangers from traffic because of poor or non-existent planning also plague the environment. There are also issues that are relevant only to specific areas of the globe, but which are important nevertheless. These include the ability to spread disease rapidly in dense urban areas, such as the SARS outbreak in Hong Kong, or flu virus threats. Animal attacks in urban areas due to incursion of humans on animal habitat, such as alligators in Florida, cougars in California, and more recently, leopards in India, kangaroos in Australia and foxes in the inner suburbs of London, are also environmental concerns. Hurricanes, tornadoes, earthquakes and floods in certain places are natural occurrences that pose dangers to developed human settlements.

All these matters are made worse when the country is developing and there is a large influx of population into major urban centers. The projected doubling of the official population in Shanghai, by 2020, for example, suggests that the allure of mega-cities may be undermined by their failure to effect environmental sustainability. The lack of adequate infrastructure and social organization to deal with growth in cities, means that environmental problems can only intensify. The case of Istanbul is typical. While the population of Turkey doubled between 1970 and 1996, the population of Istanbul increased more than fourfold during the same period (Fareri, 1996). Yet, rapid growth itself is not confined as a phenomenon to developing countries alone. Much of the US urbanized territory has been built since the 1950s as a consequence of the shifts to the suburbs and the sunbelt. This deconcentration has also been rapid. As a consequence, environmental problems from fast and often poorly planned growth abound in both the developed and the developing world.

Unique ocean formations, such as the Tampa and San Francisco bays in the US, have been almost destroyed biologically, practically bereft of valuable plant and animal life, in the wake of residential suburbanization and the deconcentration of population in their respective regions. Clear cutting of virgin forests, pollution of lakes and streams, fouling of beaches with oil, sewage or industrial waste, and emission of choking smog are but some of the environmental problems that once only typified the older areas of the Northeast and Midwest but are now ubiquitous across the US.

In rapidly growing and deconcentrated metropolitan regions, traffic congestion is so bad that it is fast approaching gridlock. It's not uncommon for commuters in parts of California or Atlanta to travel four hours by car on daily trips to and from work. While traffic congestion is an environmental concern characteristic of all urbanized areas across the globe, countries such as the US that possess the expertise could have avoided these problems through better planning and resource management.

Environmental problems of urbanized areas are highly interrelated and are often a consequence of dense development. For example, areas that have grown rapidly but which have not made adequate provision for sewage and street drains become covered over with rainwater and flooding during storms. This large scale runoff also pollutes streams, ponds and lakes in the metropolitan region and even threatens the quality of drinking water.

While toxic pollution is associated with industrial development, inadequate planning for home construction on a large scale is also the source for considerable environmental hazards. Water, solid waste and garbage pollution are problems of massive housing development, as is air pollution from the excessive use of automobiles. According to the Environmental Protection Agency, air pollution is defined as any combination of ozone, carbon monoxide, sulfur dioxide, nitrogen oxide and hydrocarbons. Although regions vary with regard to which of these constituents are the most dominant, all urban areas suffer from this kind of pollution. Its medical costs are estimated to be in the billions of dollars for individuals. Another problem of air quality involves 'suspended particulate matter', i.e., the particles of dirt or liquid small enough to be suspended in the air and breathed into the lungs. This form of pollution is also hazardous to personal health.

ENVIRONMENTAL RACISM

This concept combines the issue of racial or class segregation with the issue of environmental hazards and pollution concerns in the metro region. It is a practice of placing hazardous wastes or projects that negatively affect the environment in locations where poor and minority people dominate. Love Canal, in Niagara Falls, New York was a poor working class community that became the site of a hazardous waste dump. Over time people with housing that was built on top of this location suffered an unusually high rate of cancers and birth defects. It was only when a resident movement investigated and complained about the hazards that relief was obtained and the site was eventually abandoned because of its documented dangers (Gibbs, 1981). Other studies of the US show how hazardous waste sites are located within the vicinity of southern towns that have a majority of poor black residents. This aspect of dumping in regions of powerless people is quite prevalent and decidedly dangerous to minority groups in the sunbelt of the US (Gottdiener and Hutchison, 2000: 311).

In developing countries: '[O]n the whole, the rich insulate themselves from the worst of the environmental problems. They can obtain clean water and dispose of waste water in septic tanks; the poor, on the other hand, even when they have sufficient water, must live with the dangers of washing in, and even drinking, contaminated water. Whilst the rich find satisfactory ways of disposing of their solid waste, that of the poor is rarely removed from their neighborhoods and accumulates wherever there is space: on vacant land, in canals and rivers. The authorities build roads and plant trees for the rich, while the poor provide their own plank ways or mud paths to access their self-built houses' (Atkinson, 1996: 6).

Environmental problems exist in developing cities across the globe. Urban shanty towns are lauded for giving residents opportunities to advance themselves that they cannot find in rural areas, but these places still have open sewers that cause serious illness, especially among the children who play in the streets. See the entry on the *Ghetto*. Also, see entry on *Sustainable Urbanization* for more information on environmental concerns.

REFERENCES

Atkinson, A. 1996. 'Sustainable Cities: Dilemmas and Option.' *City*, 3–4: 5–11 June.
Fareri, P. 1996. 'Turkey: Uncertain Emblem of the Future' *City*, 3–4: 59–62 June.
Gibbs, L. 1981. *Love Canal: My Story*. Albany, NY: SUNY Press.
Gottdiener, M. and R. Hutchison, 2000. *The New Urban Sociology, 2nd Edition*. NY: McGraw-Hill.

26

Feminine Space

Society is dominated by social relations of male power. The masculine and the feminine, as cultural qualities, are related to each other in the form of superordinate/subordinate relations. Men possess power in our society that is manifested as the ability to define situations and to control social outcomes. Men are situated in the positions of leadership and control in the powerful organizations of our economy and political structure. This hierarchically structured system of gendered dominance is manifested in masculine space as well, see entry on *Masculine Space*. In contrast, the subordinate social status of women also produces environments where females have power. These are examples of 'feminine space' (Spain, 1992).

Consider the following observations by Lara Zador (2001:1):

> 'My notion of womanhood is tied to space, I have a fear of taking up too much space as though space is masculine and the more feminine I am, the less space I consume . . . My anorexic friend sent me a note apologizing for the size of the letters she used, she was sorry for taking up so much space with her words. Women only shout when the say "NO", which means no when a very private space is about to be violated – one of the only spaces women can call their own.'

As with the masculine case, the exploration of feminine space includes representational or virtual spaces. It is possible to speak of a 'feminine space' in literature, in films, in advertising. Ellen McCracken (1999) discusses how the religious space of the Catholic Church is re-interpreted by Latina authors and expropriated in the syncretistic practice of Santeria. This is a case common to women in their response to the male domination of space. Environments themselves are not changed; their symbolism and significance are only altered by the different, subversive reading of feminist discourse. The significance of such writing is that it acknowledges the importance of spatial transformation as well as symbolic re-readings in the critical practice of feminism.

The voice of women has been heard but little recognized and rarely acknowledged in architecture and urban planning. Dolores Hayden's (1981) pathbreaking book details the contribution of women to design in homes, cities and suburbs. Women's roles were defined as stay at home housewives in the 1920s, after once participating actively in the industrial labor force. This shift to the middle-class made the domestic kitchen and the single family suburban home the new environmental domain of women. Today's suburban culture, especially styles in automobiles, reflect the persistence of the mothering role for many middle-class women who also must chauffer their children to everyday suburban activities in environments relatively devoid of mass transportation. It is still possible to say that large supermarkets, shopping malls and the middle-class, single family home are examples of 'feminine space'.

According to the Matrix Collective (1984), control by women over the decoration of the single family home has enabled them to express themselves and to influence others by their environmental choices. This milieu stands in contrast to the space outside that is and remains controlled by men. As Benard and Schlaffer (1993: 338) remark about the street:

> 'Whether you wear a slit skirt or are covered from head to foot in a black Chador, the message is not that you are attractive enough to make a man lose his self-control, but that the public realm belongs to him and you are there by his permission as long as you follow his rules and as long as you remember your place.'

These spatial distinctions play a significant role in the continued socialization of young people into separate gender roles that reproduce society's gender bias. There are other disadvantages to society revealed by a spatial analysis sensitive to gender.

> 'Community planning invariably assigns the major portion of open space to traditionally male-dominated activities, such as sports. Places for mothering are rarely considered at all, and often are restricted to playgrounds. Creating safe environments for children and mothers requires some planning. In Columbia, MD, one of the totally planned New Towns in the US, pedestrian and automobile traffic are separated by the segregation of space. This feature of Columbia makes it easier for mothers to protect children at play.' (Gottdiener and Hutchison, 2000:167)

Other countries, such as those in Scandinavia, make explicit provision in public space and on public transportation for mothers with children. Their cities are safer for them than are ours.

REFERENCES

Benard, D. and E. Schlaffer, 1993. 'The Man in the Street: Why He Harasses' in L. Richardson and V. Taylor (eds) *Feminist Frontiers III*, NY: McGraw-Hill. pp. 338–91.
Gottdiener, M. and R. Hutchison, 2000. *The New Urban Sociology, 2nd Edition*, NY: McGraw-Hill. p. 167.
Hayden, D. 1981. *The Grand Domestic Revolution*, Cambridge, MA: MIT Press.

28

Matrix Collective, 1984. *Making Space*, London, UK: Pluto Press.

McCracken, Ellen, 1999. *New Latina Narrative: The Feminine Space of Postmodern Ethnicity*, Tuscon, AZ: Univeristy of Arizona Press.

Spain, D. 1992. *Gendered Spaces*. Chapel Hill, NC: Univeristy of North Carolina Press.

Zador, Lara, 2001. www.soapboxgirls.com, April.

Fiscal Crisis

Decades of population deconcentration and economic decline have cost the US city dearly by weakening its resource base. Many places no longer have enough surplus revenue to pay for basic services. For some time, administrations have relied on the state and federal governments to make up the difference in budget shortfalls. When that gap has become severe, municipal governments suffer from the condition known as 'fiscal crisis' (O'Connor, 1973; Gottdiener and Hutchison, 2000). In the UK, the decimation of the fiscal powers of local municipalities by successive governments, and the privatization and contracting out of municipal services to private providers, have been outcomes of the same trajectory. More decentralized systems, such as in France and Germany, have not been immune as center-periphery relations have come under budgetary stress in those countries as well.

The fiscal crisis of the state has affected all levels of government, not just central cities. At the federal level, however, our national government has the ability to float as much debt as it wants without answering to a higher authority. Cities and suburbs cannot do that. In the UK, local authorities (boroughs) were able to issue debt, subject to central government constraints, up until the early 1980s. The German Länder are still able to issue debt but, again, only within the constraints imposed by central government and global budget deficit limits imposed on countries that are members of the European Community. When local areas suffer from fiscal crisis, other levels of government become involved.

As a municipal corporation, a city can even go bankrupt. In the 1970s, several US cities experienced severe fiscal crises and Cleveland did go bankrupt in 1978. This event used to be more common in the 1800s as the country's economy went through periodic crises of economic depression. Formally, local authorities cannot go bankrupt in the UK. If they set a budget unacceptable to central government for the coming financial year and attempt to run a deficit, the elected councilors can be surcharged (held personally financially liable) and barred from office. In recent years, the New Labour Government has discovered 'the New Localism'. This is essentially a technocratic policy in which local authorities that correspond to 'Best Value' (the program of the Audit Commission, the national auditor of local authorities) may be rewarded by being able to keep part of capital receipts from the sale of local public assets. Local business taxation is controlled by central government, with the exception of the City of London (the financial district) which is the richest borough in the world. Unlike federal systems of government, as found, for example in the US and Germany, the impact of the fiscal crisis of the state is mediated through the agency of the central state in other areas of Europe. Its impact on local residents is no less severe, however.

Even when the extreme case of bankruptcy is avoided, as happened in the 1975 New York City crisis, the threat of severe shortfalls means that the municipality must make drastic cuts in its services. These measures, always unpopular, affect directly the local quality of life. During the 1970s, for example, firehouses in NYC were shut down, teachers were let go, garbage collection was cut back and many civic activities were simply canceled.

In the US, the economy is controlled by private enterprise, but the quality of community life is heavily dependent on local government (see entry on *Education* and *Reproduction of Labor*). The level of taxation is low compared to other industrialized countries. With profit-making only minimally regulated, cities and suburbs generally rely on such revenue generating mechanisms as property and sales taxes. The impact of the latter falls most heavily on the poor. During times of economic decline, revenue generation is severely affected. Yet, people in this country seem to prefer the present system rather than increasing tax rates for the private sector corporations to pay for public services. For decades, after the 1950s, when both cities and suburbs were strapped for cash, local administrations relied on state and federal programs to make up the difference. But, in the 1970s, when those very programs were cut back by the national government, a precipitous, severe fiscal crisis occurred.

An important factor complicating the management of a fiscal crisis is the many and varied interests that emerge during this period of austerity and government restructuring. City and suburban labor unions representing municipal and town workers fight cutbacks in employment that are viewed as necessary to fight the short fall. In Cleveland, despite strong worker opposition, the municipal unions were eventually forced to accept large layoffs of personnel and even pay cuts. Local elected officials are also placed in the hot seat by such a crisis. If the state government had been helping the city, as most of them did, they were often not given a voice in how aid was spent until, that is, a fiscal crisis bloomed. At that point, the state government usually demanded, and rightly so, a hands-on authority to help bring municipal finances back in line with expenditures. These outside state control boards that often appear whenever there is a fiscal crisis are never very popular with city residents. Yet, they are even less popular with local officials who view them as a visible sign of their own political failure.

Another interest group that becomes active during fiscal crisis, is the private sector itself. Yet, if public services decline as does the quality of urban life, those companies that can move to more healthy places usually do so. During the 1970s, for example, New York City not only lost a significant number of corporate headquarters, but trained professionals as well, all of whom decided that it was then finally time to move. In contrast, banking and financial interests usually stay. This is so because banks are heavily involved in downtown real estate and they are also the primary beneficiaries of new municipal financing arrangements that often involve higher interest rates than usual because of the crisis situation. Banks do very well during fiscal crisis, as most municipalities would prefer to restructure debt at higher interest rates than go bankrupt.

Fiscal crises are symptoms of the general decline in city economies. This pattern has been visible since the 1950s as a consequence of metropolitan deconcentration and the shift of people and industries both to suburbia and the sunbelt. Because those areas, in turn, grew rapidly, they too suffered fiscal crisis and an inability to fund adequate infrastructure and public services. The massive shifts in population began in the 1950s. It took over 20 years, propped up by state and federal programs, for the shortfalls in revenue to make themselves felt in a noticeable way. But, when that occurred in the 1970s, it became clear that both cities and suburbs suffered from the inability to provide the kind of services and a quality of life that most Americans desired. After the 1970s, cuts and scarcity prevailed and people have had to live with declining community quality ever since, although wealthier communities are always protected by their affluence. As long as we have an economic system where capital controls profits and government taxation is limited, all places within metro regions will live under the specter of fiscal strain. For this reason fiscal crises remain a threat to the urban quality of life even in the 21st Century.

In Europe, the situation has been more variegated and complex. However, the relationship between the growth of the suburbs and the tax base of urban areas throughout the period from the 1950s to the 1970s has created similar problems for the quality of urban life. Paradoxically at the start of the 21st Century, London's suburban boroughs were experiencing decline as baby boomers and young professionals colonized the inner central areas and middle-class families moved out to the fringes of the countryside. One reason for this shift is the significant cost of transportation from outlying places to and from the central city of London, a condition that is not characteristic of the US because of the heavy subsidization of highway construction and private transport in the past.

REFERENCES

Audit Commission (1995), *Local Authority Performance Indicators, 1993/94*. London: HMSO.
Gottdiener, M. and R. Hutchison, 2000. *The New Urban Sociology, 2nd Edition*. NY: McGraw-Hill.
O'Connor, J. 1973. *The Fiscal Crisis of the State*. NY: St. Martin's Press.
Smith, P. (ed) 1996 *Measuring Outcomes in the Public Sector*. London: Taylor & Francis.

Gentrification

32

This process involves the inflow of capital investment into the real estate of an already existing place in the metropolitan region whose values are depressed. Gentrification, which is a kind of urban renewal, is related to the decay of place. Both are cycles of capital investment in urban real estate. The process arises from the decisions of property owners not to invest in places when they are located in depressed areas of the city. As one observer remarks:

'The housing market tends to sort the population by income into different areas. Racism may add another type of sorting. If an area is increasingly filled by lower income residents, landlords have an incentive to not maintain their properties. If they were to invest in upgrades, they'd need to charge a higher rent to make this a profitable investment. People with higher incomes who could pay the higher rents may not be willing to live in that neighborhood. So landlords simply "milk" the decaying buildings of their rent. By putting off repairs, they can save money to buy other buildings elsewhere.' (Wetzel, 2002: 1)

The failure to continually upgrade buildings and replace the worn-out site with new cash in-flow, amounts to a process of disinvestment – a shrinkage of capital – in an area. As a space becomes more of a low-rent district, some houses may be cut up into separate rooms or apartments to increase the rental revenue. This leads to further deterioration of the housing stock and the community environment. If a declining area is close to centers of employment, the availability of cheap housing and novel aspects, such as interesting architecture and small restaurants nearby, are incentives for capital to re-enter the area and invest in real estate, thus starting the investment cycle all over again. To make investment in new construction and rehabilitation profitable, developers must be able to attract residents that can pay higher rents such as professionals (the 'gentry'). Once this process gets underway, the less affluent residents are pushed out of the area and we have a full blown example of gentrification.

Gentrification in the US and many parts of Europe is usually characterized by the conversion of apartments into condominiums (studios) and the renovation of select homes in a specific area. As more upscale residents move in, candle-lit restaurants and stores catering to people with higher incomes displace convenience and bargain shopping outlets. Rents rise as landlords realize they can attract professionals and business people as tenants. Older residents on limited incomes then have to move out. In London, for example, the predominance of owner-occupation has seen professional classes appropriate large three storey Victorian houses or developers convert them into apartments and studios. The combination of owner-occupation and the widespread cosmopolitan nature of London makes gentrification there more complex than in US counterparts (Hebbert, 1998). However, quite large housing tenure change, from low income private rental to higher income owner-occupation, has been a consistent feature of gentrification over the last 30 years.

In other European cities, competition for international sporting and cultural events, for example the Olympics, Commonwealth Games, the 'European City of Culture', city marketing and the location of cultural centers has produced a rise in gentrification of the inner city during the last ten years. The central agency of this change has been real estate interests marketing waterside developments and associated lifestyles to urban professionals. Waterside developments, whether located on rivers, lakes or oceans, appear to be a consistent feature of contemporary gentrification in many cities around the globe.

When an area gets 'gentrified', prices go up for all neighborhood services. Writing about the changes that took place in the 'Hell's Kitchen' section of Manhattan, on the west side, Michael Gwertzman focuses on the little things that became so costly to previous residents, that they were forced to move. 'He remembers eating at a restaurant . . . which served Cuban-Chinese food for $3 a plate. Six restaurants later in the same space, a new "Latino" restaurant serves the same food for $10 a plate' (1997: 2).

The process of displacement that often accompanies gentrification may result in political struggles as older residents resist the incursion of new capital. Thus, the process of dis-investment and re-investment results in cycles of decline and gentrification that afflict the housing stock of the city. Community concern and resistance accompanies these changes including the emergence of political protests and, occasionally, social movements (see entry on *Urban and Suburban Social Movements*).

REFERENCES

Gwertzman, M. 1997. *Keeping the 'Kitchen' in Clinton*. www.hellskitchen.net, accessed 25 June 2003.
Hebbert, M. 1998. *London*. Chichester: John Wiley.
Wetzel, T. 2002. 'What is Gentrification?' www.uncanny.net/~wetzel/gentry.htm, accessed 25 June 2003.

Ghetto and Racial Segregation

34

A ghetto is an area of a city or suburb occupied exclusively and relatively involuntarily by members of predominantly one social group. The term today connotes an urban area of poverty, unemployment and substandard housing.

In 1970, nine of the ten largest metro central city areas in the US had white majorities, ranging from 55% (Detroit) to 82% (Boston). Twenty years later, only Philadelphia (51%) and Boston (58%) were predominantly white. The rest of the city cores had populations that were mixed, with whites as a single group being a distinct minority. Where did the white people go? To the suburbs. Since 1950 they have been leaving the city in vast numbers. Beginning with the opening up of employment opportunities during World War II, large numbers of African Americans left the South and migrated to cities of the Northeast and Northcentral states. Record numbers, during this population shift of whites to the suburbs and blacks to the inner city, combined with overt racial discrimination in housing, led to the segregation patterns that have prevailed since that time. Declining economic prospects and shifts in the labor requirements of new jobs have left these emergent ghetto areas of the cities in distress. By 1970, the majority of Americans lived in suburbs, not cities. Because blacks could not suburbanize as rapidly or in large numbers due to racial discrimination and poverty, inner city areas with African-Americans increased their concentration of blacks. Ghettos became more extreme.

According to Cutler, Glaeser and Vigdor (1997), racial segregation in the US remains at a very high level. On average, 60% of blacks would have to move in order for blacks and whites to be equally distributed in US cities. Cutler, Glaeser and Vigdor examined segregation in US cities over the century from 1890–1990. From 1890–1940 blacks migrated to urban areas and located almost exclusively in ghettos. Between 1940 and 1970, black ghettos expanded. Since 1970 though, urban segregation has declined, especially for more educated African-Americans.

Cutler, Glaeser and Vigdor suggest and evaluate three different explanations for urban segregation. The most important factor is the involuntary segregation of ghettoization where whites took collective action either through informal or formal means to segregate blacks in particular areas. Cutler, Glaeser and Vigdor call this 'collective action racism' – including restrictive covenants, racial zoning, policy instruments and threats of violence. These factors were widespread before 1960 but became illegal after that as a consequence of fair housing laws and civil rights legislation. However, racial practices such as screening and loan biases still exist.

Another factor is lifestyle, especially for African-Americans that move north from the south. These people, like other immigrants, sought areas of the northern cities that had cultural resources they needed, such as black churches. According to the authors, African-American migrants from the south are 10% more likely to belong to an all-black church than native Northern blacks and 24% more likely to prefer a segregated neighborhood.

The third factor is 'white flight' where inner city white residents pay more to live in all white suburban communities: 'the data seem to support this explanation today as a contributing factor for the persistence of

35

segregation decades after equal housing laws were enacted.' Simply put, most inner city blacks cannot afford suburbia and those whites that can, move away to live in segregated suburban areas thus perpetuating involuntary segregation of blacks within the city.

Cutler, Glaeser and Vigdor find that, despite gains in integrated metro areas, 'there are more completely black areas in our cities than there have been in the past.' Furthermore, although blacks on average pay less than whites for urban housing, they pay relatively more for rental housing.

Over the years, urbanists have developed demographic means of measuring segregation. Until recently, two key measures have been used the 'index of dissimilarity' and the 'index of isolation'. Massey and Denton (1993) have defined these as follows:

(a) *Dissimilarity*

If blacks disproportionately reside in some areas of a city relative to whites, we say that dissimilarity between the two races is high. The index of dissimilarity measures the proportion of whites that would have to move to black areas in order for the two races to be evenly distributed. The highest level of dissimilarity is 1 or 100% of whites would have to move. According to Massey and Denton (1993), a level of 0.3 is considered low, between 0.3 and 0.6 is considered moderate, and above 0.6 is considered high.

But, dissimilarity alone does not make a ghetto.

(b) *Isolation*

'In measuring the *isolation* of blacks from whites, we want to know how much interaction there is between the races.' (Massey and Denton, 1993) An index of greater than 0.3 using the authors' index of isolation is considered isolation.

According to Massey and Denton, 'a city possesses ghettoization if the index of dissimilarity is greater than 0.6 and the index of isolation is greater than 0.3' (1993: 5).

Massey and Denton (1993: 74–7) introduce three other measures of segregation: *Clustering, Concentration* and *Centralization*. Cutler et al. (1997) found that these latter three are highly correlated to the first two and thus use only (a) and (b) above in their study. But Massey and Denton use the five measures as separate dimensions to identify a phenomenon they call 'hypersegregation':

'Not only are blacks more segregated than other groups on any single dimension of segregation, but they are also more segregated on all dimensions simultaneously; and in an important subset of US metro areas, they are highly segregated on at least four of the five dimensions at once, a pattern that we call *hypersegregation*.' (1993: 77)

Massey and Denton find that nearly one third of the black population in the US continues to live under conditions of extreme segregation: 'Typical inhabitants of these ghettos are not only unlikely to come into contact with whites within the particular neighborhoods where they live; even if they traveled to the adjacent neighborhood they would still be unlikely to see a white face; and if they went to the next neighborhood, no whites would be there either . . . No other group in contemporary United States comes close to this level of isolation within urban society.' (1993: 77)

Despite this grim evidence of both segregation and hypersegregation, data since the 1970s also reveal that there have been 'modest' declines in the level of segregation within US metro areas. According to Cutler et al. (1997), after 1970, substantial waves of Hispanic immigrants came to the US and they often mixed with blacks in low income neighborhoods. In addition, there has been some positive effects of the fair housing laws passed since the 1960s to combat racial segregation in real estate. Educated African Americans have particularly benefited from legal powers that allow them to purchase homes in formerly restricted areas of the metro region.

Racial segregation is not a problem exclusive to the US. With a significant influx of black people from the Caribbean and Africa, the UK has recently exhibited its own problems in this area of concern, which had not been experienced since the riots in the inner London suburb of Brixton in 1981. Still there are differences between the two nations. In the UK, racial composition is less diverse than in the US. In addition, racial minorities constitute only a small proportion of the total population. It is estimated that about four million racial minorities live in the UK, representing about 7% of the population, and about half of them live in London (Katwala, 2001). Major minorities include: Indian, Pakistani, black Caribbean, black African, Bangladeshi and Chinese. Racial minorities are disproportionately concentrated in major cities and large metropolitan areas. Within a city, racial minorities tend to be segregated into impoverished neighborhoods or areas of low-quality housing due in part to discriminatory practices in housing markets and economic marginalization.

Notwithstanding spatial concentration and segregation, the majority of racial minorities live in mixed areas (Daley, 1998). As in US cities however, racial segregation and racial tensions are by no means trivial in UK cities. Inexorable racial segregation, combined with relentless social exclusion and deprivation, leads to racial conflict and racially motivated riots. During the summer of 2001, for example, clashes between white and South Asian youths swept through the northern towns and cities of England, including Bradford, Burnley and Oldham. These towns, once celebrated as examples of Victorian industrial affluence and pride, have been in economic decline for decades. The disappearance of large-scale employment from traditional industries and the consequent flight to the suburbs bordering on the countryside, create employment exclusion for Asian and Caribbean youths. This heady brew has thrown the remaining urban white population into the arms of atavistic racism and its political proponents.

There is a distinct division of gheottoization in the UK however, that reflects the regional imbalance. In London, racial concentration tends to occur in large public housing estates (projects), or where there is a dominance of owner occupation, in particular suburban towns (Southall and Wembley) that have large Asian populations. These areas co-exist alongside high levels of cosmopolitanism, underpinned by the affluence of urban professionals. The contrasts are stark. Affluent finance professionals in the Isle of Dogs (part of the old Docklands close to the financial district of the City of London) live in up-scale, gated communities while being surrounded by large post-World War I housing estates that are predominantly populated by working poor Bangaldeshis. The latter came in large numbers to London to occupy the bottom of the international division of labor of the garment industry in the East End of London. A UK government report of the late 1980s, at the time when the City of London was gaining global finance status, stated that Bangladeshis had poor levels of health and educational achievement and were likely to be the occupiers of the poorest public housing (Rhodes and Nabi, 1992).

Now with increasing effects of globalization and trans-national migration patterns, often occasioned by unstable geo-politics, other countries in Europe are increasingly experiencing both the influx of racially and ethnically diverse groups and their subsequent segregation in specific areas of the metro region. Existing third generations from Algeria and Morocco, born and bred in European cities, find themselves more and more marginalized and identified closely with the problems of newer immigrants. The recent banning in France of the *hijab*, the headscarf worn by Muslim women, is symptomatic of these tensions, but also points to the long history of France's relationship with its former colonies in North Africa. The problems that have emerged, such as the high level of youth-related crimes among Muslim immigrants in the public housing estates of the outer Paris region, are remarkably similar to the US experience, a record of racial segregation that was once considered unique.

REFERENCES

Cutler, D., E. Glaeser and J. Vigdor. 1997. *The Rise and Decline of the American Ghetto.* National Bureau of Economic Research, Working Paper 5881, Cambridge, MA.

Daley, P. 1998. 'Black African in Great Britain: Spatial Concentration and Segregation' *Urban Studies* 35: 1703–24.

Katwala, S. 2001. 'The Truth of Multi-Cultural Britain.' *The Observer*, 25 November. www.observer.co.uk/race/story, accessed 10 May 2003.

Massey, D. and N. Denton 1993. *American Apartheid.* Cambridge, MA: Harvard University Press.

Rhodes, C. and N. Nabi, 1992. 'Brick Lane: A Village Economy in the Shadow of the City?' in L. Budd and S. Whimster (eds) *Global Finance and Urban Living: A Study of Metropolitan Change.* London: Routledge.

Global Cities

The term, global city, refers to the select number of cities – e.g. NY, London, Tokyo – that serve as the command and control centers of the global economy. According to Saskia Sassen (1991), these urban places are characterized by a local economy based on financial and business services belonging to the multi-national banks and corporations that directly control the activities of the economy across the world. (See the entry on *Globalization.*)

The two phenomena – global city, globalization – are not necessarily related and most often imply two different processes. Hence it is necessary to use several entries to convey the information about the changes taking place in urban locations as a consequence of the economic restructuring of world capitalism.

It is true that the major global cities are so connected to each other through the organization of international finance that they are disconnected from their national contexts. Manhattan, the City of London and the business/Ginza district of Tokyo have more in common with each other than with other cities in their respective countries. It is also true that their local economies are equally susceptible to the cycles of growth and decline of that financial sector. Thus, while they prospered in the 1980s, they suffered a decline in the early 1990s that resulted in increased job loss, foreclosures on real estate, and substantial declines in corporate taxes that help float government spending. As late as the year 2003, Tokyo is still mired in the deflation caused by the bubble-bursting trauma of its real estate crash. Thus, these places are not all powerful and, in this sense, suffer the same in manner, if not degree, from their reliance on the global economy, as do other kinds of locations.

Furthermore, now there is a new trend away from the centralization of financial activities in specific cities altogether. And this is the consequence of the very same innovations in telecommunications that have made the global city possible in the first place. 'For example, the National Associated Automated Dealers Quotation System (NASDAQ) has emerged as the world's fourth largest stock market: unlike the New York, London or Tokyo exchanges, NASDAQ lacks a trading floor, connecting half a million traders worldwide through telephone and fiber optic lines. Similarly, Paris, Belgium, Spain, Vancouver and Toronto, all recently abolished their trading floors in favor of screen-based trading' (Warf, 1996). The new configuration is centered on stock exchanges demutualizing themselves by becoming private companies owned by stockholders that could locate anywhere.

Sassen's thesis aside, the fact that there remains an international hierarchy of financial centers is the result of the interaction of still powerful external economies of scale and scope and the role of real estate in investment bank balance sheets, not simple command and control functionality (Budd and Parr, 2000). There is also a distinct hierarchy of financial functions, with many lower order activities being digitized or de-centralized. London has seen significant decline in financial services employment in the last ten years, to be compensated by growth in business services as London takes on the appearance of a rentier rather than simply a global city. Gordon estimates that 60% of employment in the London economy is accounted for by local and national and not global market demand (Buck and Gordon, 2003). Hence, the thesis that financial trading activities require the same kind of face to face interaction that produced agglomerations in the central districts of 'global cities' may now be overrated.

The global city thesis was always simplistic in the case of many cities. The City of London has a long history of being a global economic center, well before the conditions mentioned by Sassen. Its shipping and insurance companies underwrote the trade of the British Empire and its first global company, the East India Trading Company, was established in 1600 (Porter, 1998). The new information economy, with its accelerating use of all types of electronic telecommunications, possesses counter tendencies of de-centralization as well as supporting the growth of new centers, including multi-centered regional growth (see entry on page 87). In addition, the example of NASDAQ shows that this same mode of information based on electronic means of communication produces virtual networks of agglomeration without the need for a specific physical location. The latter is truly a new way of directing the world's business in some instances alongside strategic alliances among financial services providers. National competitive trajectories and not global ones still appear to be the order of the day. Globalization is connected to modernity through the agency of the metropolis, but the leap of logic into a configuration of global cities is still conceptually and empirically suspect (Budd, 1995).

The proclamation of global cities contained a thesis about the effects that the agglomeration of command and control functions would have on the local labor force and consequently the structure of the local service and housing markets. This 'social polarization' thesis was also advanced by Saskia Sassen (1991). She claimed that the processes of economic change in specifically global cities leads to a growing polarization of occupational and income structures whereby there is an absolute growth at both the top and bottom ends of the distribution and a decline in the middle. According to Sassen, the 'global city' houses the command and control centers for multi-national corporations and finance capital so that its occupational structure is dominated by financial and business services. Global cities of this kind have experienced a decline in traditional manufacturing and growth of low skilled service jobs. Consequently, the labor force increasingly consists of highly paid professionals and low paid service workers. This translates into a skewed housing pattern where areas of the city are gentrified and have become affluent enclaves while the rest of the city is declining and houses the working poor. Thus, 'occupational polarization is accompanied by growing social, housing tenurial and ethnic segregation'.

Chris Hamnett (1994) observed that Sassen made these claims on the basis of the NY and LA cases, but that elsewhere it was not true. Later it was suspected that Sassen's thesis may have held solely because of its focus on individuals. At the lower end of the social stratification hierarchy however, it is the household unit as a whole, rather than the individual, that better expresses adjustments to the economy. If we consider household income and behavior, her thesis does not even ring

41

true for the cases of New York or Los Angeles. According to Hamnett, otherwise marginalized workers living in a household may pool resources and resort to the informal economy so as to maintain their standing in the middle. Furthermore, Sassen's claims for NY and LA may have only been substantiated 'because of their very high levels of immigration and the creation of large numbers of low skilled and low paid jobs' (Sassen, 1991).

Hamnett (1994) argues against Sassen's polarization thesis: 'There is a huge difference between asserting that changes are creating large numbers of low skilled and or low paid jobs and changes which lead to a larger proportion of low skilled jobs, but not necessarily large numbers', i.e., a shift rather than just absolute growth. 'This may be true of NY and LA but in most Western capitalist countries the numbers of semi-skilled and unskilled jobs have been steadily shrinking for the last 20–30 years' (Hamnett, 1994). While evidence can be found for some relative polarization, this is very different than saying that the changes are producing large numbers of low wage jobs. The latter is not true.

Hamnett says there is much evidence that with the rise of post-industrialism, the sector of employment that is expanding is the middle-class professionals and managers. Also, the presence of an increasing share of low wage jobs in great numbers is a consequence of the large influx of low skilled immigrants, especially those that are Hispanic, in both NY and LA. Thus, according to Hamnett, Sassen mistakenly generalized from these two cities to all global places, which is a fallacy.

Cities across the globe are certainly the sites of inequality and great disparities between the wealthy and the poor (see entries on *Inequality and Poverty*; *Ghetto and Racial Segregation*). It is extremely doubtful however, that the economic restructuring creating a centralization of financial services and banking headquarters that Sassen calls the 'Global City', produces this pattern. Almost 70 years ago, the Chicago School researchers observed the same kind of polarization in their city calling this contrast 'the Gold Coast and the Slum', while over 100 years ago, Friedrich Engels documented the disparities between extreme wealth and poverty produced by industrial capitalism on the cities of England (see entry on *Uneven Development*).

Sassen is correct when she observes that banking and finance tend to be located in the downtown sections of select cities, but it is difficult to say that this particular pattern is the supreme cause of other social effects on occupational structure and housing. Places like New York, Chicago and Los Angeles in the US, have benefited greatly from liberal immigration policies during the last few decades and there is more manufacturing in

42

these areas than people like Sassen care to admit. The Greater London economy (i.e., the region of London) still employs about 300,000 people directly in manufacturing. The different taxonomies of manufacturing and services has never made any sense. In late 1998, the UK national accounts changed the classification of software from a business expense to investment. Software is both a manufacture, with physical and virtual delivery, and a service. Such definitional problems of the information economy continue to hamper adequate analysis.

Beyond these points of critique, both Sassen and Hamnett make the same mistake characteristic of other urbanists that seek to discuss the phenomenon of globalization and its effects on cities. They conflate the region with the inner city itself. For a critique of this fallacy, see the entry on the *Multi-centered Metropolitan Region* (MMR). Hamnett, for example, states that for the purpose of his analysis, the 'small number of massive urban regions' that are the locations of the command and control functions for the global economy 'shall be called world cities'. Sassen is even cruder. She simply assumes that Manhattan can stand in for the entire New York City region which, in actuality encompasses parts of three states – New York, New Jersey and Connecticut – and a total population of over 20 million people, and, conflates the famous financial district of England, known as the City of London, with the actual sprawling and immense region of greater London. Because of this particular conceptual failure, analyses of the so-called 'global city' and its social effects are quite suspect. Unfortunately, many urbanists continue to make the same misleading mistake. Often what analysts refer to as 'New York', for example, on closer examination of data, turns out to be the borough of Manhattan alone.

Now these fallacies find themselves in policy documents. Policy for the London economy has been wrongly based on the 'golden goose' principle. This states that planning and tax policy should do nothing to discourage the laying of the global 'golden eggs' by the finance, insurance and real estate (FIRE) sectors of the service economy located predominantly within the City of London, i.e., the financial district. Yet the complexity of the Greater London economy, and the dual nature that has arisen from the extension of market relations into most aspects of its urban life are given short shrift. As one observer remarks in respect to the fallacy of policies based on globalization theory alone:

43

'For the last year London has had, once again, an elected assembly and a mayor charged with producing executive strategies . . . There is a grave risk that these plans may be grounded in a mistaken understanding of the London situation and thus fail to achieve for its citizens, the egalitarian aspirations which the mayor and senior politicians espouse.' (Edwards, 2002: 26)

Thus, it is much more critical to study multi-centered metropolitan regions with regard to changes in social, cultural and economic factors on their own terms, rather than see all development emanating from some higher realms postulated by globalization theory.

REFERENCES

Buck, N. and Gordon, I. 2003 *Working Capital*. Oxford: Blackwell.
Budd, L. 1995 'Globalisation, Territory and Strategic Alliances in Different Financial Centres' *Urban Studies* (32)2 (March).
Edwards, M. 2002. 'Wealth Creation and Poverty Creation' *City* 6(1): 91–100.
Hamnett, C. 1994. 'Social Polarization in Global Cities: Theory and Evidence' *Urban Studies* 31(3): (April).
Sassen, S. 1991. *The Global City*. Princeton, NJ: Princeton University Press.

Globalization

44

Globalization refers to the increased interdependence of the world's economies shown by the circulation of information, money, people and goods across national boundaries. It is characterized by a process of decline in national ownership of major corporations to the benefit of a select number of 'transnational corporations' that operate without consideration for the implications of their decisions to specific places across the globe.

During the recent period that gave rise to the domination of the world's business by these transnational corporations, the kind of electronic transfers of money made possible by finance capital discussed in the case of the global city (see previous entry) became critically important. The globalization of portfolio investment (stocks, bonds and derivatives) has facilitated the growth of Foreign Direct Investment (FDI), one of the major drivers of the internationalization of economic activities in the last 30 years. Increased capital mobility brought about changes in the geographic organization of manufacturing production and in the network of financial markets. In particular, it made it possible for transnational corporations to seek out distant locations around the world that supplied labor for manufacturing at the lowest possible price. This 'labor sourcing' resulted, most especially, in the persisting production of cheap consumer products. Factory after factory closed in the advanced industrial countries while new plants were constructed supplying everything from steel to sneakers in places like Vietnam, the Dominican Republic and Malaysia. It is this pattern of de-industrialization, on the one hand, and exploitation of new sources of labor power, on the other, that is characteristic of 'globalization'.

Consumers in the advanced western countries, like the US or the UK, can experience this one dimension of globalization with a visit to a retailing establishment, such as a clothing store in the mall shopping center. The labels on clothing declare their origin in the low paid factories of Bangladesh, Mexico, Malaysia and the Dominican Republic. The items of clothing are all the same, only their country of origin and the sweatshops in which they were manufactured differs. In the same department store, it is also possible to acquire an appreciation for this scale of globalization at the electronics counter. Asian countries, especially China, dominate as manufacturers of goods. Consumers know nothing of the conditions under which these TV sets and stereos were made, but they do respond to their comparatively cheap prices. Aspects of globalization are also covered in entries on the *Global City; Uneven Development*; the *Socio-spatial Approach* and *Urbanization and Urbanism*, so they will not be repeated here.

Globalization, however, involves much more than the flight of manufacturing abroad. As we have mentioned, it has also been realized by the growth, scope and incredible efficiency of financial capital. Using the latest electronic means of communication in a wired-up planet, the shifting of money from one investment to another is carried out on a global scale. Much of these flows consist of transfers between different investment and commercial banks around the globe. Increased capital mobility also generated a demand for types of production needed to ensure the management, control and servicing of this new organization of manufacturing and finance. These new types of production range from the development of telecommunications to specialized services that are key inputs for the management of a global network of factories, offices and financial markets. For these reasons, the concepts of globalization and the global city are related, although it is only the social, occupational and cultural effects of the former that are acknowledged without reservation. Furthermore, according to the French economic and social theorist, Robert Boyer, although internationalization is going through a new phase, globalization is not complete and still mainly relates to finance

(Boyer, 2000). Hence, understanding the limits of what the term 'globalization' refers to remains important today.

According to Sassen (1994), there is an effect of globalization on the cities of the advanced capitalist countries that is both social and economic. In the entry on the *Global City* above we discussed the alleged social consequences of increasing polarization and found little evidence to support Sassen's view. In contrast, however, the economic consequences of globalization are well known and acknowledged. In fact, these effects are so well documented that their study predates Sassen's work as they involve the process of de-industrialization that has afflicted the advanced countries since the 1960s (see entry on *Uneven Development* for more discussion).

In the case of the UK, many of the economic effects noted by Sassen were, in fact, seen as long ago as the 17th Century, as production of manufactures switched from home to colonial sites financed by the merchant banks of the City of London (Kynaston, 1994). Still, Sassen has summarized these effects in a useful way. As she notes, due to de-industrialization and the transfer of most manufacturing jobs to countries that were formerly on the periphery and presently possess labor forces that earn a comparatively low wage, cities that were once leading manufacturing centers are now in decline. In the advanced countries, only those places have prospered that remain command and control sites for finance capital and help to coordinate the rapid exchange of capital. Thus, for example:

> 'Paris now concentrates a larger share of leading economic sectors and wealth in France than it did 20 years ago, whereas Marseilles, once a major economic center, has lost its share and is suffering severe decline.' (Sassen, 1994: 5)

Sassen argues that global investment has followed this shift and flowed into the real estate sectors of the select few global cities, thereby creating a boom in the price of housing geared towards highly-paid urban professionals. Through renovation, gentrification and new construction, the landscape of the global city has been transformed by this investment, with the old housing stock and even the old districts of the city disappearing under this speculative onslaught.

> 'We can see the same effect in the retreat of many real estate developers from the low- and medium-income housing market who are attracted to the rapidly expanding housing demand by the new highly-paid professionals and the possibility for vast overpricing of this housing supply . . . The rapid development of an international property market has made this disparity even worse. It means that real estate prices at the center of NYC

are more connected to prices in London or Frankfurt than to the overall real estate market in the city. The high profit-making capability of the new growth sectors rests partly on speculative activity.' (Sassen, 1994: 6)

However, there are significant differences between nations. The housing market in the UK for example, is affected principally by local factors such as location and transportation advantages, rather than global effects. Thus, the whole of South-East England which is the wealthiest part of the UK where the concentration of business and financial services is historically heaviest, also displays the highest housing costs. The factors driving these costs are national and regional not global.

According to Sassen, globalization also involves a different kind of economic activity than in the past. It is her remarks about this activity that are most instructive for the understanding of the current world economy and its effects on place:

'When international flows consist of raw materials, agricultural products, or mining goods, the geography of transactions is in part determined by the location of natural resources. Historically, this has meant that a large number of countries in Africa, Latin America, and the Caribbean were key sites in this geography.' (1994: 10)

Now the manufacturing sites that are most important are the ones offering cheap labor rather than resources, per se, with the exception of commodity markets, where transportation costs are still crucial. Places around the world that can control their workers, that do not have unions, that can absorb the environmental costs of unregulated manufacturing and can sustain people on limited wages, have become the key sites of production for the global economy. These facts do not sit well with the organized labor of the advanced industrial societies and there is a new tension between workers and capitalists that has been transferred to a global scale.

Furthermore, while manufacturing has certainly shifted to formerly peripheral locations, the ownership of capital has remained largely the same and centralized within the sector of the advanced industrial countries as it has always been since the advent of capitalism. Speaking about capital flows into less developed countries from the nations of the First World, or Foreign Direct Investment, Sassen (1994) notes that 'by the mid-1980s, 75% of all FDI stock and 84% of FDI stock in services was in developed countries'. Thus, little has changed under globalization conditions of production in terms of the world division of wealth. 90% of the world's income and wealth is still located in three main areas: North America, the European Union and East Asia. Similarly the bulk of

47

telephone, internet and airline traffic flows are between these three areas (Budd and Clear, 2001).

Finally, because formerly manufacturing cities in the developed countries have all experienced de-industrialization and consequent decline, it is presently necessary for them to find ways to revive the local economy. Many cities have found this a difficult task under current conditions of freely flowing capital. Investment that may pour into a location one day seems easily abandoned for competing places the next. Factories are either built or refurbished by corporations only to be shut down as their owners are bought out by other sources of capital. Locations with manufacturing that have sought to impose normative environmental regulations are told to forget such initiatives or run the risk of chasing capital away to other places. In short, the previous decades of globalization have witnessed some successes but also many hard luck stories about places abandoned by capital investment.

In sum, for many cities experiencing globalization in the form of the flight of capital and the consequent necessity of attracting new investment under present conditions of easy capital mobility, there is a pressing need to re-invent the viability of their location. Activities such as tourism and the expansion of cultural or sport offerings have taken the place, in many urban areas, of traditional manufacturing. Currently, central city locations in the US, under the persisting grip of decline and spatial competition with places elsewhere, continue to search for strategies to attract capital.

In the European context, many places that are not considered major global cities nevertheless have become quite successful at rejuvenation in recent years as new forms of economic activity and accompanying social and cultural capital locate there. Marseilles, for example, has re-invented itself as one of the most attractive locations in France, taking advantage of its port status and seaside location. The richest city in Europe is Hamburg, while it is Berlin and Frankfurt that are most often mentioned as *the* global cities of Germany (European Commission, 2003). Once a thriving port and shipbuilding center, Hamburg is now the largest trans-shipment center for goods in Europe, based on providing shipping, insurance and logistics services. Hamburg is also one of the main production sites of the European aircraft manufacturer, Airbus, that in 2003 overtook Boeing as the world's largest seller of civil aircraft. Its stock exchange only accounts for about 2% of the total German turnover and so it can hardly claim global city status, but Hamburg still remains Europe's richest city on an income per head basis.

Such differences among cities make spatial competition even more

48

intense. At the same time, organized labor continues its search for ways to tame the flighty aspect of international capital and the lack of attachment to any given place of the transnational corporations. However, this is nothing new as David Harvey makes clear:

> 'If, therefore, "globalization" signifies anything about our recent historical geography, it is most likely to be a new phase of exactly this same underlying process of capitalist production of space'. (2000: 54)

Globalization, in short, remains a period of capitalist development, as observed by Harvey, and, according to Boyer, one that is in a state of flux. Consequently, it is also a process that keeps individual locations in a state of flux as well. However, it is not, as some have argued, an entirely new and definitive phase of Capitalism.

REFERENCES

Boyer, R. 2000. 'Politics in an ear of globalization: a regulationist view' *International Journal of Urban and Regional Research* 24(2): 274–322.

Budd, L. and F. Clear, 2001. 'The Business Environment for eCommerce' in L. Harris, P. Jackson and P. Eckersley (eds) *eBusiness Stuctures*. London: Routledge. pp. 1–25.

European Commission, 2003. *Cohesion Report*. Luxembourg: European Commission.

Harvey, D. 2000. *Spaces of Hope*. Edinburgh: Edinburgh University Press.

Kynaston, D. 1994. *The City of London: A World of its Own, 1815–1890*. London: Pimlico.

Sassen, S. 1991. *The Global City*. Princeton, NJ: Princeton University Press.

Sassen, S. 1994. *Cities in a World Economy*. Thousand Oaks, CA: Pine Forge Press.

Homelessness

The homeless are those who cannot afford shelter by themselves. With no access to housing, they sleep outside or in public spaces such as streets, doorways, parks and subways. It is not uncommon to find the homeless sleeping in old automobiles, perhaps their only major possession left after losing a home (see entries on *Housing; Real Estate* for more explanation of housing markets).

Although there is generally a sharp distinction in regard to the availability and quality of housing among cities in the developed and developing countries, the problem of homelessness is a growing concern in advanced industrial societies. In the early 1990s, several observers pointed to the presence of apparently homeless people sitting on the city streets in the US, although the exact number of people could not be counted. One observer suggested that during the decade of the 1990s there were more people homeless than at any other time since the Great Depression of the 1930s (Blau, 1992). Another estimated that on any given night as many as 350,000 people in the US were without shelter (Peroff, 1987). In addition, it has been noted that squatting as well as homelessness has become increasingly more common in the cities of Europe as well as the US (Adams, 1986).

Homelessness is a growing phenomenon in Europe within countries that once possessed ambitious, publicly supported housing programs. In a 1995 report, the European Observatory on Homelessness estimated that there were two million homeless people in the countries of Western Europe. This figure included nearly half a million homeless people in the UK, the second largest figure followed by France with a third of a million. Germany had the most extensive figures among member states, with an estimate of over 800,000 homeless people. The extent of homelessness varied from country to country in Europe for various reasons including national economic situations, housing market conditions, real estate speculation and welfare policies. The impacts of the fall of communism and the rise of internationally determined and flexible labor markets have also been a common experience in Europe, resulting in increased homelessness.

Just as in the US, the problem of homelessness has worsened in the UK since the 1980s. In England for example, the number of households applying to local authorities for homeless assistance has increased from 102,650 during 1997/8 to 114,340 during 2000/1. As elsewhere, such figures underestimate the scale of the homeless problem, because young single people and childless couples are not accepted by the local authority as in 'priority need' although they have nowhere to go. For this reason, the young homeless are increasingly visible in British cities (Smith, 1999). In addition, the official figure excludes the 'hidden homeless' living in temporary accommodation. *Crisis*, the homeless charity in the UK, estimates that there are still some 400,000 people stuck in temporary housing. There is also an increasing ethnic and gender dimension to homelessness in the UK (*The Guardian*, 18 June 2004). Furthermore. the growing disparity between the urban rich and the urban poor is having an impact on homelessness in rural areas, as a recent *Countryside Agency* report notes (2004). The buying of second homes by urban professionals is pushing up the prices in rural areas, thereby excluding housing opportunities for the locally embedded population and affecting local rental markets (Countryside Agency, 2004).

In the many large cities of the less developed countries, lack of adequate and affordable housing is quite common, and the scale of urban homelessness, when compared to the developed countries, is enormous. The number of the homeless around the world is estimated from 100 million to 1 billion, depending on its definition (UNCHS, 1996: 229, 2001: 197). The lower bound 100 million counts only those who have no shelter at all (i.e., houseless), and the upper bound 1 billion includes those who are dwelling in substandard, insecure or temporary shelters without provision for the most basic services such as safe water, sanitation and drainage. Homelessness, measured either way, is a global problem, although the cold statistic itself does not accurately reveal the devastating condition of homelessness. For the many urban poor, sleeping in public buildings, parks or other public spaces may be a part of their daily routine.

In India for instance, the homeless are seen virtually everywhere: on pavements, in parks and unused water pipes, and under bridges. Some of them are lucky enough to be accommodated in night shelters provided by local governments, non-governmental organizations, or other social institutions. Persons or households under these two circumstances – sleeping rough and sleeping in night shelters – are highly visible and often stigmatized as criminals or dangerous at best. Migrants that have arrived recently in cities often double up with relatives and friends thereby disguising their lack of accommodation. A large number of the concealed homeless consist also of women and children who have run away from domestic violence and sexual abuse.

Most often the homeless population in both developing and developed countries consists of the unemployed, migrants, substance abusers, mentally ill people, racial and ethnic minorities, battered women, runaway youths and street children. However, some of the homeless sleeping in public buildings or open spaces have sufficient income to rent a room or bed. Others have homes in rural areas, but they move to cities for work temporarily during the slack season on the farm. They choose to sleep rough or in night shelters to maximize savings. Whereas the demographic profiles of the homeless are distinct, structural forces, rather than those demographic characteristics, are underpinning the problem of homelessness. In the largest cities the supply of affordable housing has fallen short of the demand due to speculation and the upward trend of real estate costs as a consequence of globalization. The issue of homelessness is increasingly a global one whose geopolitical consequences are not well understood outside developing countries. In China, the current global growth star, unofficial populations (those not officially registered) almost match that of the official populations in the largest cities. In Shanghai, one of the richest cities, the official population was about 8 million in 2003 out of a total of 15 million. Yet, the authorities in Shanghai announced planning for a multi-centered region with an official population of 15 million by 2020. Whether this new development is sustainable will depend on the scale of inflow of the landless poor attracted to the opportunities of the city that are currently in numbers larger than officials will admit (Safier, 2001).

Briefly, then, homelessness in the US and some European countries, such as the UK and those of the former Soviet Republic, is largely the consequence of welfare state restructuring and public assistance cuts. In developing countries, the constant influx of migrants funneling into urban areas where there is neither a supply of 'official' shelter nor full-time jobs creates both homelessness and shanty towns (see entry on *Slums and Shanty Towns*). Under these conditions and without any improvements in the global economy, the presence of the homeless will persist in urban areas around the world.

REFERENCES

Adams, C. 1986. 'Homeless in the Postindustrial City: Views from London and Philadelphia' *Urban Affairs Quarterly*, 21: 527–49.

Blau, J. 1992. *The Visible Poor: Homelessness in the United States*. NY: Oxford University Press.

Countryside Agency, 2004. *The State of the Countryside 2004*. Wetherby: Countryside Agency Publications.

The Guardian, 2004. 'When a House is not a Home' London: Guardian Newspapers. 18 June. http://society.guardian.co.uk/homelessness/story/0,8150,1243937,00.html accessed 22 June 2004.

Peroff, K. 1987. 'Who Are the Homeless and How Many Are There?' in R. Bingham, R. Green and S. White (eds) *The Homeless in Contemporary Society*. Beverly Hills, CA: Sage Publications. pp. 33–45.

Safier, M. 2001. 'Transforming Shanghai: Landscapes of the Turbo-Dynamic Development in China's "World City"' *City* 5(1) (April).

Smith, J. 1999. 'Youth Homeless in the UK: A European Perspective' *Habitat International*, 24: 63–77.

United Nations Center for Human Settlements (UNCHS), 1996. *An Urbanizing World*. Oxford, UK: Oxford University Press.

United Nations Center for Human Settlements (UNCHS), 2001. *Cities in a Globalizing World*. London, UK: Earthscan.

Housing

The resource, housing, is commodified and allocated by real estate markets in capitalist societies (see entry on *Real Estate*). There is a market for rental, private home and commercial real estate. Under capitalism, the type and quality of housing that can be acquired depends, like any other commodity, on the ability of the purchaser to pay the market determined cost of shelter. As with all consumer purchases, there are also loan-granting institutions available that will aid in the acquisition of goods by providing money in return for interest. In the case of private housing in the US however, the institutional framework for the provision of loans, or mortgages, is quite complicated and is regulated by the government, in addition to the usual regulation of the banking industry as a whole. Yet, the fundamental restraints remain – you live in a house and in a location that you can afford, whether you own or rent (called type of housing *tenure*). There is one difference between the arrangements in the US and other capitalist countries: Americans are subsidized in the purchase of single family homes, because the federal government allows them to make a pre-tax deduction of all interest paid on their mortgage. For this reason, renters are automatically discriminated against because no such comparable provision is available for their tax relief.

In the UK, the housing environment is similarly complicated, but the burning issues of accessibility and affordability remain, as elsewhere. Social housing is the main provider of non-owner occupation in the UK. New public housing is negligible and most public housing is being transferred from local authorities to the social housing agencies. The UK housing stock in 1982 consisted of 58% owner-occupation; 10.8% private rented; 2.2% social housing; and 29% public housing. In 2002, the respective figures were 69.8%; 9.7%; 6.6%; and 13.8% (www.odpm.gov.uk).

The owner-occupied segment of the housing market is both a source of economic growth and economic instability in the UK as the Organization for Economic Co-Operation and Development has recently noted (2004). Average house prices are 5.2 times the average earnings at present, compared to the long-term average of around 3.5. Owner-occupiers exploit their housing wealth in the UK through borrowing against the difference in their current house price and the amount of mortgage debt, called equity in the US. This has been an important source of sustaining high consumption levels, particularly in the South-East of

England (the wealthiest part of the UK). A recent report, carried out on behalf of the Treasury (the Finance Ministry) noted that the UK has experienced a long-term upward trend in real house prices, 2.4% per annum over the last 30 years. This has created problems of affordability. In order to deliver a trend in real house prices of 1.8%, an additional 70,000 houses each year in England might be required. To bring the real price trend in line with the EU average of 1.1% an extra 120,000 houses each year would be needed (HM Treasury, 2004). Despite the scrapping of tax relief on mortgage debt in the early 1990s, house prices in the UK continue to rise and housing remains the dominant form of personal wealth in the UK.

Because the value of urban land is determined by its location and not its intrinsic worth as a resource, the dependency on the type and placement of housing on ability to pay, whether subsidized by a loan or not, leads directly to spatial inequality in the distribution of people within metropolitan areas (see entries on *Inequality*; *Ghetto and Racial Segregation*). Distinctions produced by the real estate market are more complex than a simple contrast between the more or less affluent. Considerable variation in the prices for shelter results in a rather fine grained filtering process of people throughout the metropolitan region. Due to the practices of developers in suburban residential areas, for example, single family homes are clustered according to prices that may differ by only as much as $20,000. A family searching for a home that they can afford in the $200,000 price range, for example, may not be able to purchase one in a section of suburbia where homes start at $220,000 and up. Clustering is also produced by the rental market. In any given building or apartment complex, the rents are confined to a narrow range. Those that cannot bear the price in one location must search in other places until they find a cluster with available units that they can afford. In sum, the private real estate market under capitalism allocates housing according to the ability to pay, but construction and development practices cluster like-priced units so that this same mechanism leads to region-wide segregation of individuals by income (there are also racial biases that operate, see below). This clustering is not a separate aspect of location but is an intrinsic feature of the residential real estate market in the US.

REDLINING AND STEERING

These are the two most common discriminatory practices in the US. Redlining is the process by which financial institutional actors (banks, insurance companies) withhold access to resources such as mortgages and insurance policies from specific geographical areas. Mostly the poor and minorities suffer. In the UK, this term would refer to the postcode lottery which also affects education and health provision. Financial institutions track house prices by postcode and supply different levels of financing according to postcode area.

Steering is the practice by real estate agents of shunting prospective customers that are minority or poor to specific areas away from other opportunities in white and/or relatively more affluent neighborhoods. Similarly, real estate agents will market certain locations to families because of the premium paid to be situated within the catchment areas of better performing (usually middle-class) schools.

HOUSING AFFORDABILITY

People may acquire quality housing but, often, they really cannot afford it because the financial burden consumes an excessive amount of their personal income. According to guidelines from the federal government's Department of Housing and Urban Development, a housing cost burden is defined as paying more than 30% of monthly income, regardless of tenure (i.e., rental or owner-occupied). By this measure, over 28% of all US households were cost burdened at the time of the 1990 census, a figure of disturbing magnitude ('Housing Problems', www.ruralhome.org). In many urban areas, renters were disproportionately represented among those paying excessive costs for shelter. Results of this kind indicate another dimension of *uneven development* (see entry on page 165). Providing an adequate supply of affordable housing is clearly a problem in the US, as is the case in the UK. The clearest indicator of this problem, and the uneven development it personifies, is in the presence of homeless populations within metropolitan areas (see entry on *Homelessness* above).

HOUSING AND SEGREGATION

There is a dual housing market for those who can and who can't afford housing and for those who are white and those who are not.

Discrimination in housing occurs through the failure of banks to approve loans and the steering of real estate agents to specific areas or away from specific areas, and so on.

Rental units have their own aspects of discrimination, such as the behavior of landlords in refusing to rent to prospective tenants because of racial or other reasons. In the UK, social housing is subject to good tenancy agreements with the threat of eviction if these are breached. The conditions laid out in these agreements are often onerous and have more to do with social control of poorer families and individuals. Similarly, local authorities in the UK have introduced anti-social behavior orders (ASBOs) for public housing tenants. Dysfunctional families and single-parent families (the UK has the highest rate of teenage pregnancies in Europe) are excluded from housing rather than having their health and behavioral problems addressed by appropriate support agencies. There has been a perceptible shift in housing policy in the UK in the last 20 years. Housing wealth is also strongly related to greater life expectancy. Recent research in the UK exposes the following:

- the homeless have death rates which are 25 times greater than the national average;
- residents in temporary accommodation (cheap hotels that only offer bed and breakfast) have four to five times the death rate of those in housing;
- death rates for hostel residents are seven times greater;
- death rates for those sleeping on the streets are 25 times greater.

People in households who have over £100,000 ($285,000 at the time of writing) of housing equity (the difference between the current value and the amount of mortgage debt) are likely to have, on average, more than twice the life expectancy of those sleeping rough on the streets (Dorling, 2003). Housing is now a privilege not a right in almost every country, even those that once had ambitious public housing programs and a national commitment to providing adequate housing for all families (see entry on *Housing*).

HOUSING QUALITY

In addition to the issues of affordability and spatial segregation, housing can be a problem when it is not maintained or is deteriorating. Substandard housing is defined by the federal government's Department of Housing and Urban Development according to the kind of physical and structural deficiencies present ('Substandard Housing Defined', www.rental-housing.com). Inadequate shelter: may lack hot or cold water or a flush toilet, or both a bathtub and a shower; it may have heating equipment that is broken, or that has broken down at least three times for six hours or more during the previous winter; it may have no electricity, or has exposed wiring and a room with no working outlet, or, has had three blown fuses or tripped circuit breakers in a period of 90 days; it may have no working light fixtures in public areas, such as hallways and staircases, have loose or missing steps, a broken elevator or missing railings; or it may have at least five basic maintenance problems, such as water leaks, holes in the floors or ceilings, peeling paint or broken plaster, or evidence of rats, which haven't been fixed after 90 days.

A residential housing unit may be classified as 'moderate' substandard if it has one or more of the following: problems with repeated breaking of flush toilets; unvented gas, oil or kerosene heaters as the primary heating equipment; lacking a sink, refrigerator or an oven (although microwaves are now allowed); hallway problems listed above; maintenance problems listed above.

Problematic rental housing is regulated by the US federal government Department of Housing and Urban Development (HUD), which can levy fines, and is monitored by the US Census of Housing. According to one survey conducted in NYC in 1998, for example, the census found that over 20% of all rental units in the Borough of the Bronx, over 15% in Brooklyn and over 16% in Manhattan, were substandard. This is a high percentage for a 'global city' and shows clearly the quality of *uneven development* discussed elsewhere. The figures were also high compared to one of the poorest rural areas in the US, the Appalachian Region of Kentucky and West Virginia, which had over 10% substandard units in 1990 ('Housing Problems', www.ruralhome.org).

HOUSING QUALITY AND THE SLUM

See entry on the *Slums and Shanty Towns*.

According to HUD, 'The most widely used definitions of housing adequacy are based on evaluations of individual homes. But housing quality is strongly influenced by the physical and social context of the surrounding area in which the home is located. Extensive aggregation of substandard and/or informal home construction is called a slum.'

HOUSING IN DEVELOPING COUNTRIES

Urban space is highly differentiated by the quantitative and qualitative dimensions of housing conditions, such as size, location, extent of provision for basic services and accessibility. Accessibility to adequate housing is a critical issue for the urban poor. In most rapidly growing cities of the developing countries, housing is a critical problem precisely because there are too few units. In Brazil, with about 36 million households in 1991 for example, the shortage reached almost 6 million; among the existing dwellings, over 10 million units needed to be repaired. Developing countries are estimated to need 21 million housing units every year for this decade (2000–10), and the figure will increase to 25 million for the following decade (2010–20) to accommodate additional urban households (UNCHS, 1999). As elsewhere, the more rapidly growing cities tend to have a higher proportion of housing shortages.

The problem of housing is not confined to the absolute number of housing deficits. A more serious problem is the quality of existing and new housing units such as substandard housing and overcrowding. In the developing countries, a very high proportion of the urban housing stock is substandard, being built on illegally occupied land with temporary materials, no authorization, and no access to basic infrastructure and services. About a quarter of the urban housing stock in the developing countries has temporary structures, more than a third of urban housing units have been constructed without compliance with local regulations, and 13% of urban dwellers in the developing countries are cramped in areas without access to safe water, and 25% without access to adequate sanitation (UNCHS, 1999). Overcrowding is another indicator of the quality of housing. When measured by floor area per person, urban dwellers in low-income countries occupy only a sixth of the average living space in high-income countries (UNCHS, 2001, 199). The severity of housing problems in growing cities of the developing world can be illustrated by the 'hotbed' system in Calcutta, India, where two or three tenants rent the same bed in a room to use in turn over a 24-hour period (UNCHS, 1996, 217).

Given these housing conditions, informal or illegal housing is not unusual in most cities of the developing countries. For households on limited income, the possibility of owner-occupation is diminishing and informal housing including illegal subdivisions and sharing becomes an important source of affordable, if not adequate, accommodation. By relying on informal housing, the urban poor may minimize costs and maximize income. Illegal subdivisions are the main source of housing supply for the urban poor in many cities of the developing world, along with housing built in squatter settlements (see entry on *Slums and Shanty Towns*). Sharing is another type of informal housing. Recent migrants arriving in a city with the help of family members, relatives or friends tend to rely on migration networks for initial accommodation and job information (see entry on *Homelessness*). The recent migrants and urban poor settle in non-standard, poor-quality housing usually nestled on the urban periphery where public utilities and infrastructure are typically not serviced (Peattie and Aldrete-Haas, 1981). Informal settlements are not the same as squatter settlements. Although all people living in illegal settlements are commonly labeled as squatters, most are not squatters because they occupy the land with permission or implicit approval of the landowner. Unlike squatters, informal residents are not usually threatened with eviction.

PUBLIC HOUSING

Despite the presence of a private real estate market, housing can also be supplied by government sponsored programs at all levels of society from the local to the national. Using public funds, these can support the construction and or subsidy of rental housing based on economic need. In addition, subsidized housing can be constructed and run not only by government but also by unions, coops and housing associations. But government sponsored public housing is never for profit. In the UK, in the 1950s and 1960s, the construction industry was known as the regulator of the economy. If the construction grew at 2% per year, so would the economy. When there was a downturn in privately funded activity, publicly funded programs, especially housing, would fill the order books of construction firms. In this way, public housing was supported in the UK and, in turn, so was the private sector. Since the 1980s, with the decline of the welfare state in the UK, public investment in housing has been drastically cut.

Around the world countries differ greatly with regard to both the extent of units provided and the success of their public housing programs. In the advanced economies, the provision of public housing is no longer a political imperative. The growth of private housing and real estate holdings at the expense of public housing and underwritten by private finance, re-asserts the role of capitalism in the exploitation of land rents, as Adam Smith, David Ricardo and Karl Marx noted two and three centuries ago, and heralds the disappearance of the welfare state.

REFERENCES

Dorling, D. 2003. 'Housing Wealth and Community Health: Explanations for the Spatial Polarisation of Life Chances in Britain.' http://www.lancs.ac.uk/fss/apsocsci/hvp/projects/dorling.htm accessed 15 June 2004.

H.M. Treasury, 2004. 'Delivering Stability: Securing our Future Housing Needs' London: Stationery Office.

'Housing Associations' www.odpm.gov.uk.

Peattie, L. and J. Aldrete-Haas, 1981. 'Marginal Settlements in Developing Countries' *Annual Review of Sociology* 7: 157–75.

'Housing Problems', www.ruralhome.org, accessed 25 June 2003.

'Substandard Housing Defined', www.rental-housing.com/rental/substandard.htm accessed 25 June 2003.

United Nations Center for Human Settlements (UNCHS), 1996. *An Urbanizing World*. Oxford, UK: Oxford University Press.

United Nations Center for Human Settlements (UNCHS), 1999. *Basic Facts on Urbanization*. Nairobi, Kenya: UNCHS Habitat.

United Nations Center for Human Settlements (UNCHS), 2001. *Cities in a Globalizing World*. London, UK: Earthscan.

Immigration and Migration

Urban spaces have always grown and been sustained by the constant influx of new people. Historically, cities developed as people who were tied to a prosperous agricultural economy found they could sustain themselves by other means, most commonly associated with a permanent market place. As these market locations grew, so too did they attract increasingly more people from the surrounding agricultural land. This type of population shift would be considered 'migration' today, because it consists of a movement of people *within* national boundaries. 'Immigration', in contrast, refers to the movement of people *across* national boundaries. In many ways the processes of migration and immigration constitutes the very lifeblood of cities, suburbs and in general, metro regions in countries around the world.

Our task in this book has been to help define concepts in order to avoid terminological confusion. Nowhere is this need more evident than in the proliferation and confusion of terms produced by the new cultural studies discourse on immigration. Most writers, however, seem to embrace each new term thereby avoiding any need for specificity. Recently, for example, a number of writers have reconceptualized the phenomenon of immigration through the discourse of cultural studies and by introducing a number of neologisms and/or other terms that were used in the past in different contexts, such as hybridity, diaspora, transnational ethnicities and transculturation. Concise meanings have given way to semiotic confusion and jargon in much of this work (Clifford, 1997: 245). To cite one case, the concept of 'diaspora' originally referred to the forceful scattering of the Jews from the Kingdom of Judea by the Romans throughout their empire after the last of three Jewish Wars (around 80 CE). The political, punitive and forceful dimensions of the term are stripped clean by current writers that use it to refer to any ethnic group that is currently dispersed in a number of different countries as the consequence of a variety of factors over a relatively long period of time. The neologism, 'transnational', is another confusing term. Why it is used instead of the more traditional or specific concepts such as immigrant, guest worker, undocumented alien and the like, is hard to say. The concepts of de- and re-territorialization and those dealing with the different types of migrants and immigrants are clearer and much preferred, at least by the present authors. For the former, see entry on page 19.

At present there are different kinds of immigrants.

LABORERS

In Europe, gaps in the availability of domestic laborers compelled countries to make arrangements for workers to be allowed to leave their home nations on a 'temporary basis', at least in theory, and reside in the host country as a 'guest' without citizenship. This guest worker system was used by Germany extensively in the 1970s and 80s to import hundreds of thousands of male laborers along with their families principally from Turkey. In the UK, immigration from the British Empire and the Commonwealth has been a constant feature since the late 16th Century. In the immediate post-World War II period, immigration from the new Commonweath (Indian sub-Continent and the Caribbean) has accelerated as the 'mother country' cried out to fill jobs that the indigenous population deemed beneath them. Most of these immigrants settled in London and its suburbs or in other cities where labor shortages in particular sectors were acute, for example textiles. There has been successive waves of immigrants in the East of London ranging from French Hugenots escaping the revolutionary terror in the 18th Century to Jews escaping the pogroms in Central and Eastern Europe in 19th Century, followed by Bangladeshis in the mid-20th Century who were recruited for the bottom of the economic pile of an international division of labor in the garment trade (see entry on *Global Cities*).

In the US, guest worker arrangements have been made with Mexico and some Caribbean countries, such as the Dominican Republic and Puerto Rico. Large numbers of Hispanics now reside in the US as a consequence of labor needs.

Despite their alleged temporary status, guest workers have had a profound impact on European countries. The once relatively homogeneous Germans, and it is not unfair to bring up the nightmare of racial purity murders during the Holocaust by this country, now live in a multicultural society that is part Muslim with ethnic differences that are quite stark. This is especially so for cities like Berlin, Frankfurt and Hamburg that all have their large Turkish sections. The fear of growing Muslim political power in parts of Europe is not exaggerated. Most of these countries do not have a long history of tolerating ethnic minorities. Cities in the US as far north as Minneapolis and Chicago have significant Mexican communities due to the far ranging extent of agricultural businesses and their need for non-unionized, cheap workers. Hispanics currently comprise a powerful and growing voter base, although their interests remain split among constituencies, different countries of origin and party affiliations.

TRADITIONAL IMMIGRANTS

These are people who have applied for permanent entry into other nations. Often they have limited resources and so they are dependent on friends and relatives in the destination country for aid. Usually, it is these very connections that determine the success of the legal process, for without them the potential immigrant cannot be sponsored. As a result, ethnic communities in host countries continue to grow as the stock of first generation immigrants persists in being replenished by new arrivals over time. The diverse ethnic areas in US cities have kept making their mark on the urban terrain in this way.

62

PROFESSIONAL AND MIDDLE-CLASS ECONOMIC IMMIGRANTS

From the late 1970s to the present, the US and many European countries have allowed significant immigration from places elsewhere for people with advanced skills. Recently, these professional and middle-class immigrants have eclipsed traditional ones. For example, in the US at the time of the 1970 census, US-born Asians constituted about two-thirds of the Asian American population. A short time later, by the 1980 census, the ratio had been reversed as Asians from abroad comprised over 70% of the total Asian American population. More striking has been the change in the composition of this group for the US case. Increasingly after 1970, significant immigration was experienced from India, Pakistan, Hong Kong and South Korea, rather than China or Taiwan and Japan, as was the case in the past.

Michael Ames observes the following, which is typical of the experience of many city-dwellers in the 1990s:

'In Vancouver, where I live, English is now a minority language among the home languages of school children, 44.5% compared to 31.6% who speak a Chinese language in their homes, followed by Vietnamese, Punjabi, Spanish and Hindi. In fact, I believe that Cantonese is now the second most frequently spoken language in British Columbia, next to English, even though French, like English, is an official language of the country.' (1998: 2)

A similar flip-flop in population make-up was experienced in the State of California where prior to 1990, people classified as white comprised a majority. By the year 2000 this was no longer the case as mainly Hispanic and Asian populations combined with African Americans to constitute a slight plurality of the total. Such changes are clearly reflected in urban areas because of ethnic place-making which externalizes cultural diversity across the landscape. In London it is estimated that there are 300 languages spoken. At the London office of Goldman Sachs, the US investment bank, it is estimated that 49 different first languages are spoken among its staff.

The de-territorialization and immigration of Asian peoples has brought graphic changes to urban areas in the US, Canada and in the UK in particular. Re-territorialization within cities has produced new ethnic enclaves or expanded traditional ones thereby multiplying the experience of diversity. Place-making by new immigrants and their attempts at forging identities based on dual or multiple nationalities have also greatly influenced the culture of the host countries.

For the most part, this latest wave of immigration, since the 1970s is comprised of people that were relatively well educated and/or had significant resources who were looking for better opportunities of advancement abroad. They came to the US voluntarily, as did traditional immigrants. But, unlike the latter, they often retain their citizenship and ties to the country of birth. The outcome of this process has been a new kind of immigrant that is at home in many places and one possessing cross-cultural ties to people and governments in more than one nation.

According to Ames:

'What is strikingly new about the new world order, Arjun Appadurai (1990) suggests, is that it has become a kind of rapid global interactive system never seen before, filled with inconsistencies, differences, disjunctures, alienation and electronic forms of togetherness, inclusions, and exclusions . . . This introduces into the world a powerful new force of "de-territorialization": global movements, new markets, and growing diaspora of intellectuals who are continuously interjecting new peoples into nation states and new ideas into global discourses.' (1998: 1)

Although the claim that new ideas are being felt as a consequence of this movement is certainly over exaggerated, the observation that immigration on a global scale of relatively well-educated people with relatively well-paying jobs has resulted in internet traffic and modes of togetherness that are new, coupled with significant international travel to visit friends and family on a regular basis – all characteristics that differ greatly from the traditional immigrants of the past.

There is a big difference between the process of migration in the developing countries and that of the developed countries. In Europe and the US, migration from rural to urban areas occurred at the same time as industrialization. In developing countries, by contrast, migration from rural areas is occurring despite unemployment in urban areas. This is so because in developing countries people migrate based on expected income rather than actual income and because rural poverty is so great. It is the 'life lottery'. A rural worker will migrate if he/she expects his average city income will be greater than his rural income despite periods of unemployment. A solution to this kind of migration is to retain resources in rural areas and develop them further.

Rural to urban migration in developing countries is most often viewed as a problem – poverty in rural areas and lack of development leads to a rapid and uncoordinated influx into large cities that cannot assimilate newcomers, leading to an increase in slums and urban poverty. The result is increased crime, substandard housing, congestion, disease, pollution and a loosening of family bonds and loss of traditional cultural practices and values. The most common reasons given for people moving from rural areas to urban ones in the developing countries are: family needs, seeking education, and job searches. Family is most common in sheer numbers only because the family head usually moves first and then the rest of the relatives follow. By this mechanism, entire family groups have left traditional villages in the countryside of developing countries only to be swallowed up by urban shantytowns (see entry on *Slums and Shanty Towns*). Yet not all migrants to cities are the same. Different groups have different coping strategies for adapting to the city so that there is great diversity in the urban experience of migrants. There is variety in the way groups responded to the job, housing and social dilemmas placed on them. In addition, rather than having to choose between complete assimilation or some variant of an ongoing racial or ethnic orientation, there are a variety of alternatives exhibited by migrants in between the two extremes.

For researchers of immigration from rural to urban areas and/or from developing to developed countries, the basic unit of analysis is the household or family rather than the single individual. That is, in these cases, movement across space is a family affair even if the head of household, whether male or female, arrives first.

REFERENCES

Ames, M. 1998. 'Museums and the Culture of Uprootedness' Unpublished paper, University of British Columbia.

Appadurai, A. 1990. 'Disjuncture and Difference in the Global Cultural Economy' *Public Culture* 2(2): 1–24.

Clifford, J. 1997. *Routes: Travel and Translation in the Late Twentieth Century.* Cambridge, MA: Harvard University Press.

– Inequality and Poverty –

Inequality and poverty are not the same. The former is a relative condition usually measured by comparative ratios, such as the Gini or, less commonly, the Theil-L coefficient. These relate high to low levels of income obtained by people living in the same city or region. To be sure, poverty may have its relative components, but it is an absolute condition manifested in inadequacies of various social indicators, such as poor health, poor sanitation, poor nutrition, poor pre-natal care and, equally as profound, limited to non-existent opportunities of bettering the existing situation in the future.

INEQUALITY

Inequality is typically urban. Friedrich Engels noted the contrast between the wealthy and the poor in the 1850s when he visited the industrial cities of England, and novel writers of the 19th Century, such as Charles Dickens, made the same observations in their Victorian era books. Early Chicago School researchers, such as Harvey Zorbaugh in the 1920s, referred to this distinction as 'The Gold Coast and the Slum' (see entry on *Uneven Development* for a discussion on Engels and other early work). Indeed, inequality is epitomized by spatial differences in well being. Less affluent slum residents may be getting along, but take a short walk in most cities to the locations where the more affluent live and the contrast is immediately graphic. Poverty, in distinction, is as much a rural as it is an urban phenomenon. In fact, world-wide, there is more poverty in rural than urban areas. This spatial differential has historically been responsible for the essential demographic component of urbanization, namely, the population movement from the countryside to the city in search of a better life.

The entry on *Global Cities* discusses why Sassen's (1991) 'social polarization' thesis – reducing the city to dual populations, one increasingly affluent, the other mired in low level service jobs – is wrong. Further evidence comes from an English study by Williams and Windebank (1995), who assert that Sassen's perspective ignores a more relevant way of approaching changes in the occupational structure than by focusing on individuals. They argue that it makes more sense to view urban wage earners within a household context. Taking a whole economy perspective, UK data reveal that since the 1980s there has been a radical shift in employment practices with a fundamental decline in households that have only one (usually male) wage-earner. 'The stereotypical household of the male breadwinner and the wife at home has suffered a major decline' to less than 25%. While many individuals belong to families that have experienced either increasing affluence or poverty, the vast majority belong to households with two or more wage-earners. Thus the polarization, often spoken about, does not exist. But, there is increasing inequality between households with only one breadwinner and those with multiple ones. The latter are the social units that are becoming more affluent.

66

In the UK, policy-makers are increasingly drawing their attention to households who are 'work-rich' and those that are 'work-poor'. Nick Buck points to six themes that underlie inequality in the UK: changes in state benefits compared with labor market earnings; different rate of growth of earnings of different occupational groups; changes in household composition; change in the level of unemployment; increases in paid work by married women; and the changing balance of manufacturing and service-sector employment (Buck, 1991).

By adopting the household rather than the employment place as the primary unit of analysis, the process of socio-spatial polarization has been portrayed not as an increasing divide between core and peripheral employment, but, rather, between two types of households: the new 'workhouses' which not only have multiple earners but also conduct more informal work, especially of the autonomous variety; and the 'no longer working' group of households that suffer exclusion from employment and are unable to participate in the informal sector due to mitigating circumstance. Thus, part-time and other forms of so called peripheral or marginalized work cannot automatically be associated with deprivation, as the individual employment approach often shows.

Clearly, there are more than just two social spheres alive in central cities. Recent immigrants, small business owners, and a persisting segment of the middle class continue to reside in urban areas. Yet, the growing affluence and voracious high end consumption style of life pursued by the relatively well off does create the impression of a dichotomous urban terrain existing between the haves and the have-nots in the largest cities. Around the globe, the inequality gap has also been expanding. Urban places in regions like Latin America and Africa have always exhibited this duality. But, lately, with the fall of communism in Eastern Europe, inequality has appeared with a vengeance in the former Soviet societies. When China enacted capitalist reforms in the late 1980s, its social structure also developed an inequality gap. In short, there are virtually no urban places now that are not experiencing the growing difference between the rich and the poor.

Researchers in the US recently completed a four city study of inequality that confirms little to no progress in alleviating aspects of racial and income segregation (Multi-Study of Urban Inequality). Analyses of Atlanta, Boston, Detroit and Los Angeles for the period 1992–94 focused on 'How changing market dynamics, racial attitudes, and racial segregation act singly and in concert to foster contemporary urban inequality'. Most strikingly, the patterns observed in the spatial isolation of the African Americans and the less affluent were already substantiated prior to the 1990s. In effect, this most recent research effort confirms that economic prosperity and the 'changing market dynamics' of US cities in the 1990s had little effect on segregation.

Inequality is manifested in residential segregation (see entry on the *Ghetto and Racial Segregation*) which, in turn, is manifested in great differences among all school children with regard to their educational performance. Urban school systems suffer because of the concentration of poor and minority students within central cities (see entry on *Education* and *Reproduction of Labor*). On average, among all students in metropolitan areas, whites score 20% higher on standardized tests in grade school than blacks, Hispanics and Native Americans. While attention has been paid in the past to the effects of segregation on black students, it is now clear that Hispanic students are even more disadvantaged by inequality and segregation. Data from 1990 indicate that dropout rates are the highest for the Latino community. These data indicate that something much more than the mere effect of language barriers is going on – Asian students in comparable conditions do not exhibit a remarkable dropout rate. In effect, the spatial isolation of many Hispanics results in the failure of their children to obtain an adequate education, thereby, in turn, reproducing the marginal economic status of their parents.

Taking the multi-centered metropolitan region as a whole, there is an obvious inequality differential between the city and the suburbs. Life chances are enhanced for children by moving from the inner city to the suburbs, when that change can be affected. Often it cannot be because of the limited availability of affordable housing in the suburbs. Spatial differences between the city and the suburb in the US can be summarized by the following contrasts:

Suburbs	Cities
more homogeneously white	more minorities who are the majority
more homogeneously middle-class	sharp contrast between wealthy and poor
more residential	more tourism
population is younger	concentration of aging population
more retailing, commerce and industry	more high end speciality shopping
	banking and professional services
more affluent	significant numbers of poor people

Such a divide between the relatively affluent and the less well off on a regional scale is not characteristic of European metropolitan areas, despite the presence of inequality there as well (Jargowsky, 1997). Rather, the European situation is more complex because of the historic nature of many of its cities. Consequently, the settlement patterns mean that areas of deprivation are found close to areas of affluence. Housing, educational and health differences, as well as cultural and ethnic differences, sustain the inequalities between very proximate areas. For example, the traditional manufacturing district of St. Denis in the Paris metropolitan region is now populated by high-tech service firms and professionals who sit cheek by jowl with poor immigrant communities originally from Algeria and Morocco in North Africa, whose young men are mainly unemployed and thus alienated from mainstream secular society (Body-Gendrot, 2000).

POVERTY

Unlike the relative concept of inequality, poverty can be measured directly by social indicators of well being. Poverty is not only a problem of poor countries; it is found at a significant level in the most affluent societies. Since the 1980s, the number of people around the world living in poverty has increased. In the US, the census defines the poverty level as an annual income for a family of four. In 2002, the census defined poverty as at or below $17,463. Over 12% of Americans are considered to be living in poverty by this measure ('Housing Problems' www.ruralhomes.org2003). The United Nations defines this level for people living in developing counties as either $1 or $2 a day income per person. In 2001, roughly 1.2 billion people were living on less than $1 a day, that is, about 20% of the globe's total population (similar to the US level) and there were almost 3 billion people, or half the world's population, living at or below $2 a day.

Poverty can be found in rural as well as urban areas. It becomes a metropolitan problem when it is expressed spatially as a concentration of poverty stricken people in specific places. The census defines poor neighborhoods as tracts with 40% or more people living at or below the poverty line. As Jargowsky notes:

'The poor, especially minorities, are increasingly isolated in depopulated urban wastelands. Such neighborhoods exhibit severe signs of economic distress, including vacant and dilapidated housing units, high levels of unemployment, high rates of single parenthood, problems with gangs and violence, and widespread drug and alcohol use.' (1997: 143)

In the UK, the link between inequality and poverty is generated by health (Davey-Smith et al. 2002). Dorling states:

'Policies which have produced increased income inequality and poverty have helped to drive the polarisation of mortality. The geographical polarisation of health chances has been precipitated by a polarisation of life chances, in terms of employment opportunities, income and living standards. The health gap is now such that, in the period 1994–1997 in Britain, 24% of deaths of people aged 15–64 would not have occurred had the mortality rates of the least deprived decile of the population applied nationally; almost one quarter of all deaths can now be attributed to unfavourable socio-economic circumstances.' (2004)

To be sure, problems of gangs, drug and alcohol abuse, and even single parenthood among teenagers, exist in the suburbs as well. But, what distinguishes poverty in contemporary urban society is its concentration

69

at high levels within pockets of severe decline and isolation in the urban landscape. Between 1970–90 the concentration of people living in poor neighborhoods increased from 12.4 to 17.9% (Jargowsky, 1997). 'Poverty concentration is much higher for minority groups. For example, 33.5% of the black poor and 22.1% of the Hispanic poor lived in hi-poverty neighborhoods in 1990, compared to 6.3% of the white poor' (Jargowsky, 1997: 143). The cross connection between minority and poverty status is quite graphic for US cities and most troubling. Since the 1970s, there is a pattern of increasing isolation in terms of race and income within the central cities of the nation. For example, between 1970–90 the percentage of blacks in Detroit that were classified as living in poverty increased from 11.3% to 54%. New York City experienced an increase of 27%, Chicago of 21.4% and Pittsburgh of 21.7%. The concentration of poor Hispanics also increased within large central cities. New York saw an increase between 1970–90 of 18.8%, Philadelphia of 48.4%, and Detroit of 33.8%. According to the UK government, just under one in four people (approximately 13 million people) live in poverty. This figure includes nearly one in three children or around 4 million (Department of Work and Pensions, 2002). In comparison to the rest of Europe, the UK does not fare well. Over 15% of the UK population is included in the human poverty index, compared to 10.4% in Germany and 11.1% in France (United Nations, 2000). The human poverty index is measured by:

- the proportion living below 50% of national median income (Germany: 5.9%; France: 8.6%; UK: 8.9%)
- the percentage of people not expected to live to age 60 (Germany: 10.5%; France: 11.1%; UK 9.6%)
- the percentage of 16–65 year olds classified as functionally illiterate (Germany: 14.4%; UK: 21.6%)
- the percentage of long-term unemployed in the labor force (Germany: 4.9%; France: 5.2%; UK: 2.1%).

This significant and troubling increase in the concentration of poverty within central cities is the consequence of several factors including white flight to the suburbs, an influx of poor migrants and immigrants, and the shift of the economy to more professionally oriented jobs and away from blue collar manufacturing. Concentration of poor and often minority people within spatially isolated areas in the metropolitan region is considered a serious social problem. William J. Wilson (1987) called attention to the 'tangle of pathology' and the reproduction of social problems that this isolation produces. As indicated in the entry on the

Ghetto and Racial Segregation minority and poor concentration is reproduced over time as limited resources prevent people from breaking out of their economic and social constraints. Poverty is not only perpetuated but it seems to be increasing due to the failure of society to overcome this spatial isolation.

Poverty in developing countries is also increasing just as the population of urban areas around the globe continues to increase as well. Not only are cities in developing countries getting bigger, but, with growth, the absolute numbers of poor living in cities is also growing. Comparable measures of poverty are obtained from quality of life indicators that include availability of adequate housing, health care, potable water, and levels of infant mortality and population morbidity. According to a United Nations study, the percentage of poor people living in cities increased for most developing countries between 1980–93. Some examples are: Ghana – 28.3% from 23.7%; China – 10.8% from 6.0%; India – 23.3% from 19.3%; Pakistan – 28.6% from 23.7%; and Columbia – 37.4% from 35.8. Among all nations, those located in South America and Africa have the highest levels of urban poor. Furthermore, as in the case of the US, rapid economic growth in the 1980s and 90s, for places like South Korea and Indonesia, did not translate into reductions in the overall percentage of people living in poverty. In addition, as the countries of Eastern Europe abandoned communism and as the Chinese economy shifted to more capitalist features, the percentage of people living in poverty also increased and, in some cases, quite remarkably. According to the United Nations, the percentage of people living on less than $2 a day in Eastern Europe for example, increased from 3.6% to 20.7% from 1987–98 (World Bank, 2000).

Analysts of poverty are alarmed at the extent of its concentration within central cities, as we have already discussed. Other dimensions of poverty are equally disturbing. The high levels of female headed households that are poor indicates a world-wide 'feminization of poverty'. Families are broken up and children are abandoned to a life on the streets in many cities of the developing world as a consequence of this process. Women cannot cope with the dual burdens of raising a family and making a living. In the US, the increase in female headed households living in poverty since the 1980s is reflected in the deterioration of adequate opportunities for children to better themselves and in the absence of positive male role models (see Wilson, 1987). In sum, it is the social aspects of the poverty condition – specifically, the weakness of the family, the deteriorating environment of poor neighborhoods, and the limited chances for social advancement that compound the absolute indicators of poor welfare, such as high infant mortality, poor health care, malnutrition, inadequate shelter and the like – that make the persisting presence of urban poverty such a compelling issue for all societies.

RACIAL SEGREGATION AND POVERTY

There is controversy over the primary cause of the growing concentration of poverty in major US cities. Whereas some researchers attribute it to racial segregation (Massey and Denton, 1993), others insist that social and structural transformations over the last decades have played a major role (Wilson, 1987). Proponents of the latter position, although they underline social and structural transformations, do not deny the harmful effects of racial segregation on the concentration of poverty (see, e.g., Jargowsky, 1997). In the US, the urban poor in major metropolitan areas are increasingly segregated into high-poverty neighborhoods, which are also increasingly divided along racial lines. A recent study shows that the number of the urban poor living in those racially segregated, high-poverty neighborhoods commonly labeled as ghettos (predominantly African-American), barrios (predominantly Hispanic), and slums (mixed or white), almost doubled in recent decades, from 4.1 million in the 1970s to 8 million in 1990 (Jargowsky, 1997).

For the UK, the Joseph Rowntree Foundation reported:

'The proportion of "poor" families in each ethnic group: 16% of white households had a low income . . . All minority groups had a higher percentage, but the gap was quite small for Caribbeans (20%) and Indians (22%). The extent of poverty was more serious for Chinese (28%) and Africans (31%), though in the case of Chinese people, there were also more well-off households than in other groups. The new, more detailed, data confirm the previous survey's estimate that Pakistani and Bangladeshi households were four times as likely to be "poor" as white households. Pakistanis and Bangladeshis were much, much more likely to be poor than any other ethnic group. Not surprisingly, low incomes were rare among working households; more common among pensioner households; and more common again among non-working households below pensionable age. This was true in every ethnic group. But the difference *between* groups is emphasized by the fact that poverty was more common in Pakistani and Bangladeshi *working* households (50%), than in white *non-working, non-pensioner* households (43 per cent).' (Joseph Rowntree Foundation, 1998)

Urban racial minorities are vulnerable to structural changes in the urban economy taking place under the pressure of the global economy. In the process of de-industrialization and re-industrialization, the urban labor market has been increasingly polarized into low-skilled and rising high-skilled sectors. De-industrialization, including plant closing and the relocation of manufacturing, has destroyed low-skilled, blue-collar jobs which were traditionally the main sources of livelihood for urban racial minorities; by contrast, the growth of high-tech, knowledge-based industries in major cities has created job opportunities for skilled workers with educational credentials. As a result of changes in the urban economic base, urban minorities have turned increasingly to the low-wage service sector.

In addition, economic restructuring has accompanied changes in the spatial organization of work. In the US, the restructuring of settlement space since the 1950s is characterized by the general process of deconcentration (see entry on *Multi-centered Metropolitan Region*; Gottdiener and Hutchinson 2000, Chapter 5). Deconcentration is a ubiquitous leveling of industries, jobs and the labor force across space. Driven by two distinct socio-spatial forces of de-centralization and re-centralization, deconcentration has produced spatial differentiation and fragmentation. Whereas command and control functions, finance and other specialized producer services tend to remain in major urban centers (due in part to the advantages of agglomeration economies), production, commercial activities and other business functions have dispersed across space. The suburbanization of jobs – that is, the movement of jobs from the cities to the suburbs – is part of this border process of de-concentration. This spatial redistribution of employment opportunities generates a growing mismatch between the suburban location of employment and minorities' residences in the inner city. If, as is the case in most US cities, public transportation is limited in scope and service, then the inner city poor are isolated from these suburban job opportunities. Poor regional public transportation in combination with the deconcentration of employment reduces the probability of finding jobs for urban minorities living in impoverished inner-city neighborhoods.

All European cities have undergone similar processes of economic and social flight to the suburbs related to rising incomes and wealth, but also growing inequality. However, the European situation is more complex because Europe is not a single socio-economic or political entity and its countries possess differing degrees of urban re-concentration. This re-concentration is also a function of inequality, with young professionals and baby boomers appropriating the best housing in newly gentrifying urban areas in some cities (www.jrf.org.uk Joseph Rowntree Foundation, 1988.)

The socio-demographic transformation of the inner city is another important structural factor involved in the concentration of poverty in major US cities. Whereas de-industrialization and deconcentration have shaped contours of urban labor markets and employment opportunities, socio-demographic transformations have brought about changes in the urban class structure. The flight of whites to suburbia is clearly an important phase in this changing class structure and the crystallization of residential segregation. What is of more importance is the large scale migration of high-income blacks and other racial minorities out of the inner-city neighborhoods. Gone with this selective out-migration are the social buffers and role models for the less affluent. Residents remaining in the impoverished inner-city neighborhoods are 'the truly disadvantaged' (Wilson, 1987) increasingly isolated from the mainstream.

Many studies have documented the devastating effects of living in an overwhelmingly impoverished neighborhood (for a review, see Small and Newman, 2001). The harmful 'neighborhood effects' or 'concentration effects' are manifold and far-reaching, including lack of quality schools, deprivation of conventional role models, inability to access jobs and job networks, and a high risk of crime and victimization. Without doubt, racial segregation is combined with the growing concentration of poverty. In parallel with growing neighborhood poverty and social isolation, these neighborhood effects on life chances grow more severe over time in many US cities (Massey and Denton, 1993).

THE POOR AND HOUSEHOLD COPING STRATEGIES

This phenomenon is closely tied to the Informal Economy (see next entry).

Some urbanists argue that it is the household group rather than the individual that should be the basic unit of social analysis. Often people belonging to households of two or more persons behave in ways that promote the general economic well being of the group rather than individual advancement. For example, this is the argument that Roberts (1991) makes and he also claims that research on the household division of labor suggests that the group is the basic unit of urban analysis for places everywhere, not just in the third world where this argument is most obviously persuasive. Research has discovered that not all the members of a household are immediate family. Households may contain distant relatives and even friends. The collective pooling of resources does not preclude differences among members, such as conflicts between men and women.

In regard to the study of poverty, household coping strategies show that the poor do not accept their situation passively. They innovate and find ways of supporting themselves. They may engage in 'self-provisioning' which includes domestic processing or production of food, making clothes, undertaking repairs, building illegal housing or add ons. Coping strategies are closely tied to the informal economy and may include the sex trade, drugs and begging (see next entry). Household coping as a means of meeting poverty conditions in urban areas is a better way of understanding such responses than the usual emphasis on individuals alone (Williams and Windebank, 1995).

REFERENCES

Body-Gendrot, S. 2000. 'Marginalisation and Political Responses in the French Context' in P. Hamel, H. Lustiger-Thaler and M. Mayer (eds) *Urban Movements in a Globalizing World*. London: Routledge. pp. 59–78.

Buck, N. 1991. 'Social Polarisation, Economic Re-structuring and Labour Market Change in London and New York' in M. Cross and G. Payne (eds) *Social Inequality and The Enterprise Culture*. London: The Falmer Press. pp. 79–101.

Davey-Smith, G., D. Dorling, R. Mitchel, et.al.,2002. 'Health Inequalities in Britain: Continuing Increases up to the End of the 20th Century' *Journal of Epidemiology and Community Health* 56: 434–5.

Department for Work and Pensions, 2002. *Households Below Average Income 1994/95 to 2000/01*, Corporate Document Services. London: Stationery Office.

Dorling, D. 2004. 'Housing Wealth and Community Health: Explanations for the Spatial Polarisation of Life Chances in Britain' http://www.lancs.ac.uk/fss/apsocsci/hvp/projects/dorling.htm accessed 15 June 2004.

Gottdiener, M. and R. Hutchison 2000. *The New Urban Sociology, 2nd Edition*. NY: McGraw-Hill.

'Housing Problems' 2003 www.rural.home.org, accessed 25 June 2003.

Jargowsky, P. 1997. *Poverty and Place: Ghettos, Barrios and the American City*. NY: Russell Sage Foundation.

Massey, D. and N. Denton 1993. *American Apartheid*. Cambridge, MA: Harvard University Press.

Roberts, B. 1991. 'Household Coping Strategies and Urban Poverty in Comparative Perspective' in M. Gottdiener and C. Pickvance (eds) *Urban Life in Transition*. Newbury Park, CA: Sage Publications. pp. 135–68.

Joseph Rowntree Foundation, 1998. 'The Incomes of Ethnic Minorities', *Findings*. (November). London: Joseph Rowntree Foundation http://www.jrf.org.uk/knowledge/findings/socialpolicy/pdf/sprn48.pdf accessed 15 June 2004.

Sassen, S. 1991. *Global Cities*. Princeton, NJ: Princeton University Press.

Small, M. and K. Newman 2001. 'Urban Poverty After the Truly Disadvantaged' *Annual Review of Sociology* 27: 23–45.

Williams, C. and J. Windebank 1995. 'Social Polarization of Households in Contemporary Britain' *Regional Studies*, 29(8): 727–32.

United Nations. 2000. *Human Development Report 2000*. UNDP, New York.

Wilson, W. 1987. *The Truly Disadvantaged: The Inner City, the Underclass, and Public Policy*. Chicago: University of Chicago Press.

World Bank. 2000. *World Development Report 1999/2000*. NY: Oxford University Press.

75

– The Informal Economy –

The informal economy is defined as the combination of workers within urbanized areas that are 'off the books', goods produced in unregulated factories with non-unionized and undocumented laborers, goods and services produced and exchanged for barter (i.e., not cash, but in kind) and goods and services sold without regulation on the streets. In some countries the informal economy is so large as to rival the money exchanged in the formal sector.

Only recently has the presence of an informal economy in urbanized places been recognized as an important subject for analysis in its own right. Prior to that reconception, people viewing poor and ghettoized areas conceived of them in terms of economic deprivation alone. Now we understand that, in many cases, residents of areas excluded from the formal opportunities of society, nevertheless, engage in income earning endeavors that can, in some instances, result in considerable cash. Perhaps the most graphic example of the informal economy is the drug trade which amounts to billions of dollars a year in illegal, but financially lucrative transactions. Other examples extending to quasi-legal acts include the practice by legitimate businesses of paying some people for work that is off the books, such as domestic servants and/or babysitters, that are not employed with formal insurance or social security records, or the practice of using undocumented workers in otherwise legitimate businesses, such as restaurants or factories.

The issue of the informal economy is an especially important focus of third world urbanization research. As global restructuring expands in less developed countries bringing highly paid professional services, poor people drawn to the big cities find informal or casual employment as shoe-shiners, messengers, delivery persons and domestic helpers, in addition to the burgeoning demand for restaurant and other commercial laborers. In some of the newly developing countries, like Malaysia, illegal factories manufacture faux designer fashion items, such as fake Gucci or Louis Vuitton merchandise, others make imitation Rolexes and other watches that are expensive when bought in a legitimate way. Most of the time these jobs have no security and no insurance, but they provide people with the incentive to leave their homes in the rural areas and move to the large cities of the third world.

Although participants in the informal sector are not subsumed under capitalist relations of production and exchange, they are closely linked to the formal economy on a national or global scale (Portes and Schauffler, 1993). In both developed and developing countries, the informal sector is connected to the formal sector of the national and global economy through subcontracting networks and commodity chains. For instance, street vendors sell goods such as cigarettes and other branded products obtained from the formal sector; garbage collectors and recyclers are linked to the formal economy through an infrastructure that buys trash; and illegal prostitution is often one of the paramount features of a tourist economy. Around the world, formal sector firms cut labor costs by using home workers, sweatshops, and others in the informal sector that are devoid of the benefits or safeguards of formal employment.

Engaging in the informal sector is a survival strategy of the urban poor in response to insufficient job creation. In this sense, whether we are discussing developed or undeveloped countries, the informal sector is a 'refuge from destitution' (Portes and Sassen-Koob, 1987: 36). It is undeniable that many participants in the urban informal sector are marginal in their economic status. However, as in the case of off the books or illegal manufacturing enterprises, the informal economy represents much more than a mere survival mechanism of the poor. Entrepreneurs in this sector are adaptive and resilient enough to front businesses that can grow in considerable size and scope. In general the informal economy is a very significant, if only quasi legal, component of national economies for several reasons: It provides goods and services at a low price; it plays the role of a reservoir of the industrial reserve army that holds down wages for the formal sector of the urban economy; and finally, the informal sector provides migrants and indigenous city residents with channels of social mobility and opportunities for the accumulation of wealth. Consequently, there is no simple relationship between working in the informal sector and being poor, nor between the presence of such a sector and the relative wealth or level of development of the country. So many functions are provided to society by this sector that it is found everywhere. For the most part, however, we can say that the informal economy is located in the large cities and is, therefore, an 'urban' phenomenon, although not exclusively so.

The exact magnitude of the informal sector is difficult to estimate due to its elusive nature. Nevertheless, there is general agreement that the informal sector represents a growing proportion of economic activity, particularly in less developed countries. There are significant variations in the level of informal employment between and within regions. It ranges from more than 50% of the labor force in urban areas of sub-Saharan

Africa, to 30% in Latin America and the Caribbean. Within sub-Saharan Africa, the informal sector employment as a percentage of total employment represents 17% in South Africa and over 80% in Zambia (ILO 2002: 241).

One study of nine different cities in developing countries estimated that at least 40% of the labor force was engaged in this economy. In the developed countries the figures are lower, but only slightly so in many cases. According to a World Bank study in 2002, the proportion of workers was over 30% and their productivity was comparable to laborers in the official economy. Furthermore, in the developed countries of Europe, the World Bank study found that those with the most labor regulations and the highest taxes also had the most informal workers. Even in advanced economies, there are widely ranging estimates of the size of the informal economy. From 5–10% of national income in the UK and US, to 30% in Italy and 50% in Russia (*The Economist* 2004). Gordon and Sassen using employment and population data, state that the informal economy accounts for much less of London's economy, compared to New York's (Gordon and Sassen, 1992). However, given that London is a global city, a capital city; a pay resort, a financial and business center and a manufacturing region, one would expect the figure to be much higher (Hebbert, 1998).

The fall of communism in Central and Eastern Europe and the accession of many of these countries into the European Union along with the geo-political fall-out in the Balkans, the Middle East and Africa have all combined to produce an unprecedented influx of migrants, both legal and illegal into the UK and other Western European countries, such as Italy, Germany, France and Spain. Many of these people wind up working in the informal economy. In the UK, refugees tend to concentrate in London and the South-East of England. Indeed, Gordon's more recent work shows the rise of business services employment in the London economy (Buck et al., 2003). The demand for formal business services brings in its wake greater demand for cheap and often illegal labor that underpins this sector. Furthermore, in many cities of Europe, a construction boom over the last several decades has emerged in vigorous fashion. Construction is always a reliable sector for informal employment, especially prone to using immigrant labor. Immigrants and illegal refugees are also consistently found working in agriculture. Therefore, the estimates of 'off the books' workers in Western Europe seem low.

The informal sector is generally a larger source of employment for women than for men in the developing world. Studies suggest that a majority of economically active women in developing countries are in the informal sector. Official statistics tend to underestimate the size of the female labor force in the informal sector because much of women's paid work – let alone unpaid housework – is invisible and thus not counted in official statistics. The informal sector also absorbs a number of child workers. The number of child workers between the ages of 5–14 living in the developing countries is estimated to be at least 250 million (UNICEF, 2001). Most of them labor in the informal sector, carrying out a variety of work in the plantations, sweatshops, affluent households or streets. They are vulnerable to exploitation and abuse. The exploitation of children under these miserable working conditions in over-crowded cities is a global concern. Street children who work and live on the street, in particular, are the most visible manifestation of urban poverty.

The proliferation of the informal sector in major cities is attributed to the excess supply of labor created by: rural-to-urban migration; the excess regulation of the economy; and the structural transformation of the economy including changes in the organization of production (Portes and Schauffler, 1993). In the US, for example, the process of economic restructuring in the wake of increasing global competition has been accompanied by the proliferation of the informal sector, especially in large cities. The dismantling of the welfare state, the privatization of state-run enterprises, and the decline in organized labor power have facilitated the transformation of labor markets and labor practices in the US, the UK and other countries of Europe. Researchers on this world-wide phenomenon claim that the incentives to use off the books and unregulated labor remain quite attractive in cities throughout the world. These incentives often condemn itinerant workers, new immigrants and marginal populations to a lifetime of drudgery, as affluent households buy low paid personal services, cleaning, and child-minding from work-poor households. In most cities in Europe, these work-poor households are characterized by one-parent families, ethnicity, below average or substandard housing and limited educational opportunities. The working poor are also locked into an informal debt culture in which unscrupulous lenders offer loans with exorbitant interest rate payments they cannot afford. The famous former Lord Mayor of London, Dick Whittington, came to London to make his fortune in the city 'paved with gold'. Over the centuries many have followed in his footsteps to find themselves limited to the opportunities of the informal economy, but with no means to break out of its bonds. These restraints include being exploited by criminal gangs, often drawn from their own communities.

One of the ways the informal economy is organized at the level of daily life is by households. Rather than consisting of a sector of individuals, this part of the economy is better understood as comprised of families that work together to pool their resources in a highly restricted environment. In developing countries the limitations placed on people may be the result of labor and immigrant regulation or racial discrimination, while in the developing part of the world rural to urban migrants are faced with the daunting task of acquiring enough resources to survive their transition. In all cases these 'household coping strategies' are a significant phenomenon of urban life. Studying the household rather than individuals also gives researchers a better picture of how people cope with limited life chances. For more information on household coping strategies see the entry on *Inequality and Poverty*.

THE SOCIAL PROBLEM OF AN UNDERGROUND ECONOMY

The informal economy may involve activities that are not only illegal because they use undocumented workers or are off the books, they may also involve criminal acts in their own right. Illegal activities in the informal economy include drug trafficking, people smuggling, money laundering, gambling and prostitution. For this reason, the presence of an underground sector may constitute a serious social problem that jeopardizes the well being of the larger society. When criminal acts are present, their effects are widespread and disturbing to others. Hence societies are faced with a number of strong incentives to monitor and even intervene in the informal economy. At the very same time, because the service and construction industries rely so heavily on immigrant labor, both legal and illegal, to fill the low wage slots, the informal economy thrives in the developed countries of Western Europe and the US.

REFERENCES

Buck, N., I. Gordon, P. Hall, M. Harloe, and M. Kelinma 2002. *Working Capital: Life and Labour in Contemporary London*. London: Routledge.

Gordon, I. and S. Sassen, 1992. 'Restructuring the urban labour markets' in S. Fainstein, I. Gordon, and M. Harloe (eds) *Divide Cities: New York and London in the Contemporary World*. Oxford: Blackwell.

Hebbert, M. 1998. *London*. Chichester: John Wiley.

International Labour Office (ILO). 2002. *Key Indicators of the Labour Market 2001–2002*. New York: Routledge.

Portes, A. and S. Sassen-Koob 1987. 'Making it Underground: Comparative Material on the Informal Sector in Western Market Economies' *American Journal of Sociology*, 93: 30–61.

80

Portes, A. and R. Schauffler 1993. 'Competing Perspectives on the Latin American Informal Sector' *Population and Development Review*, 19 (1): 33–60.

United Nations Children's Fund UNICEF. 2001. *Beyond Child Labour, Affirming Rights*. New York: UNICEF.

Masculine Space

Spaces within our built environment are gendered (see entry on *Feminine Space*). Places that can be characterized as 'masculine space' facilitate the expression of male-biased activities and power. Produced by material as well as non-material aspects of society, gendered spaces exhibit biases towards one or another sex. Aspects of the material environment, such as masculine associated theming in a sports bar, help define the space according to dominant gender use. Behaviors that are socially acceptable within that same space, or which are not easily sanctioned according to gender, comprise the non-material social practices that also help define dominant gender use. Together these two dimensions articulate with social practices creating a 'gendered space'.

Masculine spaces are places where traditionally men have congregated more commonly than women and where males are at a distinct advantage regarding the deployment of power. Bars are excellent examples, as are sports stadiums, although places like restaurants where men and women act out typical dominant/subordinate social roles also qualify. The offices of white collar labor have long been associated with male dominance and can also be considered masculine spaces. In fact, in most of the corporate world, if not virtually all of it, men resist the 'feminization' of office décor and interior design. A final and graphic example of a 'masculine space' would be any public mass audience facility within which the equal numbers of bathrooms for the sexes painfully obscures the fact that women need many more times the amount of bathroom space when they are among a crowd than do men. The pathetically long lines of women outside their restroom at up-scale classical concert halls illustrates this negative bias perfectly.

There is an implicit understanding that the domestic realm is a feminine space while places of action and public meeting are masculine ones (see entry on *Feminine Space*). Yet, typically male gendered spaces have recently been under attack by female attendance and transformation (Petty, 2003):

'To a great extent, the Western male has been driven out of spaces once considered exclusively male. The workplace, the pub and the club are all spaces that have seen an increasing level of female participation and inclusion.'

According to this report, however, the increasing 'bisexuality' of previously male-gendered spaces has contributed to the redefinition of maleness that reinforces excessively masculine traits.

'The erosion of the exclusively male space of the past and the failure to redefine new, healthy spaces for men has led to a redefinition of masculinity that is overtly sexual, aggressive and, at times, violent . . . The ideal male, no longer the SNAG (Sensitive New Age Guy) of the mid-nineties, is now the aggressive 'new lad' popularized by such magazines as *Maxim* and *FHM*, and re-enforced through sports culture, schools, television and music.' (Petty, 2003)

Now, as real masculine spaces retreat under social pressure to have them accommodate both sexes, virtual masculine spaces of a certain, exaggerated kind have proliferated in movies, magazines, virtual video games, 'extreme' sports and on television (see for example, Comedy Central's *The Man Show*, as well as all the ultra-violent or extreme video games on the market that are played through the home TV set). One cannot be physically present in these virtual spaces, but they do reproduce the exclusively male discourse, albeit in an exaggerated and, most certainly, an alienated fashion. Petty concludes the assessment of the disappearance of masculine spaces in our society with the following:

'This is not a call for exclusive men's clubs, segregating boys and girls in the classroom, or creating a new gender hierarchy. It is, however, a cry for constructive definitions of masculine identity, and the provision of venues (cultural, literary, political) in which men are encouraged to examine their masculinity in honest, unclouded terms. The disappearing man is being replaced by what is increasingly becoming a walking penis with fists. A troubling site indeed.' (Petty, 2003)

The above observations are interesting precisely because they introduce the important concept that spaces in our culture are both real and virtual (see entries on *Nightlife and Urban Nightscapes*; *Socio-spatial Approach*). However, the claim that, actually, existing environments are increasingly bi-sexually controlled, may be an exaggeration. Societies still invest men with the power to dominate. That fact alone implies that, in most spaces, it is male-biased activities and influence that will prevail. Thus, the creation in society of spaces that are uniquely feminine or which cater to the sensitivities and needs of children, for example, remains an important consideration in social planning.

REFERENCES

Petty, Jordan *Entrepot*, 1 (1 January 2003).

Models of Urban Growth

BURGESS MODEL – CONCENTRIC ZONES

Ernest W. Burgess developed a theory of city growth and differentiation in the 1930s based on the social Darwinist or biologically derived principles that were common in the work of Robert Park and Roderick McKenzie (see entry on *Chicago School*). According to Burgess, the city constantly grew because of population pressures. This, in turn, triggered a dual process of central agglomeration and commercial de-centralization; that is, spatial competition attracted new activities to the center of the city but also repelled other activities to the fringe area. As activities themselves located on the fringe, the fringe itself was pushed farther out from the city, and so on. Thus the area of the city continually grew outwards as activities that lost out in Central Business District (CBD) competition were relocated to the shifting periphery.

In Burgess' theory, the city would eventually take on the form of a highly concentrated central business district that would dominate the region and be the site for the highest competitive land prices, while the surrounding area would comprise four distinct concentric rings: zone in transition, zone of workingmen's houses, residential zone, commuter zone.

Research shortly after Burgess unveiled his model, in the 30s and 40s, contradicted his theory and questioned the concentric zone hypothesis. Many people to this day still think of the city in Burgess' terms with a large central district that dominates the surrounding area constituted as

83

rings. This is quite remarkable when we acknowledge that shortly after Burgess published his theory it was questioned by more accurate conceptions of how urban regions grew that were based on better research. As indicated in several entries of this book, city-dominated thinking is deeply entrenched in urban studies, even if it is a fallacy (see entry on *Multi-centered Metropolitan Region*).

HOMER HOYT – THE SECTOR MODEL

Published in 1933, Hoyt's model was also based on Chicago but it contradicted Burgess' work. His sector conception of space was derived from a study of changes in the land prices within the city of Chicago extending back 100 years. Hoyt argued that cities were carved up, not by concentric zones, but by unevenly shaped sectors within which different economic activities tended to congregate. These were produced by competition for locations within a capitalist market in real estate that translated the functional needs of business into land prices. Hoyt further argued that manufacturing and retailing, in particular, had the tendency to spin off and away from the center and agglomerate in sectors that expanded outward, while leaving other economic activities behind in a more functionally specialized central business district. This conception is quite accurate today, although Hoyt's general approach is limited because it remained city-based.

CHAUNCY HARRIS AND EDWARD ULLMAN – THE MULTIPLE NUCLEI MODEL

Harris and Ullman, like Hoyt, were essentially correct in conceiving of the development of urban space as consisting of irregular sectors and centers rather than concentric zones under pressure of real estate competition among users with different needs. However, both of these alternative models assumed that the CBD, or the central core of any city would remain dominant. They did not foresee the way the entire metro region would experience functional specialization (see section on the *Multi-centered Metropolitan Region*).

Harris and Ullman argued that the spin offs of activities from the CBD would take the shape of separate centers rather than sectors radiating from the central core. These smaller centers were conceived as 'homogeneous urban districts' and they remained organized around a CBD of some kind. In their model, unlike Burgess, no regular pattern could be found where spin off districts were located in relation to each other.

The entry on the *Multi-centered Metropolitan Region* argues, in contrast to all city-centered approaches, that the separate centers are functionally differentiated and not linked to the larger whole. Malls are not placed around the region at random, they are located by their developers according to marketing or service areas that have nothing to do with the CBD but are dependent, instead, on the population distribution of the entire metro region. For Burgess, Hoyt, Harris and Ullman, and I should add many urbanists today, the CBD remains an all purpose shorthand concept for economic concentration within a city. This view of urban space is false. Multiple centers are spread throughout the metro region and are produced and sustained by regional, national and global modes of societal organization.

CENTRAL PLACE THEORY AND GROWTH POLE THEORY

European urban and regional economists and geographers have been influenced by the work of two German regional scientists, Christaller (1933) and Lösch (1945), who are credited with the invention of central place theory. At its simplest, central place theory offers an explanation for two kinds of urban phenomena: the existence of an urban hierarchy, i.e., the ranking of cities from ones with the most functions and importance to those with the least; and the spatial structure of the urban system – in other words, the relationship between different cities in a region (Evans, 1985). Originally based on a study of Southern Germany that was predominantly rural, central place theory has been weak on explaining the existence of an urban hierarchy in industrialized economies. Despite criticism and re-working, central place theory in the context of other theoretical developments does offer insights into the formation of Multi-centered Metropolitan Regions (MMRs, see entry on page 87) and the earlier variant, Polycentric Urban Regions (PURs) once used in Europe. Its other utility has been to explain the hierarchy of financial services offered within the urban system of a country (Parr and Budd, 2000).

Another of the important concepts emerging from work in Europe has been that of French theorists in advancing the concept of 'regional growth poles' and development strategies using this perspective. A growth pole is defined as:

'a set of industries capable of generating dynamic growth in the economy, and strongly interrelated to each other via input–output linkages around a leading industry (or propulsive industry).' (in the original French meaning) (Richardson, 1978: 165)

The concept of the natural growth pole (defined in abstract economic space) derives from the work of Perroux (1945). Influenced by the work on innovation by the Austrian economist Schumpeter, Perroux viewed growth within an economy as stemming from domination and disequilibrium, in other words uneven development (see entry on page 83) (Parr, 1999). Influenced by Perroux, a subsequent generation of economists developed growth pole strategies for many urban developments around the world. 'New towns' in the UK and the French equivalent, *les grandes ensembles*, are examples of growth pole schemes whose central purpose was the deconcentration of urban areas. The subsequent relative failure of this form of urban policy in a European setting is based on many causes. Part of the problem is that the original Perroux model was focused on inter-sectoral or inter-industry linkages and little or no consideration was given to the external effects of the flow of goods and people across an urban region. The latter is currently the key factor of spatial development as a consequence of globalization, along with transport and computer innovation.

In sum, central place theory, despite limitations, states that individual centers exist within a wider system and are characterized by complex interactions (as in a Multi-centered Metropolitan Region). Growth pole theory focuses solely on the internal workings of the pole and not its external relationships within a wider region. There are limitations to the applications of central place theory, the most dominant being that it deals with spatial equilibrium at a specific point in time, whilst growth pole theory is concerned with dynamic change over time. There are further objections concerning the range of economic activities covered by central place theory, and the spatial-hierarchical structure implies few levels of centers. However, as Parr (1973) demonstrates, many of these objections can be overcome. In doing so, these approaches open up rich possibilities for exploring the Multi-centered Regional – or Polycentric Urban Regional – perspectives in a European context.

REFERENCES

Christaller, W. 1933. *Die Zentrlaen Orte in Süddeutschland*. Jena: Fisher.

Evans, A. 1985. *Urban Economics: An Introduction*. Oxford: Blackwell.

Lösch, A. 1945. *Die Raumliche Ordnung der Wirtschaft*. Jena: Fischer.

Parr, J.B. 1973. 'Growth Poles, Regional Development and Central Place Theory' *Papers in Regional Science*, 31, 174–212.

Parr, J.B. and L. Budd 2000. 'Financial Services and the Urban System: An Exploration' *Urban Studies* 37(3) 593–610.

Richardson, H. 1978. *Regional and Urban Economics*. Harmondsworth: Penguin.

Multi-centered Metropolitan Region

The form of settlement space known as 'the city' is about 10,000 years old. Classically, it consisted of a central area with a relatively high population density surrounded by a supportive space of agricultural production. This bounded city form remained virtually unchanged until the period of capitalist industrialization during the 19th Century. At that time, the creation of two distinct classes, the workers and the capitalists, split the population with regard to wealth. Affluent families established homes away from the city in the hinterland, while retaining a place in town as well. Furthermore, when the forces of profit-making were extended to a capitalist market in real estate, speculators began immediately to stake out land outside the central city for sale. They encouraged prospective buyers to use whatever means of transportation available at the time to commute to work. Horse-drawn carriages were eventually replaced by crude steam powered passenger trains, then electrical trolleys and finally the automobile itself for transportation to and from outlying areas. At each stage of urban development, the boundaries of settlement were pushed further away from the city center. Throughout this early period of 'suburbanization', however, the areas outside the urban core were always attached to it through economic dependency for money making, working-class jobs, commerce, and participation in 'high' culture, i.e., art, music, fashion and the like.

Some urbanists still claim that modern day suburbanization is the result of the mass production of the automobile. Cities like Los Angeles are celebrated as landmark places of sprawl created by this means of transportation. Yet, nothing could be further from the truth. Analysts that rely on such technological determinism, still a common misconception, are always wrong because they fail to think in terms of social organization. Political, economic and cultural, as well as mere technological forces always work together to create significant changes in society. Mass suburbanization really began in the years immediately following World War II in the US. It was a product of powerful forces unleashed by government programs and economic prosperity that transformed ordinary workers into a 'middle-class'. In the end, this profound demographic shift of people from the central cities to the outlying areas created a new form of space that is not the city. We call it the *Multi-centered Metropolitan Region*, or MMR, and it is as qualitatively different from the traditional city as was the city itself from its predecessors 10,000 years before that (see entries on *Models of Urban Growth*; *Socio-spatial Approach*; see Gottdiener, 1994; Gottdiener and Hutchison, 2000; Gottdiener and Kephart, 1990). Among its distinguishing characteristics is the way the classical downtown has spun off its many functions to other centers so that each is more functionally specialized than in the past. Our urbanized regions now possess multi-centers, some of which are dominated by the function of consumption, or white collar office operations, or manufacturing of some kind, or residential life or recreational and leisure activities. The traditional central city still exists and still remains important in its own right, but it is much more specialized as a place of business and consumption, as well as having a population that is much less representative of the society as a whole.

We can only wonder why urbanists today discuss the features of the new spatial form, such as independent industrial parks that are centers of employment in their own right, or, the immense spaces of consumption, known as suburban malls, that draw people, not only from many surrounding cities, but even from other states, while retaining a discursive focus on 'the city', as if the central core still retained the same overarching importance as it once did prior to the 1950s. Most urban analysis is now out of date because of this failure to recognize the transformation of settlement space to the new form of multi-centered and regional multi-functionality. We continue to see books with the word 'city' in the title – *Understanding the City*, *City Builders*, *City Culture*, *The Postmodern City*. Such a proliferation of terms having the word 'city' as a suffix, makes its meaning impossible to pin down, because the word itself is no longer a spatial but a metaphorical concept. Urbanists have created a great terminological confusion by their own inability to sort out the concrete from figures of speech. They write about the global city, the dual city, the informational city, the divided city, the fragmented city, the analogue city, the digital city, the sprawling city, or the edge city. These terms are simply wrong. They apply an attribute, such as the increasing use of digital means of communication, characteristic of settlement spaces that are now regional or even national and international in scope, to some imputed center, a 'city', that just does not exist. We no longer live in a spatial form of centrality, like an edge city, but a sprawling region of development with many separate centers each with their own levels of functional specialization.

The multi-centered metropolitan form of space was produced in part by powerful government programs. Two, in particular, are quite deterministic and, in their own way, much more significant than the role of the automobile itself. After the depression of the 1930s, the US government launched ambitious housing programs to help both the banking and the home construction industries back to recovery. Among other aspects, the government allowed a 'home owners' interest rate deduction on taxes. It still exists today and means that people who own their own homes but who carry a mortgage of some kind can deduct the full interest on their payments from their pre-tax income. They don't pay taxes on their mortgage interest. This is a direct subsidy to anyone that can afford to buy their own home. It is also a great incentive to become an owner rather than a renter, *if you can afford* to do so. Renters that cannot, get nothing in the way of a break on their taxes. Because rentals are more characteristic of the traditional city, and home ownership more characteristic of suburbia, government housing programs clearly worked to disperse or deconcentrate the population and to promote living in a single family, suburban home.

A second program does involve the automobile, but makes it the means of suburbanization, rather than the cause, in opposition to the claims of technological determinists. During the 1950s, the US government decided to build a criss-crossing web of 'interstate' highways allegedly to facilitate military transportation should the country ever be attacked. This 'National Defense System of Highways' act, passed in 1956, led immediately to the carving up of the nations hinterland by the asphalt and road construction industries, and created the opportunities for speculators to rush in and develop real estate. Massive and sprawling single family home construction, on land that was once only valued for agriculture, and tied together by newly minted highways with high speeds soon followed. Industry, commerce and even cultural or leisure activities, along with once compact urban population, dispersed on a mass basis throughout the expanding metropolitan region, and then re-coalesced into separate and more specialized centers. Gas powered vehicles became the means by which locations were connected across this ever expanding sprawl of settlement space.

In Europe, there has been a revival of interest in Polycentric Urban Regions (PURs). The distinction with a Multi-centered Metropolitan Region is that the former consists of a 'a set of neighbouring but spatially separate regions' (Parr, 2004: 231), whereas the latter is not as spatially separate because of improvements in transportation and communications. Some British researchers claim that PURs are a variant of Multi-centered

Metropolitan Regions (Champion, 2001), but the effects of sprawl and clustering so characteristic of US metro regions have yet to be fully recognized as important in Europe. In the UK, Birmingham conforms to the latter, but like Greater Boston in the US, it developed from the former. There are numerous examples of PURs in the rest of Europe, including the Randstaat in the Netherlands and the Ruhr in Germany. Given the density of populations in most of Europe, there are strong attempts to spatially separate different urban areas as a matter of government policy. Also, planning restrictions tend to apply where ribbon developments along rail links would tend to produce spatial coalescence between urban regions. The European Commission is actively seeking to encourage the growth of planned PURs as the policy solution to sprawling regional development (European Commission, 1999). In the US, in contrast, multi-centered regional development is the consequence of a failure to establish regional planning.

The growth of a multi-centered metropolitan region takes place through the twin processes of *de-centralization* and *re-centralization*. The same processes can be said to underlay the development of PURs, although suburban sprawl and independent suburban clustering is much more extreme in the US. *De-centralization* means the overall and absolute reduction in the numbers of people and activities from the traditional city. It involves not simply the dispersal of actions, but of social organization. With de-centralization comes a different way of connecting people through social as well as technological means. The general leveling of population density itself is referred to as *deconcentration*.

At the same time that de-centralization took place, the linked process of *re-centralization* also occurred. By the latter is meant the reformation of activities and people in relatively more concentrated spaces with an attendant mode of connection that reflects closer proximity. Thus, both de-centralization and re-centralization have their own distinct features of social organization. The building up of population centers after dispersal is referred to as *reconcentration*.

One important reason why more urbanists do not take the multi-centered metropolitan region as their basic unit of settlement space instead of the central city is because the US census has yet to abandon its city-centered terms for urban forms. Yet, there has already been considerable evidence from the census itself over the years to suggest that we have passed over to another type of settlement space. By the 1970s for example, the census revealed that more Americans were living in suburban regions outside the central city than in the city itself. Other data confirmed that economic functions were also dispersing. Between

1948–82, for instance, the census used a category, the Major Retail Center (MRC), to capture 'large concentrations of retail stores within metropolitan areas'. These were centers in both cities and suburban regions. For the latter, they were invariably malls of some kind. The emphasis on centers and clusters existing *outside* the city but within the metro region was important, however, the census discontinued collecting data with this designation 'because of the high costs of defining the areas' (US Census Bureau, www.census.gov).

At present, the main census category that includes the regional basis of settlement space is the Metropolitan Statistical Area, which does not really convey the complexity of that space and also still retains an emphasis on the traditional central city that is no longer deserved. Metropolitan Statistical Areas for the 2000 census together include about 93% of the US population – about 83% in metropolitan statistical areas and about 10% in micropolitan statistical areas. (In the previous census, 1990, the same classification only included 80% of the total population.) Of the 3,142 counties in the US, 1,000 are in the 362 metro stat areas and 674 are in micro stat areas. 1,378 remain outside the classification.

In the US, the regions of Houston, Phoenix, AZ and Las Vegas, are good examples of the new form of space. Elsewhere, in Europe for example, London, Amsterdam, and Paris, are also good illustrations, as are São Paulo in Brazil and Hong Kong. Houston, for instance, has a downtown, but it is functionally specialized in financial and business services. It is virtually deserted at night. Commerce takes place at several large shopping malls dispersed throughout the region and the same is true for light industry and manufacturing which can be found in industrial parks or similar districts. Even places like New York also illustrate the new form of space, although that form is harder to see in this case. To be sure, Manhattan represents a traditional city center that still functions much like the core districts of the past. Yet, even so, it is only one place of highly concentrated activity. The New York City region is home to over 20 million people and encompasses parts of the states of New Jersey and Connecticut, as well as New York. People in many areas of this region, such as Northern New Jersey or Long Island, live their lives without ever necessarily having to visit Manhattan. If they do, it is for the kind of special occasion that resembles tourism. They can shop, work and engage in leisure activities close to their homes and in specialized centers spread out within this immense region. The same can be said for residents of Chicago, Atlanta, Los Angeles, and other large population concentrations in the US. To speak of these agglomerations as 'cities', the way many urbanists still do, is to ignore the basic reality on the ground one that consists of a new form of settlement space with many centers that are functionally specialized and tied together by a variety of communication and transportation modes.

For more discussion on the new form of space, see the entries on *Models of Urban Growth* and *The City'*, in particular the discussion of the relationship between growth pole theory and central place theory, which appears to set theoretical markers for the emergence of this form. For discussions that illustrate the way the traditional city still differs from other forms of space and is still important, see the entries on the *Pedestrian and Automobile, Globalization* and *Nightlife and Urban Nightscapes*.

REFERENCES

Champion, A.G. 2001. 'A Changing Demographic Regime and Evolving Polycentric Urban Region: Consequences for the Size, Composition and Distributions of City Populations' *Urban Studies* 38: 657–77.

Gottdiener, M. 1994. *The Social Production of Urban Space, 2nd Edition*. Austin, TX: University of Texas Press.

Gottdiener, M. and R. Hutchison 2000. *The New Urban Sociology, 2nd Edition*. NY: McGraw-Hill.

Gottdiener, M. and G. Kephart 1990. 'The Multi-nucleated Metropolitan Region' in R. Kling et al., *Post Suburban California*. Berkeley, CA: University of California Press.

Parr, J.B. 2004. 'The Polycentric Urban Region: A Closer Inspection' *Regional Studies* 38 (3): 231–40 (May).

US Census Bureau, *Guide to the 2002 Economic Census*, www.census.gov, accessed 25 June 2003.

92

Neighborhood

This concept, perhaps more than any other with the exception of community, is interpreted according to diverse ideological conceptions and/or agendas of planning. As in the case of *community*, these interpretations have little to do with actually existing places (see entry on *Community*).

The apostles of the *New Urbanism*, Duany and Plater-Zyberg (see entry on page 96), for example, invoke the organicist ideology of the Chicago School, regarding 'natural areas' (see entry on *Chicago School*).

'Like the habitat of any species, the neighborhood possesses a natural logic that can be described in physical terms. The following are the principles of an ideal neighborhood design: (1) the neighborhood has a center and an edge; (2) the optimal size of a neighborhood is a quarter mile from center to edge; (3) the neighborhood has a balanced mix of activities – dwelling, shopping, working, schooling, worshipping and recreating; (4) the neighborhood structures building sites and traffic on a fine network of interconnecting streets; (5) the neighborhood gives priority to public space and to the appropriate location of civic buildings.' (LeGates and Stout, 2003: 208)

Patently so, this is not a neighborhood that we can recognize as existing, but one that some planners wish realized through intervention. Yet the concept of 'natural area' as conceived by the Chicago School was based on research of that city at the time – the 1920s. It referred to a neighborhood that was culturally homogeneous or where one ethnic/racial group clearly dominated, such as Chinatown, Little Italy or Hunkey Town. This concept was closely tied to another, the 'ethnic enclave' or a neighborhood with a large population of residents that share the same ethnic/religious background, usually resulting from a high level of foreign immigration. Cities of the US period prior to the 1960s were characterized with neighborhoods very much like these. Since that time however, forces operating to disperse and mix populations throughout the multi-centered metropolitan region, as well as a drastic falling off in mass immigration, have created sections of urban areas that are ethnically and socio-economically diverse or mixed, if not racially so. (For a discussion of the persistence of racial segregation in US and UK cities, see entry on the *Ghetto and Racial Segregation*).

Perhaps the most influential thinker in regard to the concept of the 'neighborhood' as a distinct feature of the larger regional array, was Jane Jacobs (1961). When she wrote her classic book, *The Death and Life of Great American Cities* urban planners and architects were laboring under the spell of the International Style (see entry on *Postmodern and Modern Urbanism*) and replacing large sections of cities with dense, high rise developments. Jacobs decried this development and claimed it would actually destroy the modern city, not revive it. History has, in some measure, born her out. According to one observer, '[Jacobs] celebrates the seemingly small things that make a city work well for its residents: the presence of people on the street deters crime; a mix of shops and housing makes a neighborhood both convenient and lively . . . cities are ecosystems that can be smothered by rigid, authoritarian planning; . . . busy, lively sidewalks help cities thrive as safe, healthy places . . . good urban design mixes work, housing and recreation' (Walljasper, 2002).

Many contemporary architects and planners remain influenced by Jacobs' idea that city vitality is based on a healthy neighborhood street life (see entry on *Urbanization and Urbanism; New Urbanism*). Neighborhood vitality, according to the New Urbanist approach, requires a balanced mix of functions – housing, shopping, civic institutions and open space. Pedestrian circulation (the necessary 'human scale' that is sought for in this approach) is encouraged through a mix of streets and open space with conveniently located service centers.

The problem with understanding the *imagined* neighborhood of balance and centrality envisioned by urban planners is the same as that of idealized conceptions of community. Some researchers now argue that neither term captures the social ties of contemporary urban residents because today people possess networks that are less dependent on any particular space. This situation is considerably different than at the time Jane Jacobs was writing. Cyber-tech means of staying in touch were not yet invented. Now social contact no longer requires neighborhood proximity or physical communion. This concept of 'community without propinquity' was discussed in the entry on *Community*. Although the claimed effects on society of ICT, i.e., digital information and communications technology, by contemporary academic avatars of change are clearly overrated, today the cell phone and the internet along with the ubiquitous use of the automobile as opposed to public transportation, allow people to remain in close contact with a network of friends and family that are spread out across metro regions (Graham, 2004).

Neither the New Urbanists nor the network researchers however, deal with the need of a localized space that is used as a resource for people marginalized by our society. New Urbanists profess ideas that only the relatively well off can afford. Networkers and social scientists that extol the alleged power of ICT to change our lives also focus on the behavior of people with sufficient resources to 'network' across the regional realm and can afford computers. Both approaches are also biased in favor of males and professional people. Marginalized segments of the society, in contrast, need neighborhood and community relations more. This is especially true of mothers and children. 'Children's environment is not restricted to home, home yard or playground; the whole neighborhood acts as a stage that either affords or restricts children's activities' (Kytta, 1997: 41).

Children are actually among the largest consumers of public outdoor environments. Yet, their needs are often ignored by planners and developers.

'In western Europe the possibilities of children to move around freely have narrowed down during the last decades. In a large survey carried out in England, a dramatic decrease of the freedom of children to move around was found between 1971 and 1990. The researchers of the study have been worried about the so-called "pattery children", overprotected children who are not active and independent in their environments. If the contacts with the environment are regulated by adults, how does that affect the emotional and cognitive level of children's relationships in the environment?' (Kytta, 1997: 42)

According to comparative studies, children have fewest daily journeys outside the home when they live in cities, compared to rural or small town areas.

Another group of people that need fully functioning neighborhoods are those that are restricted either financially or because of age or disability. Minority people that are poor and cannot afford cars need neighborhoods and close-in access to services. So, too, do the elderly, if they cannot drive. New Urbanists seem to go too far when they prescribe balanced and fully functioning enclaves for all people in the metro region, especially in the face of so much evidence from network researchers that point to a 'spaceless' neighboring style, yet, their conception is quite appropriate for less powerful segments of our society. In this sense, vital neighborhoods are important for everyone because they play an important role in the life cycle. See next entry on *New Urbanism*.

REFERENCES

Kytta, Marketta, 1997. 'Children's Independent Mobility in Urban, Small Town, and Rural Environments' in R. Camstra (ed.) *Growing Up in a Changing Urban Landscape*. The Netherlands: Van Gorcum and Co. pp. 41–51.

Graham, Stephen (ed.) 2004. *The Cybercities Reader*. UK: Routledge.

Jacobs, Jane 1961. *The Death and Life of Great American Cities*. New York: Random House.

LeGates, R. and F. Stout (eds) 2003. *The City Reader, 3rd Edition*. UK: Routledge.

Walljasper, J. 2002. 'Jane Jacobs: Defender of the Urban Neighborhood' *Conscious Choice*, www.consciouschoice.com, accessed 25 June 2003.

95

New Urbanism is an intellectual movement of architects and planners that is opposed to the normative growth patterns of our society exemplified by suburban sprawl and restrictive residential enclaves. Among the principles they advocate are, on the one hand, a return to citizen participation in the planning process and, on the other, the conception of plans that involve the three forms of neighborhood, district and corridor.

> 'Explicitly rejecting the dominance of specialized professionals such as zoning lawyers and civil engineers, New Urbanites involve every stakeholder in the planning of a neighborhood, via no-holds barred brainstorming sessions (charettes) that emerge with practical, physical designs. The Charter of New Urbanism states, "We are committed to re-establishing the relationship between the art of building and the making of community, through citizen-based participatory planning and design".' (Fichman and Fowler, 2003: 18)

New Urbanists call for an abandonment of present day growth patterns. They seek to reshape the multi-centered metro region into localized places that are based on community *with* propinquity, despite trends to the contrary. Some of the adherents, like Andres Duany, Elizabeth Plater-Zyberk, Jaime Correa, Steven Peterson, Barbara Littenberg, Mark Schimmenti and Daniel Solomon are known as the *New Traditionalists*, because they seek to return urban living arrangements to human scale communities that are pedestrian-oriented, much like an idealized version of the small US town. Above all, this was a place, for them, where people sat on their front porches and interacted with neighbors and were able to get to work or go shopping on foot as well as by car. Following the ideas of Lewis Mumford and Jane Jacobs, the cornerstone to building an urban community involves active street life.

New Urbanists build up urban space according to neighborhoods, districts and corridors. 'The ideal neighborhood they envision is small – a five minute walk from center to edge. It is diverse, containing a balanced mix of dwellings, workplaces, shops, parks, and civic institutions such as schools and churches . . .' It has 'a center dominated by civic buildings and public space, and an edge of some kind' (perhaps defined by fields and forest; perhaps by a highway or rail line). Land use in their ideal neighborhood articulates with a system of pedestrian-friendly and transit-oriented transportation corridors that offer residents opportunities to walk, cycle, drive or take public transit to work, school, shopping and entertainment . . . This vision stands in sharp contrast to the predominant suburban pattern today: sprawling, auto-dependent, homogeneous areas lacking in public space and without clear centers or edges' (LeGates and Stout, 2003: 207).

The second component to this vision is the concept of the district. It is a functionally specialized space that nevertheless supports diverse and complementary activities. For the New Urbanists the basic planning premise of 'modernism' that required complete segregation of different economic functions is now dead. Because of de-industrialization, few urban areas contain factories today. Thus, cities are no longer afflicted by the noise and pollution of a manufacturing society that modernist planners sought to isolate from the general public through segregationist principles of zoning. The fact that cities today remain severely afflicted by the noise and pollution of auto traffic does not escape the purview of New Urbanist planners, but they do not attribute the latter inconveniences to the tradition of modernism.

The final concept promoted by this approach is the 'corridor:'

> 'The corridor is at once the connector and the separator of neighborhoods and districts. Corridors include natural and man-made elements, ranging from wildlife trails to rail lines. The corridor is not the haphazardly residual space that remains outside subdivisions and shopping centers in suburbia. Rather, it is an urban element characterized by its visible continuity. It is defined by its adjacent districts and neighborhoods and provides entry to them.' (LeGates and Stout, 2003: 211)

New Urbanism is fundamentally opposed to the present pattern of suburban sprawl. But, because it is driven by the ideas of architects and planners, it commits the physicalist fallacy. People will not behave as planners direct them to merely because some architects have conceived of a spatial design that promotes a certain pattern of behavior. Thus, Duany and Plater-Zyberg promoted housing with street access porches inspired, as they were, by small town sociability. In new developments with porches, such as Celebration in Florida, the increase in sociability among people who do not know each other, has not materialized. Making good neighbors requires much more than a theoretical architectural scheme. Simply because Duany and Plater-Zyberk constructed a development that looked like a community did not mean that the people who chose to live there would create a community. They have behaved, instead, much like affluent suburbanites everywhere and retained their spatially diffuse social networks.

With their emphasis on human-scaled neighborhoods, the New Urbanists reveal an obsession with the idealized European city, as well as the American small town, that is more imagined than real. As discussed, most people today possess strong social networks that are deployed throughout space using the telephone, the cell phone, the internet, and, most especially, the automobile. While balanced and fully functioning neighborhoods would help many people in both cities and suburbs, such as the elderly and the minority poor, they are not necessarily the kind of spaces most people would use if they were available (see entries on *Neighborhood*; *Community*).

The latter point is underscored by concrete evidence from the negative experience of projects that have implemented New Urbanist ideas. Consider the following case from San Diego (see also the entry on *Sustainable Urbanization*).

In September, 1986, the City of San Diego purchased a 14-acre abandoned Sears store and surrounding parking lot for $9 million. Responding to the principles of the New Urbanist Charter, the city opened up the development planning process to include input from local residents and their representatives. Stringent land use and design criteria were written into the proposal for redevelopment that included plans for a 3,000 sq. ft. community center to be erected on the site along with commercial buildings.

The project, known as Uptown District, was an example of the New Urbanism also because of its emphasis on pedestrian scale and its inclusion of ample public space. While malls and some theme parks have expropriated pedestrian scale, they do not make provision for public space as the New Urbanism advocates.

'What we tried to achieve', said Michael Labarre, principle architect, 'was the creation of a series of architectural images that worked together but do not give the sense that this was just one giant project built at the same time. We tried to provide a sense of streetscapes and a sense that the project is a diverse gathering of architectural images built over a number of years' ('Unsprawl Case Study' www.terrain.org, 2003: 3).

There are other pedestrian and community friendly aspects of the design:

> 'The project places all residential parking underground, using a network of pedestrian-only streets around a central park. The redevelopment is anchored by a large supermarket, yet the grocery store has only a minimal sign on the arterial road, is not adjacent to a large parking lot (since it is underground) and is designed to be "inconspicuous". There is also residential housing available in this mixed use complex.' ('Unsprawl Case Study' www.terrain.org, 2003: 3)

Despite these well thought out intentions and dutiful observance of New Urbanist ideals, the project has not been as successful as proponents predicted. Commercial enterprises have largely failed in the project. There is great turnover among the stores.

Advocates of the New Urbanism do not fault their ideas about a return to a pedestrian scale as being better and more attractive. Instead they continue to fault the automobile as the prime villain in the failure of the project. Yet, their ideas were supposed to neutralize the need and consequently the attractiveness of the auto. Instead, people have not been shopping as much in the project's commercial outlets, preferring instead to use cars to travel to better venues elsewhere. In short, the New Urbanism is not a solution that works given current social values, despite all its advocates' promises. Given the current spatial form of a multi-centered metro region, it is difficult, if not impossible, to defeat the automobile and the convenience it offers.

One of the worst offenders in the UK is the internationally known architect, Richard Rogers, who appears to think that the experience of smaller European cities can be directly mapped onto the complex patchwork topography that is London. The reification of neighborhood and its imagined community is redolent of the architectural determinism and failed modernism of the 1960s which believed that the building of Pruitt-Igoe in St Louis and Ronan Point in East London would transform the socio-economic circumstances of poorer residents in themselves. As the official spokesperson of the *Urban Renaissance*, a government sponsored report on UK urban policy, Rogers states: 'Urban neighbourhoods must become places where people of all ages and circumstances want to live. We have to increase investment and incentives to steer the markets towards them for lasting regeneration. And we must all take responsibility for the process of change, combining strengthened democratic leadership with an increased public participation' (Department of the Environment, Transport and the Regions, 1999). How to avoid the ill effects from the intoxicating mix of deconcentrating, de-centralizing and re-centralizing forces, combining with the agency of powerful real estate interests, segmented labor markets and differential access to housing and its associated wealth effects is not addressed in this paean to New Urbanism with its reified notion of 'neighborhood'.

New Urbanism is a healthy response to the problem of massive suburban sprawl and the related and negative transformation of central city life. Yet, its advocates are so enamored with the false determinism of architecture and planning schemes that they have forgotten the physicalist fallacy, which they easily commit. Transforming patterns of

New Urbanism

development requires much more than architectural visions alone. Political and economic changes in the way our society operates are also important, maybe even more basic to the need for change that we now possess. A more holistic and politically motivated approach seems called for. Fighting both sprawl and urban decay at the same time by political means is the characteristic of another perspective, the Sustainable City Movement (see the entry on *Sustainable Urbanization*).

REFERENCES

Department of the Environment, Transport and the Regions, 1999. *Towards an Urban Renaissance: Final Report of the Urban Task Force*. London: Stationery Office.
Fichman, M. and E. Fowler 2003. 'The Science and Politics of Sprawl: From Suburbia to Creative Citybuilding' Unpublished paper, York University.
LeGates, R. and F. Stout (eds) 2003. *The City Reader, 3rd Edition*. UK: Routledge.
'Unsprawl Case Study: Uptown District in San Diego, CA 2003. www.terrain.org/unsprawl/1/index.html. accessed 25 June 2003.

Nightlife and Urban Nightscapes

100

Night activities are one of the key ways central cities can be differentiated from suburbia and rural areas. *Night as Frontier* (Melbin, 1987) was the first book to systematically examine the colonization of the night-time by urban dwellers. There are several factors behind the process. Electrification illuminated the built environment chasing away the darkness and marking an extended period of urban activity that contrasted with rural life. Agriculture was bound by the day/night rhythm. When electric lights became ubiquitous, urban social activities were able to transcend nature.

Illuminated night-time in urban areas signified socializing and consumption. People visited each other in their homes or went out to purchase food and drink. Restaurants and bars were open until the local authorities declared a closing time. Throughout the industrialized countries, the hometown hour when bars were supposed to close varies considerably to this day. In London, for example, last call in most public houses, is at 11:00 pm, but new legislation in 2002 allowed some variation, while in the city of Buffalo, New York, closing time is 4:00 am. Consumption activities have expanded so effectively in advanced industrial societies that we can now speak of '24 hour' cities – the extended zone of space and time dedicated to unrestricted availability of consuming experiences. While many cities talk about this feature as an aspect of proposed redevelopment schemes, it is really only the Las Vegas region that can truly be called a 24 hour place.

Illumination also affected production. Factories could run all the time, if necessary. In fact, the 24 hour cycle is completely compliant with current union demands of an eight hour work shift. Las Vegas casinos, which are heavily unionized, discovered that it was much preferable to keep open all the time and accommodate three shifts of workers, rather than extending two shifts by having to pay over-time wages. It is said that the bars in Buffalo, New York remained open until four in the morning precisely because that was the end of the night-time shift at the steel plants. Work started up again at 6:00 am and the bars could have a respite until that shift ended in the afternoon. In short, production and consumption, which are always related, were tied together by the colonization of night-time. These work and leisure activities gave urban areas an ambiance completely lacking in areas more tied to the rhythms of agriculturally oriented or suburban life. The film *Taxi Driver* is an excellent visual representation of that late night feeling experienced only in a big city that has expropriated the daily cycle.

Chatterton and Hollands (2003), extend this analysis of the night-time further by arguing that the central city, or downtown, in particular, has increasingly become a late night place of consumption, play and hedonism for young adults. Increasingly too, new consumption venues are constructed that facilitate these activities. These spaces where people meet to drink, dance and socialize are called 'nightscapes', and they are now common features of large cities. Both cash-starved urban governments and profit-hungry global corporations have discovered that there is an immense critical mass of young adults eager to party at night. Increasingly, alcoholic products further differentiated from ordinary beer or wine, such as hard lemonade or coolers, are produced for this market, and 'chic' venues are constructed that sell them. Both the products and the spaces are manufactured by global corporations that franchise these operations.

So successful has been this new market of young adult consumption, that cities now consider catering to it as part of a general redevelopment scheme for depressed urban areas. In some places, the production of nightscapes, which includes permissive regulation by local authorities, marks one of the few successes of campaigns to bring people with money to spend back to the city center. Many urban places now have these relatively unique, youth-oriented, ludic districts of drink, dance and sexually-oriented leisure. In fact, after several years of advertising itself as a 'family destination', Las Vegas ad campaigns in 2003 are strictly designed to dispel that orientation and to proclaim that the area is a place of play for young adults. The current ads state quite boldly that 'What happens here, stays here'. Giant discos have been constructed by many of the casinos that cater to the all-night young adult market, including such names as 'Studio 54'. Currently, and in keeping with the Las Vegas style, these new nightscapes compete with each other through theming and environmental design.

The relatively recent transformation of the night-time terrain to a place of communion and consumption is quite remarkable. Once bars were characterized as seedy and, quite frankly, 'deviant', if not 'subcultural'. Mainstream and middle-class people never ventured downtown after hours to 'hang out', unless they were looking for activities outside the normative. Today, many downtown districts of large urban areas remain relatively deserted, except for these 'down and out' places. However, in locations where there has been a revitalization of the city center, nightscapes catering to young adult consumers have led the way. Using the techniques of branding products and theming environments, corporations have transformed these spaces to accommodate an expanding market of active consumers that seem to be up all night. Rather than a place on the margin, or a space of deviance, the nightscapes are now ordinary, mainstream locations where the business of buying and selling goes on as elsewhere and urban dwellers can talk with some pride about a '24 hour' city.

Exactly how this transformation from seediness to trendiness occurred is instructive because it illuminates the interplay of capital and space. In the early 1990s a dance club, the *Ministry of Sound*, opened in London. Now it is the largest global dance record label in the world. Through the use of theming, branding and franchising, global corporations create environments that tie in activities such as dancing with the consumption of alcohol, fashion, and the commodification of 'cool'. The *Ministry of Sound*, like other operations, is no longer just a place to dance, it is a global brand that sells many different kinds of merchandise. A second logic of corporate merchandising is the segmentation of markets. All young people are not alike in their musical preferences, fashions or tastes for drink. Global corporations segment these markets or follow the rifts in consumer practices to design different products for actually existing subcultural segments. Alcoholic beverages are a good example. One company, such as Anheiser-Busch, the largest beer producer in the world, makes several different brands and markets them in different ways. Advertising is the key to creating this virtual product diversity. In reality, all market segments are serviced by the same manufacturer. Only the brand names differ. Companies that create nightscape venues also construct places that seem to differ from each other in appearance. In this way, franchising the night-time does not always mean that businesses are in competition with each other. They may all belong to the same corporation and are merely appealing to different market segments.

The result of all this profit-making activity is a proliferation of consumer places downtown and an explosion of the night-time population, something that depressed cities collectively thought impossible just a decade ago. As elsewhere, with regard to the effects of globalization, it has been the local, independently-owned venues that have suffered from this juggernaut. Yet, Chatterton and Hollands (2003) make an excellent point in their analysis of the phenomenon. By applying a Gramscian cultural studies framework, we become attuned to the fact that there is a *mainstream* that is corporately controlled, but there are also *residual* and *alternative* spaces in the locational array. Antonio Gramsci argued that any society undergoing change does not simply shift from one state to another. There are elements of the old regime that remain and these are the *residual* aspects of society. In the case of clubbing, not all original venues shut down simply because new, flashy locations were built. Nightscapes contain a mix of the new with the old; consumers can still find, in most places, those residual and locally owned spaces that have 'character', as long as seediness, for example, isn't picked up by one of the global corporations and marketed as a theme, that is.

Along with the mainstream and residual dimensions, Gramsci argued that there are always forces of opposition appearing in any society undergoing change. In fact, according to the Gramscian perspective, it is precisely the oppositional activities that often lead to change itself. For the case of clubbing, market segmentation by giant corporations can never hem in alternatives. Youth subcultures are much too robust and original for that outcome because those subcultures are authentic expressions of identity issues. Consequently, nightscapes are also populated by places that cater to lifestyles or modes of symbolic expression that see themselves as alternatives to mainstream patterns of consumption. These locations are also added to the mix of the nightscape. In sum, within any of the areas that have a viable night-time, there are places of corporate control, franchising and market segmentation, and, there are also places that are locally owned and ones that cater to alternative lifestyles. As with other aspects of culture, this mix of diversity means that consumer practices and symbolic definitions will always be in a state of flux, much of it being quite healthy and innovative. As long as city administrations nurture these nightscapes and prevent powerful corporations from obtaining complete control, the central city will remain attractive to a wide variety of people. In some cases, however, such as the transformation of 42nd Street in Manhattan, the mix of venues was obliterated in favor of a mini-version of Disneyworld and for the sake of the tourist industry alone. In that case, it is understandable when observers lament the passing of 'authentic' city life.

REFERENCES

Chatterton, P. and R. Hollands 2003. *Urban Nightscapes: Youth Cultures, Pleasure Spaces and Corporate Power*. London: Routledge.

Melbin, M. 1987. *Night as Frontier*. NY: The Free Press.

Overurbanization – The Primate City

104

Advanced industrial societies, such as those in Europe and the US, have urbanized over an extended period of time. Under such conditions agricultural areas remained relatively stable and city development occurred with a measured pace. While all of these societies have large cities there is, nevertheless, a hierarchy that speaks to a *balanced growth* of urbanization. This means that populations within urbanized places exhibit a full range of ranks from many small cities to a lesser number of medium-sized places and, finally, a select few urban areas that are huge. There are several advantages of such balanced urbanization including the availability of many alternative locations for businesses and residences, increased manageability of urban administration, and comparative strength of the economy in its mix of sectors, including agriculture.

In contrast, the pattern and process of urban growth in many developing countries is characterized by *overurbanization* where all the negative effects of city growth experienced by developed countries are magnified many times. Overurbanization is a socio-spatial process of excess population concentration in urban areas beyond the capacity to provide basic services and housing infrastructure to urban dwellers. Overurbanized cities lack jobs, education and healthcare facilities, and other necessary resources to support their growing urban population (Bradshaw and Schafer, 2000). According to a World Bank report:

> 'Far more people have migrated to urban areas than could be absorbed, and despite large investments in urban infrastructure, the result has been a severe strain on urban services and labor markets. In most developing countries, this strain is reflected in highly dualistic urban systems, where islands of high income "modernity" coexist with shanty towns and slums. The permanence of the new peripheral urban settlements has not been adequately recognized, and municipal financing and management have not received the attention they need. As a result, little has been done either to deal with the appalling inadequacy of essential services, such as sanitation, in these settlements, or to assist the large part of the urban economy that consists of small-scale and informal production activities, which operate at low levels of productivity.' (1991)

Overurbanization is often evidenced by the presence of *primate cities*. Within such countries there are vast rural areas and then one or two immense urban regions, while cities of an intermediate and smaller size are completely lacking. Often, as in the case of Thailand, there is only a single primate city like Bangkok. This pattern is the opposite of the kind of balanced urbanization characteristic of advanced industrial societies. The presence of primate cities, or urban primacy, indicates 'a lack of economic, political and social integration in any given system of cities' (Kasarda and Crenshaw, 1991: 1). The lack of balanced city-size distributions is thought to represent a symptom of underdevelopment and uneven development. Resources and values of the country including power, wealth, social institutions and opportunities are excessively concentrated in these primate cities. They create a type of vicious cycle. As the only place for urban opportunities, they persist in drawing increasingly more people thereby preventing the growth of other smaller cities.

Urban problems related to overurbanization are alarming and increasingly serious in recent years. Overcrowding in primate cities is a common problem that strains resources and the ability of places to provide adequate sanitation and basic social services. Overurbanization distorts the allocation of productive resources such as labor. Regular full-time, year-round jobs are relatively rare, yet there is a massive supply of labor in overurbanized cities. Given the limited economic performance of the developing countries, it is not unusual that job creation is very slow and the rate of unemployment is very high. In addition to an abundant reservoir of surplus labor which depresses all wages, underemployment is also a problem in third world cities, such as temporary, casual, or seasonal labor. Under-utilized labor may even disguise the full magnitude of unemployment and the crisis of development. Another aspect of overurbanization is the glaring lack of supply in the provision of urban infrastructure and collective consumption commodities, such as housing, education and healthcare. The urban poor, without political and economic power, are spatially concentrated in the most disadvantaged areas where they are neglected by local and national governments in the provision of basic services. For more discussion see the entries on *Inequality and Poverty; Slums and Shanty Towns.*

In many cases the pattern of overurbanization and the creation of primate cities is a consequence of a colonial past. When countries were colonized, an urban infrastructure was developed in only a select number of locations while the interior was left to be exploited for its natural resources alone. Over time, the primate city became a magnet drawing huge numbers of people off the land and into the city in the hope of obtaining some measure of wealth. Despite the abandonment of colonial regimes, overurbanization remained as a process and continues to this day.

Future prospects for these immense regions do not look good. Almost half the world's population is now urban and by about 2015 the majority, over 5 billion people, will live in urban settlements. Most of the population growth of cities has taken place in developing countries. Approximately 55 million people are now added to the urban population of developing countries every year. Since 1970, the number of 'million' cities (those with populations between 1 and 10 million) in Africa, Asia and Latin America has more than doubled. Once started, the massive movement of people to primate cities does not stop, despite the hardships that are encountered there because of poverty and the like. Now overurbanization in developing countries is occurring even in the absence of broad-based economic growth. The least developed countries are experiencing some of the highest urban growth rates: Africa has the highest urban growth rate of all world regions, at over 4% per year (World Bank, 1991).

Exacerbating this problem is the way many of the primate cities in the third world fit at present into the global economy. Despite their severe problems, they are viewed almost exclusively as sites for cheap labor. As noted above, the over-supply of eager workers keeps all wages low. Misery and disrupted family life are commodified in the struggle for work and then exploited by companies manufacturing inexpensive goods for global export. As the World Bank reports:

'In the cities high levels of urban inequality, poverty, unemployment and underemployment are inefficient in terms of social welfare but they are very efficient to meet the needs of both local and transnational industrialists seeking relatively cheap labor.' (1991)

For more information, see the entries on *Globalization; Inequality and Poverty; Slums and Shanty Towns.*

REFERENCES

Bradshaw, Y. and M. Schafer 2000. 'Urbanization and Development: The Emergence of International Nongovernmental Organizations amid Declining States' *Sociological Perspectives*, 43: 97–116.
Kasarda, J. and E. Crenshaw 1991. 'Third World Urbanization: Dimensions, Theories and Determinants' *Annual Review of Sociology*, 17: 467–501.
World Bank, 1991. *Urban Policy and Economic Development.* Quoted in 'Urbanization and Development in Africa' (1999) Bergen, Norway: Chr. Michelsen Institute publication.

Pedestrian and Automobile

Called upon to name the most essential *experiential* contrast between the city and the suburb, it would have to be that of the pedestrian and the automobile. Clearly the difference between living in a high density residential building that is surrounded by other high density buildings in contrast to living in a single family, suburban home also typifies the difference between the city and the suburb. However, in this latter case, once inside these distinct structures, everyday life is quite similar. This is not the case with being on foot versus in a car while negotiating the built environment. A pedestrian and a driver or passenger in a car experience urban culture in completely distinct ways.

Low density suburban living is automobile oriented. Houses have driveways for access. It is often difficult for someone visiting most single family suburban homes from the street to find the path leading to the entrance. A door is clearly visible from the road, but getting there means expending some effort in discovering the small and restricted path to it in between the large expanse of front lawn. By coming to this same house in a car, the environmental signs of access are much clearer. Just drive up the driveway. Upon getting out of the car, there is usually a cemented or finished path of some kind that leads directly to the door. Suburban houses also have garages that are conveniently located and often part of the home itself, unlike the high rise residences in the city. Many suburbanites treat the garage as an extra room. Most commonly it is used for storage; sometimes with so much collected junk, that there is no room for the car itself. People in the suburbs periodically try to weed out some of this crap by holding 'garage sales', which is another, typically suburban experience.

Suburban living means commuting everywhere by car. Certainly, city residents also commute. They may even have as long a ride to work on public transportation as people in the suburban areas have by car. But, there are distinct differences between a ride in an automobile and one using public transportation. In a car everyone has a seat. The driver usually has created a kind of comfort zone in and around her/his place. There are cup holders that may contain a favorite coffee mug, CD and cassette players with an extensive selection aboard of things to listen to while driving that range from music to books 'on tape'. There is a radio for news, usually about driving conditions, or some other kind of entertainment such as music or sporting events. It has long been established that the modern automobile is an extension of the home living room with its padded seats, entertainment center and conveniently placed things to drink or eat.

The influence of US culture in Europe has been profound, accelerating since the end of World War II, from *les blue jeans* and James Dean look-alikes as the youth icon of 1950s France, to the Britney Spears and Beyoncé aspirants from Glasgow to Gdansk. The material transformation that has accompanied this cultural beat has been the automobile and its role in suburbanizing Europe's cities and, by extension, the means of fulfilling the dream of modernity through an escape from public transport. Many of Europe's cities do not suit the automobile because, with the possible exception of Berlin and Paris, most cities have not been laid out in a planned fashion. Londoners are well served by radial public transport links, but car ownership is still pretty de-rigueur for getting across the metropolitan regions. For those growing up in 1950s and early

1960s Europe, the memory of buying the family's first refrigerator and the first car was the right of passage to modernity.

The influence of the automobile and catering for it, in what the late architectural writer, Reyner Banham, called the 'Second Machine Age', has been profound in UK planning circles, despite the recent fashion for sustainable cities (Banham, 1963). However, the distinction between the US and Europe is that in the former, jobs as well as homes have been de-centralized to the suburbs whereas in European cities, it has tended to be homes alone leading to longer commuting times from work to home (Hall, 1998). In the British case, the particularity of the housing market means that residential location corresponds to the classic Alonso model of transport costs/housing costs trade-off (Alonso, 1960). That is, access to the automobile means that larger but lower cost housing in the suburbs can be accessed.

In contrast to the suburbs, living in a large city, such as Manhattan, means doing things on foot. One estimate claims that Manhattanites walk several miles a day just by taking care of their necessary tasks. There is a pedestrian culture and social etiquette that must be obeyed even when an individual is pressed for time and walks rapidly to a destination. The busy city street is a miracle of crowd behavior where strangers scurry to and fro without so much as a single clashing incident. People twist and turn, like sails in the wind, to avoid any serious bumps with others as they make their way in the crowded two lane traffic of pedestrians. Contact is often made, in fact, it is unavoidable, but it is done in such a manner as not to be perceived as a violation of another's personal space. Most often, a simple 'I'm sorry', uttered quickly after contact that might be considered something more than ordinary brushing by, is more than enough to prevent the flow of traffic from being interrupted by someone who feels they have been slighted or abused. A similar, highly structured dance within a large crowd of strangers characterizes riding in public transportation. Here, unlike the private automobile, people have to accommodate themselves to the physical presence of strangers and often under conditions of crowding where individuals are squeezed together within a confining space. No panic, no offenses, no confrontations ensue from such scenes, despite the fact that, under any other circumstance people would never allow strangers to come so close. When public transportation is this densely used, women can suffer abuse from unwanted touching and they have to take special care. But, much more often than not, the ride is uneventful, because etiquette is obeyed.

City life is comprised of strangers that come together in close proximity and personal space is redefined to accommodate close quarters and even a kind of touching that would never be tolerated by these same individuals under other circumstances. When public transportation is not jammed to the bursting point with humanity, people can often find seats and then a different repertoire of interactive ploys become involved. The key idea is not to make eye contact with others that are close by. A common device is to deploy a newspaper or book while riding so that glancing around at others can be avoided. Any visitor to a large city that takes public transportation immediately gets the impression that the place is populated by avid readers. They also experience the feeling that residents could not care less that anyone else is around. This kind of blasé attitude is very characteristic of city life (see entry on *Nightlife*).

Two keen observers have established the critical importance of pedestrian life for city culture, William H. Whyte (1988) and Jane Jacobs (1961). Whyte did film studies of people on the streets of Manhattan. He documented how the sidewalks were a kind of public space. Most pedestrians simply used them to get from one destination to another, but Whyte noticed how some people met acquaintances on the street and stopped to chat with them. This 'schmoozing', as Whyte called it using the Yiddish expression, was an important interactive dimension of city life. Whyte documented how certain parts of the city-scape came to be points of schmoozing, while others were left for their primary function of facilitating pedestrian traffic. In a sense, schmoozing is a basic form of social interaction. It reinforces friendship ties, it enables people to catch up on news about acquaintances and even close friends, and it binds together individuals that know each other in some way. It is as essential to urban life as is meeting other inhabitants at more formal places like restaurants and bars. With the discovery that schmoozing was a frequent and obviously important mode of interaction, Whyte established that the city street was a crucial public space in its own right and also one that was very typically 'urban'.

Jane Jacobs' writings were equally significant in pointing to the role of pedestrians in enriching city life. For Jacobs, the ideal city neighborhood is one that has a mix of residences and commercial establishments open late into the night. Her model was the place where she lived in Manhattan, a section called Greenwich Village, which was a lively area of diverse people including many single women. Jacobs observed that the streets were always filled with pedestrian traffic because of both the comings and goings of residents and also the clientele of the commercial businesses in the neighborhood. Street crime was comparatively low in this section of the city and violent crimes were almost unheard of there. Jacobs argued effectively that this feature was the direct result of the active pedestrian scene (see entries on *New Urbanism; Urban Nightlife*). There were simply too many people out at all hours of the day and night to allow the committing of a crime. Jacobs believed that, if the city could be made safe for single women and children, then it would be able to compete with the more family friendly places in the suburbs and people would not abandon it as they had been doing during the 1950s and 60s when she was living in Greenwich Village. Whether or not she was correct about this aspect of her argument, she did explain why crime was low in the area. Deserted spaces allow the necessary opportunity to victimize others that criminals require. Lively street scenes filled with pedestrians at all hours not only deters crime, but it is the very hallmark of a healthy city.

Suburbanites have given up a pedestrian existence and, it must be observed, that they have done so with relish. They love their cars. Most single family homes have two-car garages. In the 1950s, when mass development was occurring outside US central cities, new suburban residents adopted the station wagon as the family car. Husbands may have commuted to work using a variety of means, including public transportation rather than autos, but the suburban mom had her station wagon to shop for groceries and drive the kids around. Later, in the 1960s and 70s, the typical vehicle became the van. The term 'soccer mom' also appeared at this time. Now, suburbanites of all kinds can be observed careening around corners in huge SUVs, or 'sport utility vehicles'. These trucks that were once modified for off-road driving have evolved considerably from their original functions and are now the staple of commuter life outside the city. They are no longer used for their original purpose and have, instead, replaced the station wagon or van as the vehicle 'soccer mom's' feel safe in and which are used for the full range of suburban functions from commuting to work to shopping and chauffeuring. The British suburban experience is similar. In the London metropolitan region, it is estimated that traffic flows 30% faster during school holidays. On school days, in contrast, much needed two-way streets become one-way as offspring are drooped off in a variety of vehicles, often less than a mile away from their homes.

If a suburban family has teenagers then, invariably, they may have their own cars too. In affluent areas, homes have three and even four car garages. Vehicles are parked in and around the house. A visit to town court also reveals the price that parents pay for adhering to the norm of teenage driving. Many cases involve youngsters that have committed traffic infractions of serious kinds, such as excessive speeding. Even more troubling are those incidents when teenagers are arrested for drunk driving thereby violating several different kinds of laws at once. For quite some time in the US, auto fatalities have been the leading cause of death among suburban teenagers.

Cars have become so important to US life that their use has affected cities themselves. The same imperative operates in may parts of Europe, particularly the UK. It is quite extraordinary to document just how much space in our urban areas is devoted to the automobile. Highway construction has ripped cities apart. More often than not they have destroyed the urban social fabric by cutting neighborhoods into parts that are then isolated from each other. Perhaps the best example is the effect that the construction of Robert Moses' Cross-Bronx Expressway had on the everyday life of that borough (see Berman, 1988). Making it easy to travel by car from one end of the Bronx to the other, also destroyed communities across the Bronx by bisecting the borough in half. One result was massive apartment abandonment as people moved elsewhere to more stable neighborhoods. Years later, this part of New York City still suffers the effects of decline precipitated by the highway project. Urban places reeling under the negative effects of several decades of economic decline have also become auto dependent in an excessive way. Commonly, administrations and planners have sanctioned the demolition of under-utilized office and commercial buildings within central cities for the construction of parking lots. In this way, it is believed that, by making the downtown more friendly to car-oriented suburban residents, they will come back in numbers sufficient to revive the urban economy. It is quite remarkable to contemplate just how much space many cities have devoted to parking lots, especially the medium-sized ones that have been in decline, while, at the same time, destroying buildings with historical significance that were basically sound and could have been renovated.

At the policy level, the love affair with the car has ended in many UK cities. Built up humps, narrowing of already narrow streets and traffic light re-phasing comprise many of the traffic management measures. In 2002, the newly elected Mayor of London introduced a charging scheme for traffic entering the CBD of London. The revenue raised was to improve public transport, in particular increasing the number of public transport buses. The charge rate at the time of writing is £5 (about US$9). The impact, so far, has been a reduction of traffic by about 30%. However, the deterrent effect has been more powerful than anticipated, so that less revenue has been raised to pay for more public transport, and there is little overall effect on the level of car ownership in the London metropolitan region. As is the case in the US, people living in the outer

112

suburbs of UK cities have little choice but to use cars for everyday activities like traveling to work and shopping, due to the lack of public transportation.

Lastly, it is important to observe just how special the pedestrian experience really is for people that have lived their lives in suburbia. There is something extraordinary about being part of a pedestrian crowd and among strangers that share similar goals and do so in a pleasant way. People experience the pleasure of the pedestrian mass on trips to theme parks, such as *Disneyworld*, where they have to abandon their cars as the first condition of entrance. The enjoyment of being on foot and liberated from the automobile is not usually noticed, but it is there. So effective is the switch that shopping malls and, even, Las Vegas casinos have structured their internal spaces to recreate the city scene. *New York-New York*, *Paris*, *Caesars Forum Shops*, the *Venetian* and *Bally's*, on the Strip all use a manufactured and simulated pedestrian urban milieu as a means of producing their themes and stimulating both gambling and shopping. The attraction of the city, made safe by simulation, by charging admission and by aggressive surveillance is also clearly in evidence on a visit to the theme park, *CityWalk*, which is part of Universal Studios in Los Angeles. Other themed environments around the country use similar urban-style simulations to promote their own brand of consumerism. For this reason cities will always be important culturally, and this fact is not realized any more intensely than in the philosophy of the 'new urbanists' who wish to rewrite the landscape of suburban America on a more human and pedestrian scale (see entry on *New Urbanism*).

The attraction of the 'real' urban experience for many Europeans is the dystopian dark side of cities; their social undergrowth, their culture of negotiation between good and evil, dark and light. Many European New Urbanists would take this sense away, reproducing an imagined and mono-cultural civic culture designed solely for conspicuous consumption by the affluent (see entry on *Nightlife and Urban Nightscapes*).

REFERENCES

Alonso, W. 1960. 'A theory of urban rent' *Papers and Proceedings of the Regional Science Association*, 6: 154–9.

Banham, R. 1963. *Theory and Design in the First Machine Age*. London: Architectural Press.

Berman, Marshall, 1988. *All that is Solid Melts Into Air*. NY: Penguin Books.

Jacobs, Jane, 1961. *The Death and Life of Great American Cities*. NY: Random House.

Whyte, W.H. 1988. *City: Rediscovering the Center*. NY: Anchor Books.

113

Planning – Cities, Suburbs, Metropolitan Regions

The earliest cities developed for the most part with chaotic street systems and land uses. Enterprises and residences were located wherever the owners decided they should be. Yet, the classic civilizations did engage in forms of planning. Often building was carried out according to some overarching symbolic scheme belonging to the religious beliefs of the people. During the medieval period in Europe and in some places in Asia, cities were built with planned fortifications in the interests of self-defense. When capitalist industrialization appeared in the 1800s, first in Europe, then in the US, new conceptions of how to guide city growth emerged that replaced the rationale for religious thinking or defense. Some of the most notable ideas in the 19th Century sought to overcome the ills of pollution and public health crisis so characteristic of the industrial town under capitalism.

One important 19th Century thinker was Ebenezer Howard. He viewed the industrial city as simply too large. It had lost its human scale. He proposed, instead, that new development follow a *garden city* approach that melded factory construction with countryside living. The garden city, then, represented the best of city and country living. Howard's approach gave rise to the *new town* movement in England which resulted in construction of factory centers located outside the large cities. In the US, both Garden City, Long Island, New York, and Baldwin Hills, outside of Los Angeles, California were built on this model during the early part of the 20th Century.

Historically, the first steps in the direction of modern city planning can be traced to practices establishing districts within which certain rights of citizens were legally curbed. In the late European middle ages, slaughtering places for cattle were located on the outskirts of town so that offensive odors would not permeate the city. During the 1700s in Boston the segregation of the storage place for gunpowder away from the city center was one of the first recorded acts of *zoning* the separation of social functions in separate land use districts (Gallion and Eisner, 1980). Early zoning was confined to the

114

regulation of business locations that were either a public menace, such as gunpowder, or public nuisance, such as slaughterhouses or laundries. In 1876 the State of California ruled that the 'County of San Francisco could regulate the placement of slaughter houses, the keeping of swine, the curing of hides or the carrying on of any business or occupation "offensive" to the senses or prejudicial to the public health or comfort, in certain portions of the city'. Slowly, through various rulings, the power of communities to regulate land for the general welfare became established as law.

According to Gallion and Eisner (1980: 185):

'One of the most important legal decisions in the history of zoning was the Euclid case (Village of Euclid, Ohio v. Amber Realty Company, 272 US 365) in 1926. In his decision, Justice Sutherland of the US Supreme Court pointed out that each community had the right and the responsibility to determine its own character, and as long as that determination did not disturb the orderly growth of the region or the nation, it was valid use of the police power.'

This decision made it clear that communities which were incorporated municipalities with their own powers over land could determine the nature of development through zoning limitations. They could do this provided they also allowed the greater region, within which they were located, opportunity to grow.

During the 20th Century, the technique of *zoning* became increasingly more important. Based on modernist principles that like activities should be located near one another and that manufacturing and residential functions should be separated, zoning partitioned land use according to each. Modernist planning used a zoning scheme that guides development into separate spaces according to residential, commercial, industrial and transportation functions (see entry on *Postmodern and Modern Urbanism*). Once planned out, it was then left to the private market in land to attract potential developers. In the US, planners only have the power to draw up such schemes and offer advice in guiding growth according to zoning regulations. They cannot interfere with the way businesses and people utilize the land within those zoning categories. While public officials have the power to approve or disapprove proposed projects according to land use regulations, invariably they all support growth because of its benefits to the area. In fact, many jurisdictions believe they are in competition with each other for the attraction of new business. Consequently, they try to be liberal in the application of regulations.

Land use planning in the US is carried out by a local government office:

115

'In many cities the officials employed are few in number and the commission may have no regular staff. Then the city engineer or clerk is largely responsible for drawing up plans. In large cities there is usually a well qualified staff. Matters that fall within the legal responsibility of planning commissions are the *comprehensive plan*, *zoning ordinances* and *subdivision codes*, but there is also a coordination function that is needed in places that are growing. Some large cities or suburban regions have a separate zoning board and that administrates the land use code.' (Gallion and Eisner, 1980: 192)

The planning departments of municipalities adopted a practice after the 1950s of drawing up *master plans*. This comprehensive approach was made necessary because cities could not develop without taking into account what was happening in their regions. Planners turned to the collection of concrete data on existing land uses and assessed precisely how much space was devoted to the various zoning categories – light manufacturing, heavy industry, single family residences, multiple family residences, parking spaces, roads, parks and forms of public property. Once the inventory was complete, a plan for future growth based upon present and anticipated needs was developed. This approach is called *master planning*, and it became an accepted practice of municipal governments in the US. The master plan could then be aggregated with other such schemes for regional development.

Despite the development of comprehensive techniques for monitoring and predicting land use needs, planners in the US have few powers to realize their schemes. They are limited by the activities of the private market in land. Developers and real estate speculators are well known for being able to get around the obstacles of planning prescriptions. Furthermore, with very few exceptions, regional and comprehensive planning that fosters cooperation between cities and suburbs does not exist. In short, most places lose out to single minded and narrowly focused developers by increments. One small exception leads to another until the basis of comprehensive planning in an area is eroded completely. For this reason there have been a number of well thought out critiques of planning in our society. Increasingly, people concerned about the lack of coordination for growth and the problems of regional sprawl have developed alternative approaches.

In the UK, the desire for sustainable housing, that is, those that are environmentally friendly in the use of materials, is thwarted by the power of private developers. Demands by planners that private housing development should include a certain percentage of social housing for key public sector workers (e.g., teachers, nurses etc.) are rarely fulfilled or, if so, only at the margins. In the over-heated private housing market, developers can undermine these pressures. Moreover, private developers and speculators have built up large land banks that they exploit at appropriate moments in the growth cycle. Thus, the situation in the UK is similar to the US as growth interests have a way of requiring planning to rationalize the development process and then, at the same time, get around its limitations in order to turn a profit by violating aspects of the plan (see also the entries on *Sprawl; Sustainable Urbanization*).

PLANNING CRITIQUES

In the 1980s, Anthony Downs published a series of planning critiques. Downs sought to return to the ideas of Ebenezer Howard and balanced urbanization. However, rather than focusing on the concept of the 'garden city', he was obsessed with the positive aspects of an idealized Western European town. In particular, he was an outspoken critic of suburbia. According to Downs, the norms of living in single family homes and a reliance on the private automobile had to be abandoned. Furthermore, Downs called for a governance structure that would integrate the needs of the city and the suburb, i.e., regional government, in place of the separate municipalities that we now possess.

To replace the current arrangements of living and working, Downs turned to his idealized version of the European urban model:

> 'It featured high-density residential settlements, high density workplaces, tightly circumscribed land use patterns that prevent peripheral sprawl, and massive use of heavily subsidized public transit systems for movement. These traits are only possible under a governance system that centralizes power over the land use patterns in each metropolitan area in a single governing body with authority over the entire area.' (Downs, 2003: 256)

In short, Downs' prescriptions, when addressing the case of the US, led immediately to a well-known dilemma. With very few exceptions, local governments historically refused to surrender any power to make room for regional governance. This is especially true for control over land use regulation, because it is precisely that power which provides local governments with revenue. Despite the power of local authorities being reduced by successive British governments since the late 1970s, in contrast to the US case, full blown regional government and appropriate revenue raising powers have not fully developed in the UK. Partly, this is the consequence of a British fear of federalism and partly a resistance to planning. The relatively newly formed Regional Development Agencies (RDAs) now function as business-led organizations that coordinate economic development on a regional scale in place of government planners. Yet, there are dissenters to this situation. National employers' organizations (the Confederation of British Industry, the Institute of Directors) claim that the current planning system is undermining the competitiveness of UK businesses. Consequently, there are pressures to de-regulate the planning system and increase the powers of the RDAs from coordination to full legal authority.

Despite Europe's historical record of publicly supported urban planning, there continue to be other pressures for moving to a more 'American-style' of privately led development in order to be economically competitive. For example, the US economist, Robert Gordon, cites the differences in the productivity performance of the US compared to European economies as being produced in three sectors: wholesale, retail and financial services. He states that, if planning controls were looser in Europe, then the benefits of allowing the building of many Wal-Marts in suburban shopping malls would increase productivity (Gordon, 2003). That European societies may not wish to choose this option appears to have passed over Gordon's head.

Another source of planning critiques emerged in the 1990s with the appearance of the New Urbanists (see entry on page 96). Above all other considerations, they were opposed to the pattern of regional sprawl and sought to return dwelling spaces to a more human scale. Two architects that are outspoken advocates of the new approach, Peter Calthorpe and William Fulton, outlined a program recently that provides an alternative to sprawl:

> 'What is the most appropriate scale for urban planning? The home? The street? The neighborhood? The city? Or the entire metropolitan region? These authors argue that every element of the planned environment interacts with every other and that planners embracing the New Urbanist conception should follow a holistic, ecological approach that harmonizes the intimate scale of the neighborhood with the metropolitan scale of the region.' (Calthorpe and Fulton, 2001)

Thus, their ideas are complementary to the conception of settlement space as a multi-centered metropolitan region. In fact, they have called for residential developments within the region to be built at higher densities than at present, that are then surrounded by greenbelts. These mini-centers would resemble Garden Cities with a mix of service and light manufacturing functions so that people could use alternate means of transportation.

In this regard, Calthorpe and Fulton claim they oppose modernist principles of planning such as zoning codes. They no longer see the need for strict separation of social functions arguing, instead, that contemporary, 'post-industrial' society possesses cleaner and less obtrusive modes of production which can, therefore, be located close to residential centers.

As in the case of Downs' proposals, Calthorpe and Fulton's vision of mixed use regional development also requires massive and new state control of local areas:

'The idea that a region can be "designed" is central to the Regional City.' They call for 'an active role on the part of central governments, especially in the provision of transit systems, open-space, and development financing' (Calthorpe and Fulton, 2001). But here they conceive of 'regions' as reifications. This is a monolithic view that fails to understand how multi-centeredness means flexibility and functional differentiation. They assume that different centers can be easily aggregated and that all regional functions can be objectified. This is the kind of conception typical of planners that cannot see beyond the fallacy of thinking in *physicalist* terms alone.

Calthorpe and Fulton conceive of the landscape as resulting from existing planning codes. They critique the present form of planning by insisting that these are out of date and based on modernism. They fail to account for both how the market in real estate and how government programs have produced regional sprawl. They are so enamored with the power of the planning profession, even in light of its immense failure, that they cannot see how plans and codes have been constantly circumvented by real estate development and how suburbanization looks the way that it does because for generations the federal government subsidized home ownership and highway construction.

Can planners really do anything when capitalist political and economic institutions are so strong? The failure of planning in the US is not just about the strength of the real estate market, it is also about the immense investment of suburban and urban governments in retaining their control over land. Planners have no power because local governments will not let them have it. They are retained solely in an advisory capacity. This is supposed to be a reflection of democracy because it implies that experts should not have the final say regarding what our landscape should look like. But, in practice, this arrangement leaves an opening for special interests that they enjoy and take advantage of with immense relish. Even the advisory role of planners is thus subverted. The European position is similar as noted by one British planning writer:

119

'Yet the local planning process is no level playing field allowing all the participants an equal chance of success. Rather it is a highly political activity controlled by various policy processes, each of which may suit particular interests better than others.' (Adams, 1994: 177)

This state of affairs does not mean that no planning takes place in the US and elsewhere in the world. Considerable design and adherence to zoning codes occurs on a daily basis. Planning agencies work constantly to control growth as best they can by monitoring it and by providing local government with advice and recommendations. Zoning itself remains a powerful tool that often still does reduce the negative effects of environmental nuisances.

Critiques, like that of the New Urbanists, provide people with ideas about how to make the process better. This is especially important today when we have experienced the negative effects of regional sprawl. Another approach, known as *advocacy planning* is also available (see entry on *Urban Politics and Suburban Politics*). It proposes that planners work closely with local citizens to effect change. By encouraging participation and by disseminating correct information about growth and its effects, advocacy planners can acquire a constituency of concerned citizens that can then translate their values into political influence. New Urbanists, with their practice of 'charettes' seek the same stimulation of local citizen participation. The basic idea is that an informed populace will opt for better planning and put pressure on government to improve the environment. This is an end that planning can realize, if we let it.

REFERENCES

Adams, D. 1994. *Urban Planning and the Development Process*. London: UCL Press.

Calthorpe, P. and W. Fulton 2001. *The Regional City: Planning for the End of Sprawl*. Washington, DC: Island Press.

Downs, A. 2003. 'The Need for a New Vision for the Development of Large US Metropolitan Areas' in R. LeGates, and F. Stout (eds) *The City Reader*. London: Routledge. pp. 256–66.

Gallion, A. and S. Eisner 1980. *The Urban Pattern: City Planning and Design*. NY: D. Van Nostrand.

Gordon, R. 2003. 'Five Puzzles in the Behavior of Productivity, Investment and Innovation' Unpublished paper, Department of Economics, Northwestern University.

120

Postmodern and Modern Urbanism

The concepts of a 'postmodern' city and, relatedly, a 'postmodern' urbanism have been weakly argued, despite the popularity of the term postmodern and its more specific applicability to a type of architecture. Urbanists claiming a postmodern perspective simply translate mundane observations into their own special language that at times are just silly neologisms or at other times are references to specific postmodern concepts that may be out of place. For example, is it really necessary to observe with Ed Soja that the tall buildings located in downtown LA provide a panopticonic gaze? By using this term, does that make Los Angeles a 'postmodern city' in the way that other cities with tall buildings are not? Is the concept of 'panoptic' used correctly? Is this roof view anything like the engine of surveillance designed by Jeremy Bentham and elaborated as a strategy of power by Michel Foucault? Then why are there only tourists on top of the Empire State Building and other skyscrapers, instead of the police?

According to Robert Lake (1999), the attempts by some Los Angeles geographers to characterize that city as 'postmodern' illustrate instead why the very concept can have no meaning at all:

> 'The neologisms not only mimic the modernist's external perspective but indeed reduce the vibrancy of agents to mere caricatures. Their neologisms (protosurps, holsteinization) invoke visions of the city's residents as cattle, mind-numbed serfs unable to alter, improve or control their lives . . . "Postmodern Urbanism" may reveal the failures of postmodernism, or it may simply be a case of doing postmodernism badly. Far from succeeding in their intended role of provocative hypothesis-generators, . . . [T]hey offer generalization by cartoon, perhaps inaugurating an R. Crumb school of urban analysis.'

121

These criticisms aside, the key issue raised by any analysis wishing to compare modernism and postmodernism within the urban context is not to claim that some entire city or region is either modern or postmodern, but to discuss how modernist or postmodernist aspects are manifested in space.

Before we can discuss 'postmodernist urbanism', it is necessary to consider what 'modernist' ideas have to do with urban places.

MODERNISM

When capitalist industrialization transformed cities in the 19th Century, people began to speak of 'modernism', that is, the articulation of technology, democracy, architecture, consumerism, and city life. One aspect was the social transformation of people that had migrated from rural areas to occupy dense residential districts and assume the rank of the working class (see entries on *Urbanization and Urbanism*; *Overurbanization*). Another was the way 'high culture', that is, the arts, opera, drama, writing and even cuisine and fashion, became centralized in a few large cities, first in Western Europe, such as Paris and Vienna, then, much later, in New York, Berlin, Moscow, St. Petersburg, London and Mexico City. This 'elite' or hierarchical ordering of culture was most characteristic of modernist ideas, just as it was also believed that by living in select 'cultural capitals', like Paris, people could participate in a modern life.

With regard specifically to urbanism, modernism was exemplified by a movement of architects and planners in the period between World War I and World War II in the 20th Century. The French architect, LeCorbusier, and the German architects, Walter Gropius and Mies van der Rohe, articulated a school of design, known as the International Style, which expunged all local cultural traits and all superfluous surface elements from buildings. Instead they conceived of construction in geometrical forms, especially the rectangle, that would use the most up to date technology of heating, lighting and building materials. Furthermore, their designs were placed in new land use patterns by modernist principles of planning that stressed zoning of like functions into segregated districts, an emphasis on transportation corridors (the automobile was favored over public transport, while the pedestrian street was discouraged), and a preference for high rise skyscraper buildings surrounded by open space. This International Style was so influential that practically every city after 1940 with room to build witnessed the construction of these monolithic skyscrapers, especially in the downtown districts, while zoning became a key tool of urban planners everywhere. There is another aspect to this legacy. One of the most overlooked effects of modernism is the role of the metropolis in explaining globalization. The British literary and cultural theorist, Raymond Williams (1989), describes the connections between modernity, the metropolis and globalization through the agency of urbanization, and Anthony Giddens states that globalization is a radicalizing of modernity (1990) (see entry on *Globalization*).

POSTMODERNISM

Without question, the era of postmodernism was ushered in as a critique of modernist architecture in the 1970s, as described by Charles Jenks, despite the appearance of the term much earlier. As David Harvey (1989) has argued, when the LeCorbusier inspired low income housing project of Pruit-Igoe in St. Louis was demolished in the 1970s because of its social failure, the era of modernist architectural ideology was also brought to an end. From that time, the International Style was picked apart by talented architects seeking to free themselves from the rigid dictates of that school. Michael Graves and Frank Gehry in the US, and Rem Koolhaus and Norman Foster in Europe, were some of the exponents of a new style that became 'postmodern'. In one way or another their buildings abandoned the slavish adherence to the sharp edges of modernist geometry and replaced it with flowing designs that included a return to embellishment of the exterior. Influences from many particular cultures were also reintroduced as design elements. Rather than a skyline of rectangular skyscrapers, downtown sections of cities began to possess buildings with peaked, triangular or multiple-leveled roofs, more ornamentation on the exterior of buildings and explosive or deconstructionist features that reconfigured their iconic, rectangular shape.

Modernist city planning was also attacked, principally by the New Urbanists (see entry on page 96). Followers of this school said that the current land-use planning of cities and suburbs which relied on the modernist principles of zoning was now outdated. The spatial segregation of social functions, the death of the sidewalk in suburbia, the downtown street grid, were all elements of the International School approach and remained its major legacy. In their place, the New Urbanists sought to integrate formerly separated and specialized places. They conceived of urban life as transpiring within pedestrian-oriented neighborhoods that were within easy access to full service districts and which were, in turn, connected to transportation corridors that relied more on public means than on the automobile (see entry on *New Urbanism*). Advocates of this style were decidedly anti-modernist in their belief that society should return to a more 'human' environmental scale and that traditional design elements of homes, such as porches and pedestrian-friendly sidewalks, allowed people to socialize and thereby strengthen their local communities.

Other critics pointed to the differences in ethnic settlement patterns between cities in the past and those of today as examples of the change from modernism to postmodernism. According to Paul Delany (1994), with regard to Vancouver in British Columbia, Canada, the new pattern is de-centered and multi-cultural instead of densely settled and relatively more ethnically homogeneous. In describing this change, Delany cannot resist using some of the bothersome neologisms of postmodernists:

> 'The old pattern had homogeneous neighborhoods of difference. The new pattern has *hybridization* and *transcultural* mixing of many ethnic cultures. Residentially, ethnic groups are highly dispersed, with no sharp demarcation lines between neighborhoods; and the at-large election of city councilors [in Vancouver] has prevented the emergence of the ethnic brokerage politics typical of older cities like Chicago and New York.' (Delany, 1994)

Some observers have focused on the creation of themed and simulated environments as exemplifying key aspects of postmodernism within cities and regions (Gottdiener, et al., 1999; Gottdiener, 2001). Las Vegas, in particular, is singled out because of these attributes. 'One might say that Las Vegas has turned itself into a sin city and sim city at the same time' (www.transparencynow.com/vegas, 2003). Other aspects of the Las Vegas region that are postmodern include the presence of an economic base in mass casino gambling, as opposed to the modernist period's characteristic of an economy based on value-generating activities and the fact that it is successful as an airport based tourist destination. While the Las Vegas region has only one and a half million permanent residents, its airport handles over 20 million visitors a year. Almost exclusively these tourists are drawn to the area because of casino gambling and the spectacular themed resorts that offer it.

Now many other urban areas across the US and elsewhere are exhibiting aspects that might be classified as postmodern. Ethnic diversity is increasingly replacing the once homogeneous cities in places like Europe. Both casino gambling and theming, or simulation, are more common as elements in local economies and landscapes. Mass media and the internet have changed culture and made it more accessible to people everywhere. Most important, however, is the observation that, unlike those urbanists that claim there is a new 'postmodern' urbanism, cities and regions actually contain both modern and postmodern elements in a mix of uses, designs and outlooks. It is this intersection of the singular ideology of modernism, as a mode of urban design and planning, with elements that challenge this ideology in concrete ways, that most characterizes urban areas today. Breakdowns of cultural hierarchies in the arts, in dominant social classes, and in modes of popular culture and entertainment also create a 'logic' of culture that is no longer modernist in intent.

If some observers choose to call this new mix 'postmodernism', that is quite appropriate. However, the claim by a few urbanists that this or that city is a regional example of 'postmodernism' cannot be defended. Furthermore, what is depressing for many European scholars is the manner by which postmodernism has become a catch-all term to describe processes that remain not clearly understood. Many of these are effects of current social dynamics and growth that are still not fully formed in their consequences. By claiming that we suddenly have this or that kind of 'new' configuration or 'new' phase of capitalism, intellectual relativism and its consequent laziness can be defended. The writer on Los Angeles urbanism, Mike Davis, for example, describes the attempt to appropriate the Bonaventure Hotel as part of postmodern discourse in comparison to the master planner and architect of 19th Century Paris, Baron Haussmann:

'This profoundly urban impulse, inspired by unfettered financial forces and a Hausmannian logic of social control, seem to me to constitute the real *Zeitgeist* of postmodernism. At the same time, however, it reveals 'postmodernism' – at least in its architectural incarnation and sensibilities – as little more than a decadent trope of massified modernism, a sympathetic correlate to Reaganism and the end of urban reform.' (Davis, 1988: 87)

Here, as elsewhere in the works of Davis and some others, the concept of postmodernism is utilized in a 'shoot from the hip' style of writing that cares little for historical or theoretical specificity. The 19th and 21st Centuries are conflated in the above quote, as are the economic social formations of Feudalism and Advanced Industrial Capitalism.

125

REFERENCES

Davis, M. 1988. 'Urban Renaissance and the Spirit of Postmodernism' in E. Kaplan (ed.) *Postmodernism and its Discontents*. London: Verso. pp. 79–87.

Delany, Paul (ed.) 1994. 'Vancouver: Representing the Postmodern City' Vancouver: Arsenal Pulp Press. www.sfu.ca/~delaney/pomointro1.html accessed 6 July 2003.

Giddens, A. 1990. *The Consequences of Modernity*. Cambridge: Polity.

Gottdiener, M. et al. 1999. *Las Vegas: The Social Production of an All American City*. Oxford, UK: Blackwell.

Gottdiener, M. 2001. *The Theming of America, 2nd Edition*. Boulder, CO: Westview Press.

Harvey, D. 1989. *The Condition of Postmodernity*. Oxford, UK: Blackwell.

Lake, Robert, 1999. 'Postmodern Urbanism' *Urban Geography*, 20 (5): 393–5.

www.transparencynow.com/vegas.htm, accessed 6 January 2003.

Williams, R. 1989. *The Politics of Modernism*. London: Verso.

The issue of preservation has become increasingly important for cities and for developing countries that are experiencing globalization. It encompasses a variety of different circumstances that have in common the desire to protect the built environment because of its historical/cultural importance from deterioration, demolition, redevelopment, social upheavals and simple neglect.

PRESERVATION IN URBAN SETTINGS

The built environment of metropolitan regions is also an historical repository of architectural constructs that represent an irreplaceable cultural heritage. Often cities develop and recondition themselves in order to attract new investment, especially after disturbing periods of decline, by removing 'old' buildings in order to offer open land for new projects. This 'creative destruction' is one aspect of real estate under capitalist land market conditions (see entry on *Real Estate*). In some cities, older buildings that are under-utilized are removed simply to provide parking spaces in the hope of attracting suburban residents to visit downtown. Buffalo, New York tore down the Frederick Larkin office building, one week in 1960, in just such an effort. It happened to be designed by Frank Lloyd Wright, the most famous and most influential American architect. The Larkin was the only office building of Wright's ever built. Once it was removed, it was gone forever. It is precisely because of such retrospective knowledge, and a growing appreciation for past architectural projects as social heritage, that the issue of preservation within cities has become so important.

According to Anthony Tung:

'The universal factor which causes cities to erase their own patrimony is the allure of a better future. With industrialization, an extraordinary global phenomenon occurred: during the twentieth century, cities across the world, at different stages of development, of different historic cultural characteristics, were seduced by the appeal of modernization and in the name of a somewhat illusionary future embarked upon what we might today describe as a global wave of eradication of architectural patrimony. International experts estimate that something on the order of 50% of humankind's historic architectural heritage was erased in 100 years.' (cited in 'In the Cause of Architecture: Interview with Anthony Tung' www.archrecord.com, 2003: 1)

Experts on preservation, like Tung, who calls 20th Century urban development a 'culture of destruction', fail to see how the logic of capitalist real estate operates to undercut the social value attributed to landmark buildings. He is a critic of modernist ideology (see entry on *Postmodern and Modern Urbanism*), but he is not a critic of capitalist real estate markets. As he argues, 'Can we conceive of an urban environment that is pluralistic but not fractured and schizophrenic? Can we invent a contemporary architecture that is a true cultural expression of modern life, yet relates with respect, with civility, to the architecture of the past? I think a question of the ethic of architectural planning emerges: how do we build new life-enhancing environments without simultaneously being destructive?' (2003: 1).

Because of its confrontation with the profit motive and the recycling of urban land, preservationism requires government support, even sponsorship, and intervention in the private market. In 1966 the US Congress passed the National Historic Preservation Act (Public Law 89–665) that gave legal powers to lower levels of government and Native American tribes to preserve aspects of the environment deemed 'socially' significant. Resources were directed towards 'financial and technical assistance', providing leadership in retrieval efforts, the administration of federally owned historic sights, and guidance to non-public-owned places of cultural value. Furthermore, under the Secretary of the Interior, a register of National Historic Places would be composed and regulated that were part of the country's heritage. Properties meeting the criteria under the act were designated 'National Historic Landmarks' and preserved with the help of public funds.

In 1996, efforts towards preservation were given a boost when the federal government issued Executive Order 13006, *Locating Federal Facilities on Historic Properties in Our Nation's Central Cities*. It directed government agencies to use landmark facilities whenever possible, thereby channeling resources into their upkeep. Promoting the renewal and use of already existing structures, rather than the demolition of the 'old' in order to build something 'new', is the essence of preservation efforts.

GLOBAL CASES

Cities around the world have a special need to preserve and sustain the built environment because in almost every case they are located in areas with a long history that is embodied in architecture. Preservation, in the face of the need for economic development becomes important to third world nations that are being forced to modernize, but do not want to lose

127

their cultural and historical heritage. Preservation is also important in developed countries with a long history. Often, the primate city of the country, such as Bangkok, Thailand or Helsinki, Finland, is also a concentrated depository of the nation's heritage. The challenge for these places, as it is in the US, is to identify those structures most worthy of preservation, while also fostering the construction of new and distinctive projects. This task is somewhat easier for the US, because of its relative recent founding, than it is for areas of the world that have been settled for millennia.

Preservation is usually accomplished through municipal planning once the power to preserve is accorded to local government. Those structures worthy of attention must be identified in a democratic manner so that citizen involvement, as well as the participation of local historians and planners, is important. As material from the plan of Copenhagen, Denmark, states:

'The interest in urban preservation does not only focus on individual buildings, but increasingly on whole urban environments and city-scapes. This may involve overall developments that form an entity with a characteristic building pattern and joint features. Or it may be concentrations of individual buildings of high preservation value. It may also be buildings that, together form distinctive features.' ('Urban Preservation' 2003)

Expanding the definition of historical preservation, Dolores Hayden's work (1995), advocates broadening the concept of heritage to include public art, spatial struggles, the inclusion of diverse perspectives, especially from minority and gendered community representatives, and the relationship between landscape and public memory. To the principal question of 'what buildings to preserve?', Hayden adds, 'whose history should be preserved?' thereby advocating diversity in the historical preservation movement. From this perspective, the participation of citizen groups in the process of sustaining the urban environment becomes a critical factor.

Hayden's work, however, is trivial compared to the global issues raised by efforts of UNESCO to determine 'world heritage' sites. These are not only places designated for preservation within countries, but also cities themselves under the more recent program of designating 'cultural capitals'. The alleged positive aspects of allowing political issues to be part of the preservation/heritage equation trumpeted by Hayden, turn into mixed benefits when viewing the politicization of world heritage issues from UNESCO. One of the key issues involves the globalization of values assigned to places that determine worthiness of obtaining heritage designation. In practice, these judgments most often represent the interests of politically powerful actors belonging to the United Nations, including those from less developed countries such as Saudi Arabia as well as the hegemonic western nations. Local and weak perspectives are not acknowledged by the UN's activities most often because UNESCO ignores them. Furthermore, the 'cultural capital' program of UNESCO has been co-opted by city boosterism and promotes consumerism and tourism at the expense of local culture itself where the past is reconditioned as a form of nostalgia that is then commodified (Munansinghe, 1998). The commodification of nostalgia and a themed version of the past also characterizes those sites that are 'representations' of historical places, such as Williamsburg, VA.

The key issue raised by the preservationist movement is in regard to the articulation of values that then determine which sites are worthy. In the main, there is a failure to acknowledge diverse norms and differences of value that, if recognized, would empower less advantaged, more localized cultural interests. According to Tunbridge and Ashworth (1995) this problem involves the 'dissonance of heritage'. In many cases, these values express the norms of hegemonic western cultures. They also have been co-opted by consumerism and the promotion of place to the extent that one observer refers to the preservationist movement as a 'heritage industry' (Hewison, 1987). Among other things, the commodification of heritage can be seen in the mechanical reproduction of 'old fashioned' house furnishings and architectural components, such as doors or windows under the sign of *nostalgia*.

Perhaps the best and one of the earliest illustrations of the value dilemma embodied by global preservationist efforts is the Venice Charter of 1964 and its effects.

Meant to provide protection for historical sites in European cities that were facing renovation and re-development, it privileged the kind of building characteristic of Western Civilization, namely, monumental structures that were architecturally significant from the perspective of European aesthetics. City spaces and, in particular, historically significant areas within the city and the active neighborhood culture of the street itself were all ignored in favor of a focus on individual buildings (Appleyard, 1979). Subsequent 'charters' drafted in global meetings in different parts of the west broadened the definition of cultural worth, but retained the Eurocentric perspective on aesthetic values that so-called peripheral countries, like Sri Lanka and Cambodia, now struggle against. The fact that local preservation interests in these areas must fight against UN as well as first world designs, makes this effort very difficult. Despite such international control, for example, fanatical Muslims in Afghanistan were able to destroy millennia old giant rock carvings of the Buddha in the 1990s, while UNESCO remained active in that part of the world. Once destroyed, such totally priceless manifestations of a world-class culture cannot be retrieved.

REFERENCES

Appleyard, D. (ed.) 1979. *The Conservation of European Cities*. Cambridge: MIT Press.

Hayden, D. 1995. *The Power of Place*. Cambridge: MIT Press.

Hewison, R. 1987, *The Heritage Industry*. London: Methuen.

'In the Cause of Architecture: Interview with Anthony Tung' 2003. www.archrecord.com, accessed 7 July 2003.

Munansinghe, H. 1998. *Urban Conservation and City Life*. Oulu, Finland: Oulu University Press.

Tunbridge, J. and G. Ashworth 1995. *Dissonant Heritage: The Management of Past as a Resource in Conflict*. NY and London: J. Wiley & Sons.

'Urban Preservation' www.urbanpreservation.org accessed 20 July 2003.

Real Estate

The buying and selling of land, whether it is developed or not, is a major force in the production of space (Lefebvre, 1991; Gottdiener, 1994). Capitalism extended its relations of profit-making to the ownership of land and its market turned that asset into 'real estate'. Agricultural land is a natural resource and its value depends on how fruitful the location is for the production of useful products. The value of urban land, in contrast, is entirely contained in its attributes of location. It has little intrinsic value, unlike farmland, except for its potential as a place where societal activities can occur. Consequently, urban land acquires its value, in part, through society. Its worth depends on the collectivity. For example, it is possible to buy a piece of property within a city or suburb, just hold it while other pieces of property are developed, and then sell it at a higher price than bought without making any improvements at all. The greater price obtained is the product of collective societal activities in the adjacent area. Real estate is only one of a few select commodities with this characteristic that has been made possible by the extension of capitalist relations to the market for land. Gold and diamonds are similar; they increase in value without any apparent effort on the part of the owner, although, like land, they can also lose value if the market declines. Other commodities, such as new cars, lose value the moment they are purchased.

When an individual buys a suburban home, for example, the value of the property is primarily in the house not in the land, although the latter can be priced at a significant fraction of the overall cost depending on circumstances. Yet, the value of this one property depends considerably on how well the neighbors maintain theirs. If the houses in the surrounding area decline or become unattractive, for whatever reason, all properties in the suburban development are affected. When an individual buys a condominium (apartment) in the central city, he/she is not purchasing the land exclusively at all, only the commodified shelter of the condo (apartment block). The land is owned collectively by all the condominium residents and they are all equally responsible for its maintenance. In sum, even developed real estate, not just land itself, contains within its valuation, under capitalist conditions of a free market in property, a proportion that is directly tied to the collective actions of others.

The collective component of metropolitan real estate's value is privately expropriated in a capitalist society. This is a basic contradiction of capitalism. Some of that value, of course, is recovered for the collective good by our system of municipal taxation. Property tax is the key way many school systems in capitalist societies are financed. Taxes on real estate also help support metropolitan services. Taxing the value of land, however, is quite limited as a measure of public finance precisely because there is so much resistance to the idea in a capitalist society. Even single family home owners seek to make a profit from the ownership of their houses when the time comes to sell. Consequently, the private expropriation of the collective value of metropolitan real estate results in a perpetual fiscal crisis of local government because the latter does not have powerful enough fiscal tools to make people pay for the maintenance of the collective environment (see entry on *Fiscal Crisis*). In capitalist societies there is always considerable tension between property owners and local government. The former seek to retain as much of the increase in the value of their real estate as they can, while the latter seek to tax that increased value in order to advance the public good by maintaining and improving the environment. While it makes objective sense for all citizens to support the public sphere in this regard, it is precisely a contradiction of capitalism that private interests tied to profit-making in property overpower these obvious collective considerations. Individual real estate owners hate property taxes.

Real estate under capitalism has both a structural force and forms of agency that combine to make it the most powerful factor influencing the shape of metropolitan regions. Aspects of agency, such as the behavior of real estate agents, are easy for most people to see and understand, but the dimension of structure is also clearly important, as it is so for all other aspects of advanced capitalism, and it is a great deal more difficult to comprehend. The French philosopher, Henri Lefebvre (1991), has written the most important works for understanding the significance of real estate as a component of social structure in advanced capitalism. Our economic system is dependent on investment flows that have their ups and downs. Crises develop at both ends of this cycle leading to social and personal problems. According to Lefebvre, investment of land is a separate structure from that of investment in industry and commerce. Its behavior differs thereby leading to a separate investment cycle of prosperity and decline. Most investment is in the industrial sector, or what Lefebvre calls the 'primary circuit of capital'. When people seek other means of making money, they invest in real estate, or the 'second circuit of capital'. Lefebvre argued that, because these two circuits are slightly out of sync, money-flows into real estate are significant because it represents the development of land, which is not easily convertible to liquid assets.

This second circuit affects capitalism in two distinct ways. First, during periods of first circuit decline, money shifts to the second circuit. This appears as excessive development of land and speculation that is detrimental to the environment. Second, when the first circuit is about to recover, it cannot do so quickly because the money invested in the built environment is not easily converted back to cash. Eventually, when this does occur, real estate values plummet and, by connection, so too do municipal and metropolitan revenues dependent on property taxes. In short, the *structural* aspects of real estate investment are significant for understanding the uneven development and problems of the built environment under capitalism. These processes include the way in which land is both a form of fixed capital which gives rise to the production of the built environment; and circulating capital which gives rise to a set of financial flows that stem from rents and change in capital values of the built environment. Land is, thus, a peculiar and multi-faceted part of capital, in that its use and exploitation includes many residual elements from feudal times. In the contemporary context, we find that the majority of personal wealth holding in the UK and US is in housing and that over 95% of the wealth in both countries is accounted for by real estate.

Forms of agency are also important in understanding real estate markets and their spatial effects. There are at least six different types of actors in the production of property:

Speculators – they purchase land hoping it will increase in value without improving it. Due to the collective nature of urban land's value, as discussed above, all other categories of agency also include the component of speculation in them.

Developers – they buy real estate and then construct aspects of the built environment for sale, such as houses, factories, office buildings, retail shops, mini-malls and giant malls. Sometimes developers also retain ownership and rent out property, as in the case of malls, but, most often they simply sell off their projects and move on to another vacant piece of metropolitan land that is ripe for speculation or development.

Homeowners – they acquire shelter, either through single family, multiple family or condominium home purchases that are also held for future gain on property value.

Local politicians – they may not own local property, but they are very active in its development because city finances depend so heavily on the real estate tax. Unfortunately, campaign contributions from land developers are also the primary way local politicians acquire money to run for or stay in office.

Large corporations – these are the least connected to local individuals but are often the most powerful forms of agency. Corporations that decide to invest in a location, and spend money to finance the development of land for factories, marketing centers, office buildings, or any one of the various forms of consumer outlets, such as big box department stores. They may work closely with local developers or may have in-house people that specialize in land development and construction. In any case, their actions to invest or to disinvest, such as by closing down a factory, have a great impact on local areas.

Banks and other financial conduits – this last category is as important as the one before it. The private market in real estate depends for its lifeblood on the channels that allow money to flow into and out of it as investments and/or purchases. In many advanced capitalist societies the financial sector is so developed that there are numerous ways to invest in land. This fragmentation of conduits for profit-making is typical of capitalism and its regulation is quite difficult. There are mortgage companies, real estate trusts, holding companies, bonds, secondary mortgage lending, commercial loans, savings loans, and more. People can work in the area of real estate investment full-time or part-time. In the aggregate, the sector of finance capital involves both considerable jobs and profit under capitalism and investment in land is one of its principal activities along with the flow of money into the primary circuit.

One fallacy that was widely spread among urbanists derives from the writings of Logan and Molotch (1987) who maintained that there was a special class of people with interests in real estate, called the *rentiers*.

According to this approach, rentiers formed a 'growth machine' that worked full time to promote the development of land. This is a false way of viewing the phenomenon of real estate under capitalism. We have seen how many different ways there are to invest in property, how attractive that investment is and how many types of people are involved in the second circuit. To be sure, pressures for 'growth' are always strong under capitalism. But, it is clearly a mistake to attribute those pressures as originating from a select group or collectivity linked together by a single purpose. The second circuit of capital is fragmented both structurally and with regard to agency. Many different types of people invest in land in order to make money. Often they conflict with each other and there is always competition. This makes profit-making in the second circuit of capital a complicated and often contentious affair. The metaphor of a 'machine' completely misses the mark.

Financial innovations on a global scale further undermine this contention. In fact, the growth machine perspective seems particularly ignorant of the field of financial economics, in general, and, more curiously, as it relates to real estate investment, in particular. Changes in the nature of finance, such as disintermediation (direct access to finance rather than through the intermediary of a bank) and securitization (creating financial instruments to be bought and sold on the basis of changes in the value of an underlying asset such as an office block), on a global scale now exacerbate the real estate cycle as a whole range of financial investors enter and leave the market. Most of the proximate causes of the East Asian Crisis in 1997, for example, were not just global capital flows, but, more specifically, over-investment in speculative real estate in the case of Thailand and over-production of other parts of the built environment (factories, warehouse and infrastructure) by international financial capital (Berry et al., 2001).

Even within particular city regimes that advocate growth, it is wrong to assume the monolithic view that only a single rentier class is in control. The city booster movement in the UK, that is, those promoting cities like Manchester as a candidate for holding the Olympics and Liverpool as a European City of Culture, is heavily represented by real estate interests. They seek to exploit returns from developing derelict downtown sites, through building apartments, offices and shops close to the new sporting and cultural sites. However, the flow of finance into these kinds of development come from manifold sources and are not just part of some specific mode of social agency called a 'machine'.

Countries like the US have never had a rentier class to begin with and advanced capitalism did away with such a specialized group in most countries a long time ago. There is no singular elite present in metropolitan areas, because that concept is a simplistic fiction, but there is always pressure for investment in land, and the actions taken under that pressure by those forms of agency that temporarily wield power, are not always helpful to the public good. A study of the long history of land ownership and its relation to capitalist development in the UK reinforces this point:

'The evidence presented in the preceding chapters – in terms of theoretical, economic analysis, of the empirical study of the economic relations of landownership, and the ideologies and political struggles with which the different group of landowners were associated – indicate that there is no single group, based on landownership by capital, which can be said to be a distinct and coherent fraction.' (Massey and Catalano, 1978: 186)

We have a built environment that constantly changes, grows as well as declines, and there is little the public sector can do to control it. Development is always a contentious affair. Understanding metropolitan growth requires attention to both the factions involved and the way capital ebbs and flows through the fragmented institutions of the second circuit which currently are increasingly more complex in their opportunities for capital investment. In the US the 'growth machine' perspective remains popular, but, echoing the observation of Massey and Catalano above, it is probably because of its simplicity rather than its truth.

REFERENCES

Berry, J., S. McGreal, L. Budd, and P. Scholes 2001. 'Relationships between Financial and Property Markets in the Asia-Pacific Area' *Pacific Asia Property Review*, 7 (2): 113–25.
Gottdiener, M. 1994. *The Social Production of Urban Space, 2nd Edition*. Austin, TX: University of Texas Press.
Lefebvre, H. 1991. *The Production of Space*. Oxford, UK: Blackwell.
Logan, J. and H. Molotch 1987. *Urban Fortunes*. Berkeley: University of California Press.
Massey, D. and A. Catalano 1978. *Capital and Land*. London: Arnold.

135

Slums and Shanty Towns

A slum is a concentrated, densely settled area where housing is inadequate, residents are poor and community functions are lacking.

Although the emphasis is usually placed on the presence of deteriorated housing, because that is the most visible element, slums are afflicted by inadequate public services, poor medical and educational care, and a general neglect of its population by the larger society. Consequently, a slum is an area of inadequate housing *plus* inadequate community services, private sector stores, professional offices such as doctors, and the like. Slum populations are invariably racially and economically deprived. Generally health problems are compounded by overcrowding and the lack of both cheap and fresh food and professional medical assistance in the area.

Slum settlements represent over 30% of urban population in all developing countries. In some cases, the Middle East and Africa, the population is as high as 60%.

SLUMS AND SQUATTER SETTLEMENTS AS A PERCENTAGE OF URBAN POPULATION

City	% of City Pop
Latin America	
Bogotá, Columbia	60
Mexico City, Mexico	46
Caracas, Venezuela	54
Rio de Janeiro, Brazil	20
Middle East and Africa	
Addis Ababa, Ethiopia	79
Casablanca, Morocco	70
Ankara, Turkey	60
Cairo, Egypt	60
Asia	
Calcutta, India	67
Karachi, Pakistan	44
Manila, Philippines	35
Jakarta, Indonesia	26

Source: 'World Population Growth and Global Security' 1983.

SHANTY TOWNS – INFORMAL HOUSING

Shanty towns can be slums, but they are also different. They are sections of the city within which people have moved in 'unofficially', i.e., the people are squatters, and have constructed housing using informal means and found materials.

The shortage of affordable housing for low-income urban households in the developing countries, coupled with the massive rural to urban migration, has resulted in a proliferation of these squatter settlements (UNCHS, 1999). Often the sheer number of urban migrants in the developing countries is too great for either the private or public sector to provide adequate housing or shelter, and thus many families end up in squatter settlements. Shanty towns have many names all over the world – *favelas* (Brazil), *bustees* (India), *barriadas* (Mexico), *poblaciones* (Chile), *villas miserias* (Argentina), *bidonvilles* (Africa), *kampungs* (South Asia). Despite different names, these squatter settlements have many features in common, including frequent public health crises, crime, crushing poverty, and no future for the next generation because few countries provide them with schools.

There is also another face of shanty towns. Due to inadequate housing, many of the residents have jobs, including a large number that are either part-time and/or in the informal economy (see entry on page 76). Not all the housing is put up by the family that lives there. Many of the individuals who build these settlements are real estate entrepreneurs. The majority of shanty town dwellers live in rental housing (Datta, 1990). The urban poor find cheap rental accommodation in shanty towns despite impoverished living conditions. Shanty towns are often the only places where the working class can find affordable housing. Informal settlements with predominantly rental accommodation are common in many cities of Latin America where the demand for cheap rental accommodation far exceeds the supply and where controls on the quality of housing are negligible (UNCHS, 1996: 218). In general, shanty towns continue to grow because they are where the increasing numbers of poorly paid urban workers and rural migrants to the city can obtain shelter. It is precisely within these squatter settlements that socio-spatial networks flourish and provide new arrivals to the urban region with access to jobs and other personal assistance.

Visual images of informal settlements are bleak and observers may assume that these are defeated, disorganized neighborhoods. Although social problems, such as limited urban services and infrastructure, persist in most informal settlements, case studies show that these are vital and viable communities. Many shanty towns possess a robust social order (Aina, 1990). A common conception is that life in these places is totally peripheral to the vibrancy of the urban economy. The marginality of shanty town inhabitants, however, is largely a myth (Perlman, 1976). Many shanty towns support robust economies in themselves including areas of real estate investment. They often are the location for small-business enterprises started by urban migrants. Shanty towns may also be the sites for small and medium-sized factories. In addition, recent penetration of multi-national corporations as part of the restructuring of the global economy has brought the support of subcontracting in the developing countries (Safa, 1987). This phenomenon of vertical disintegration creates new manufacturing jobs and helps local entrepreneurs while integrating shanty towns into the global economy.

In fact, the development literature contains a debate among researchers with regard to what features of shanty town life are positive or negative. Janice Perlman (1976) for example, lists at least six positive functions of these areas. Shanty towns provides (1) free housing; (2) reception centers for migrants; (3) employment in family and cottage industries; (4) mobility within the city so people can locate closer to their jobs; (5) a sense of community and social support during times of difficulties; and (6) rewards for small scale entrepreneurs that invest in building shanties for real estate speculation.

'Despite their visual disarray and clear spatial distinction from the rest of the urban grid, squatter settlements are both highly organized within themselves and highly integrated into the rest of the housing system. There is tremendous diversity within shanty towns with regard to income, education, occupation, and material and size of dwelling units.' (Perlman, 1976)

Yet, not all researchers accentuate the positive aspects of these places. In the past many developing countries viewed shanty towns as unsightly and dysfunctional. Now we know that shanty towns do serve positive functions, but they also have many problems and that the best policy is simply to improve them as much as can be done. According to Sarosh Anklesaria (2002):

'One fourth of the urban population of India today lives in slums, under inhumane conditions. These shanty towns, common to many cities of the developing world, are characterized by low-quality housing and lack of physical infrastructure. With little access to clean drinking water and sanitation, the inhabitants face a constant threat of disease. In a typical slum, houses are built of mud and plastic sheets. Streets and alleys are often no more than seven feet wide and double as open sewers. Despite these conditions, the slum population of India doubles every ten years.'

Many of the slum dwellers are employed but they do not invest in their housing because the settlements are considered illegal and can be demolished at any time. They live there because they cannot find any other affordable alternatives. The official response to these slums used to be demolition and eviction of squatters. But, this simply resulted in the slum relocating elsewhere because the need for cheap housing in India remained. 'Then relocation schemes attempted to move the illegal squatters temporarily to makeshift camps while five to six storey apartments could be built. But this proved to be both capital intensive and socially inappropriate. The residents could not adapt to these dwellings and simply resold their flats and moved back to the slum. Such projects failed to help those who needed the housing most'.

The latest approach in India uses a community asset based plan. The idea is to improve shanty town districts, rather than replace them, so that living conditions there become adequate. Working with the existing community infrastructure, services are improved. Most importantly, government programs in India construct underground sewers because these are probably the one improvement that the dwellers need. Another policy feature allows squatters to buy the land where they are living. This provides the economic incentive for improvement of housing. Finally, improvements in transportation infrastructure that service the shanty towns enable the workers to continue to hold down jobs in the formal economy. In short, policies that improve shanty towns have replaced those that sought to tear them down.

REFERENCES

Anklesaria, S. 2002. 'Improving Urban Shanty Towns' *Architecture Week*, 21 August 2002.

Aina, T. 1990. 'Shanty Town Economy: The Case of Lagos, Nigeria' in S. Datta (ed.) *Third World Urbanization*. Stockholm, Sweden: HSFR. pp. 133–48.

Datta, S. (ed.) 1990. *Third World Urbanization*. Stockholm, Sweden: HSFR.

Perlman, J. 1976. *The Myth of Marginality: Urban Poverty and Politics in Rio de Janeiro*. Berkeley, CA: University of California Press.

Safa, H. 1987. 'Urbanization, the Informal Economy and State Policy in Latin America' in M. Smith and J. Feagin (eds) *The Capitalist City*. Oxford, UK: Blackwell. pp. 252–74.

United Nations Center for Human Settlements (UNCHS), 1996. *An Urbanizing World*. Oxford, UK: Oxford University Press.

United Nations Center for Human Settlements (UNCHS), 1999. *Basic Facts on Urbanization*. Nairobi, Kenya: UNCHS Habitat.

'World Population Growth and Global Security' 1983, Washington, DC: Population Crisis Commission.

Socio-spatial Approach

The socio-spatial approach to urban analysis is the consequence of a paradigm shift that took place beginning with the late 1960s (Lefebvre, 1991). Prior to that time, the dominant view of urban processes among sociologists and geographers was called 'human ecology' (see Gottdiener, 1994; Gottdiener and Hutchison, 2000). Ideologically biased, human ecology grounded the relationship between social and spatial processes in a biologically based metaphor borrowed from the plant and animal kingdoms. Urban patterns of population dispersal and development were viewed as an *adjustment* process to the environment that is organic and adaptive rather than being the product of class, race and gender-based social relations stemming from a complex mode of social organization. Human ecology therefore, with its emphasis on adaptation, was particularly inadequate to the understanding of urban conflict during the 1960s and the long period of de-industrialization that has occurred since that time as a consequence of changes in the world capitalist system.

By the 1980s, with a solid record of publications among urbanists in a variety of disciplines, an alternative approach, called the *new urban sociology* emerged. Because this term has so many variants and was ill-specified, the paradigm of the 'socio-spatial approach' was introduced in the 1990s (Gottdiener and Hutchison, 2000). See also the entry on *Real Estate*. The key concept of the new paradigm in urban studies is that the form of settlement space is related to the mode of organization of the economy. This does not mean that clearly defined stages of urban growth are directly correlated to exact stages of economic development. It does mean that important and key spatial patterns which define the *spatial* organization of society are associated with specific aspects of the cultural, political, social and economic features of the correlated mode of *societal* organization. According to this socio-spatial approach, the stages of urban development are related to changes in the political economy of society. For the case of the US, urban forms emerged and became modified because of phases in the development of capitalism. The following chart summarizes these trends:

140

Stages of Capitalism	Stages of Urbanization – for US
Mercantile-Colonial Period (1630–1812)	Colonial Waterfront City – Boston, New York, Philadelphia, New Orleans, San Francisco
Industrialization Period (1812–1920)	Industrial City – Chicago, Akron, Cleveland, Pittsburgh, Detroit, Atlanta, St. Louis, LA
Monopoly Capitalism (1920–1960)	Metropolitan City and Suburbs – Manhattan, Chicago, Denver, Minneapolis, Boston
Global Capitalism (1960–present)	Multi-centered Metropolitan Region – NYC, LA region, Las Vegas region, Phoenix, Minneapolis – St. Paul, Dallas – Ft. Worth

Most histories of this development, prior to the paradigm shift, make the claim that land-use pattern changes were the result of changes in transportation technology. For example, the suburbanization of contemporary US land-use patterns is commonly blamed on the mass introduction of the automobile. This is an old and out-dated view. More accurate is the understanding that real estate is developed constantly, especially in the US, as investment is attracted there from other possibilities. With a free market operating in land, developers and speculators use whatever technological means available to pursue growth. Thus, suburbanization was already quite evident in the 1800s and cities always spun off other centers whether transportation was dominated by horse-drawn carriages or the steam locomotive.

After the 1930s, when US capitalism had matured into a fully formed industrial economy, and, especially during World War II, cities began to assume functional specializations. Some, like Los Angeles, Detroit, Buffalo and Baltimore, were dominated by manufacturing. Others, like New Orleans, Atlanta and Seattle were more specialized in trading and commerce. Places like Boston, NYC and Washington, DC were oriented towards services, although the mega regions like NYC and Los Angeles scored high on all major economic functions.

This functional specialization of particular metropolitan regions was further differentiated within the areas themselves so that the central city became only one center in a regional array and it specialized in specific activities while other centers specialized in separate functions. After the 1960s, and especially today during the present period of global capitalism and limited domestic factory work, large central cities are functionally specialized in business and financial services while other centers within

141

the metro region emphasize shopping, light to heavy manufacturing, back office business operations, trading and commerce.

The socio-spatial approach argues that development patterns in the US involved two different but related shifts of population and economic activities that were massive and historically unprecedented in scale. The first was a shift to the suburbs that accelerated on a mass basis after the 1940s. The second was the shift to the sunbelt that accelerated after the 1960s. In both cases, the war efforts since World War II had a great deal to do with providing both the infrastructure and the economic resources for these transformations to occur. According to the socio-spatial perspective, land-use development is as much a product of the interventionist state and state policies as it is of economic investments and resource development. This is what is meant by a 'political economic' approach to urban growth.

Another aspect of the socio-spatial approach is the explicit recognition that social life is comprised of classes and of other social divisions that are important, such as those of race and gender. For Karl Marx and Friedrich Engels, the industrial city of the 1800s, especially the ones found in England, such as Manchester, were the best places to study the *extended relations* of the capitalist system, just as the factory was the best place to study the organization of capitalist production itself. Engels (1973) interpreted city life, not as a species adaptation to the environment, but as a class adaptation, specifically as the way the different social logics of entrepreneurs and workers played themselves out in a space dominated by the private real estate market. Everything was determined by cash. All values, ideas, beliefs and preferences were translated by the market place itself into consumption choices that were limited by budgets. Those that could afford more, got more. Those that had little, had little choice about bettering their quality of life.

According to this socio-spatial approach, urban life was not an adaptation by a species to an environment, but the production of forces and choices, of structure and agency, as individuals belonging to distinct social classes found ways of living and consuming within their means and within the system of capitalist industrial production. Now we understand that the spatial arrangements of urban areas are also the product of racism and in many places, such as suburbia, they have embedded within them relations of gender domination as well.

Within the urban environment produced by the capitalism of the 1800s, Engels also observed the many social problems resulting from social inequalities and the uneven distribution of wealth. Families that could ill-afford all their children, abandoned some of them to the street

142

where they had to fend for themselves. It was not uncommon to see urban 'waifs' selling matches or shining shoes and living without families in the squalid areas of the industrial towns. There was also terrible pollution from the factories and large areas of substandard housing. Public health crises were common and, because of inadequate or non-existent medical care, the infant mortality rate among the urban working class was quite high. Today urban areas still have to deal with the negative effects of an unequal distribution of wealth through various public programs, such as subsidized housing. These *public policies* are restricted by the current *fiscal crisis* of the state, which is an ongoing condition in societies organized around private enterprise (see entry on *Fiscal Crisis*).

The socio-spatial approach of Friedrich Engels (1973) also observed how the city represented a great contrast of the rich and the poor living almost side by side. There were areas of the city where immense wealth was concentrated. Ideas at the time explained this stark difference as something belonging to the natural order of things, much in the way the approach of human ecology ignored class differences. It was believed that people received their rewards according to their individual worth and their hard work. Engels, however, explained the very same pattern of inequality in terms of the uneven development endemic to capitalism itself which heightens differences among a population because of differences in purchasing power within a society based on the market alone.

Today the socio-spatial perspective possesses a core principle beyond those characteristics provided by Engels. Metropolitan development patterns are the result of investment flows in land. Whether a business simply requires a location in order to commence work or buys land in order to develop housing and/or commercial structures for profit, both the level of investment and the forms it takes in the real estate market remain the key ways cities and regions grow. For this reason, the socio-spatial perspective pays particular attention to real estate as the 'leading edge' of growth (see entry on *Real Estate*). According to the theorist, Henri Lefebvre (1991), it is this aspect of the economy that results in the production of space. The real estate sector of society constitutes a separate circuit of capital where money can be made, not in the manufacture of things for sale, but in the ownership of land that can then be sold as is, or developed and sold at some later time when the social wealth of the surrounding area has made that investment more valuable. This quality of wealth creation in the second circuit of real estate is quite different from the way capitalist investment returns a profit in the primary sector of manufacturing. We owe to Henri Lefebvre (1991) the insights that have

143

enabled the socio-spatial perspective to advance the argument that space itself is an important factor in metropolitan development and one that is governed by a logic of profit-making at some variance from the way capitalists in the primary circuit make money (see entry on *Real Estate*).

Accordingly, the socio-spatial perspective has the following aspects:

(1) It is possible to use standard categories of political economic analysis, such as profit, investment, rent, class exploitation, and the like, in the analysis of urban development.

(2) The second circuit of capital, investment in real estate, follows a cyclical pattern of growth and decline that is somewhat at variance with the primary circuit of industrial production. Consequently, analyzing the development trends of society requires specific attention to both circuits and the relationship between them. These aspects of analysis are much more complex than the simplistic approach of urban ecology or other forms of urban sociology, like the Chicago School.

(3) All social activities are also about space. Space is an integral factor in everything we do. Understanding this idea means that, when we explore built environments, we must pay as much attention to the way space helps define our behavior as other variables of a social or interactive kind. Attention to the spatial aspects of human life means that design and architecture all play an important role in the way people interact. Cities are different, for example, in part because of differences in their spaces.

(4) Spatial environments contain signs and symbols. They are represented in peoples' minds, as mental maps, and in the conception of the city by politicians, police and ordinary residents. This space has a meaning, therefore, to everyone that lives in it. Sometimes the representation of space is commonly accepted by diverse individuals. Other times, people conflict over the meanings of space and the definitions of what is acceptable behavior in particular places. These aspects are an important part of metropolitan culture. They can be present in both cities and suburbs. In the past, the representational aspects of space have been ignored by urban analysts. For the socio-spatial approach, in contrast, the symbolic and cultural dimension is extremely important.

(5) Finally, the approach highlights the important role government plays in space. Politics defines metropolitan boundaries. Conflicts about these lines in abstract space often lead to serious political problems, if not war when they occur on a national scale. Governments also

transfer wealth across spatial boundaries. This kind of public investment is important to the general well being of places. When a government channels money from one region under its jurisdiction to another, we say this is a *transfer of value* in space. This mechanism is behind the production of uneven development when it is perpetrated by the private sector. When the public sector is involved, it is also uneven development, but the presence of government policies also means that there may be some genuine injustices at work. For these reasons, the role of the state in space is an important aspect of the socio-spatial approach.

REFERENCES

Engels, F. 1973. *The Condition of the Working Class in England*. Moscow: Progress Publishers.
Gottdiener, M. 1994. *The Social Production of Urban Space, 2nd Edition*. Austin, TX: University of Texas Press.
Gottdiener, M. and R. Hutchison 2000. *The New Urban Sociology, 2nd Edition*. NY: McGraw-Hill.
Lefebvre, H. 1991. *The Production of Space*. Oxford, UK: Blackwell.

Sprawl

Ever since suburbanization became a mass phenomenon in the 1950s, urbanists have lamented the pattern of sprawl characteristic of that growth in places like the US and Canada. Sprawl is usually defined as 'haphazard growth' of relative low density over an extended region, with residential units dominated by single family homes. It implies a lack of planning and often results in the duplication of public services, such as policing, fire fighting and elementary education. This condition is curious because local administrations invariably possess planning staffs that engage in drafting comprehensive schemes for the direction of growth. In at least one study, this contradiction was explained as a social problem because of the way both local politicians and developers circumvent guidelines with regional sprawl as the result (Gottdiener, 1977). Sprawl is planned because it is, in part, the direct result of federal government subsidies that encourage this kind of growth – the tax subsidy on single family homes; the subsidy of highway building (see entry on the *Suburb and Suburbanization*).

The attack on sprawl by critics over the years however, is also an attack on suburbia – especially the pattern of single family homes on separate plots. Critiques of sprawl never link the two except in negative ways, but the popularity of the pattern of settlement in suburbia counters whatever undesirable effects are imputed to sprawl. Despite the collective costs of regional development, an overwhelming majority of suburbanites prefer their way of life over central city living. The issue raised by the sprawl pattern of growth is one of private satisfaction versus its social, collective costs.

Despite the frequent attacks on sprawl, negative and haphazard growth in distinction to comparatively orderly but low density development is hard to distinguish. According to one significant study, Los Angeles, which is often cited as the epitome of a sprawling metropolis, actually has less of it than does Portland, OR, which is often cited for its tough anti-growth laws. The city with the worst sprawl is Nashville, TN, a place that is rarely cited as an example of anything except as a center for country music (El-Nasser and Overberg, 2001). Consequently, there is much confusion about this term, especially among those urbanists that assert critical points in order to advance a kind of analysis condemning current patterns of growth. Some Los Angeles geographers for example, point to the pattern within their region of single family homes stretching for many miles as uniquely representing sprawl (see entry on *Postmodern and Modern Urbanism*). But, in actual fact, the LA area is quite dense because almost all the houses are on small lots. By contrast, in the Northeast and Midwest, houses tend to be on much larger lots and, therefore, their densities are much lower. Yet, the Midwest, in particular, is rarely cited as an offending region when it comes to this phenomenon.

Much of the problem of sprawl is the consequence of rapid growth within our largest metropolitan regions. A projection from the Maryland Office of Planning stated that from 1995–2020 'more land will be converted to housing in the region surrounding the Chesapeake Bay than in the past three and a half centuries'.

'In greater Chicago, in the two decades from 1970 to 1990, the consumption of residential land grew an amazing eleven times faster than the region's population.'

'In greater Cleveland, land consumption has been growing even while population has been declining. Since 1970, the regional population has declined by 11%, while the amount of urbanized land has grown by 33%.'

In the Sunbelt things are the same even though these cities have a net increase in population. Phoenix 'is reported to be developing open land at the rate of 1.2 acres per hour. Indeed, the geographic reach of Phoenix is said to be equivalent in size to Delaware'.

Atlanta has grown in population at a rate of 2.9% since 1950. Almost all of this growth has been in the suburbs.

In 2001 a comprehensive study of metro regions in the US measured the extent to which there was excessive and spread-out low density development. This feature was taken as an indicator of sprawl, although the actual failures in planning for more dense and serviceable growth were not studied (El-Nasser and Overberg, 2001). Using an empirical index for the measurement of sprawl, the study uncovered the following:

A boom in population doesn't necessarily trigger sprawl. In fact, sprawl can occur when the population in a metro area is shrinking, for example, in the Buffalo, NY region since 1970.

Topographic and environmental features limit sprawl. Los Angeles is hemmed in by the ocean and the high mountain range to the north. Las Vegas development is restricted by access to water. The Southeast, in contrast, has few such physical limitations. So, for example, 'Unrelenting sprawl along interstates 85 and 20 is creating a "string city" that stretches 600 miles between Raleigh, NC and Birmingham, AL' (El-Nasser and Overberg, 2001).

Contrary to the common perception of the west as having the most egregious examples of sprawl, 16 of the most sprawling metro regions are east of the Mississippi River. Four of the top five are in the Southeast: Nashville, Charlotte, Greensboro and Atlanta. In the southwest, growth is more orderly than the east because development in the former is tethered to water lines. In the east, builders can go just about anywhere in a metro region and find a water supply. At the same time, the easy availability of cheap land in the southwest has enabled many smaller metro areas to expand and increase sprawl.

Turning to the case of the UK, despite the planning system, and, in particular, the Green Belt policy in London and the South-East of England to contain outward metropolitan growth, sprawl has turned the Greater London area into a Multi-centered Metropolitan Region. Even with a commitment to build only on brownfield sites, the pressure for speculators to develop greenfield areas held in their land banks is intense, particularly as housing prices in this part of the UK continue to grow at unprecedented rates (at the time of writing). Cheshire and Sheppard (1989) estimated that, if all planning restrictions were scrapped, the urbanized area of the South-East would expand from 19–28% of the region. Yet, at the same time, housing prices would only fall by some 3–5% as plot sizes increased. Thus, before speculative development gets out of hand in the UK, the need for a more considered perspective, that would engage the socialization of gains with the management of any consequent tendency to sprawl, would have to form part of a policy to scrap the Green Belt around London (Edwards, 2000). Still, no such policy ever existed in the US.

Lack of regional government and the fragmentation of regions into many local governments can abet the sprawl pattern in the US. Many European countries have highly developed systems of regional government. Yet, even with dedicated systems of planning in place and possessed of wide-ranging powers, the imperatives for sprawl still exist because many of these are non-spatial (Marcuse and van Kempen, 2000). According to a US national survey, 'when voters were asked to name the most important problems in their community, sprawl and traffic tied for first place with crime and violence. Each was cited by 18% of those surveyed. Issues such as education and health and medicine trailed far behind' (El-Nasser and Overberg, 2001).

For over a century people have been fleeing the central city in search of lower density and a more 'suburban' lifestyle. Now people living in these same areas of the metro region are calling on government to prevent the very sprawl that their moves created. This distinction is the most trenchant contradiction of metropolitan growth patterns today (Duany, Playter-Zyberk and Speck, 2000):

Sprawl is implicated in the following social problems:

- social isolation and obesity – people driving everywhere;
- asthma and global warming – automobile emissions;
- flooding and erosion – too much pavement;
- the demise of small farms – real estate speculation and regional development;
- extinction of wildlife and the unbalancing of nature.

With regional, low density development producing increasing costs to local residents throughout metropolitan areas, residents have begun to fight against sprawl.

'Since 1997, 22 states have enacted some type of land-use law designed to rein in sprawl. In 1999 alone, law-makers introduced 1,000 bills in state legislatures, and they passed more than 200' (El-Nasser and Overberg, 2001). The political issue of controlling sprawl is now known as 'smart growth' rather than the previous term of 'growth control'. Smart growth candidates are active across the country in local contests (see entries on *Sustainable Urbanization; New Urbanism*). Others are opposed to smart growth and controlling sprawl because they see it as a device to control the housing market. Developers prefer no restrictions and their organized representatives claim that the issue of sprawl is overblown.

As communities debate what to do about sprawl, they continue to support it. People continue to prefer to live in suburban areas adjacent to more urbanized ones rather than in the city itself.

THE EXAMPLE OF PORTLAND, OR

Claimed as the best example of the positive effects of growth control and anti-sprawl, the truth of Portland, OR is much different and the area experiences only limited success. According to El-Nasser and Overberg (2001):

'In 1973, Portland established an urban growth boundary to stop development and preserve open space beyond a certain line. The boundary encouraged denser development inside it . . . However, Portland's sprawl index puts it roughly in the middle of the list of big metros. One reason: Growth is escaping the control of the Portland Metropolitan Council, a regional board of three counties and 24 cities that set up the boundary. Growth is occurring to the south in Salem, OR, and to the north across the state line in Vancouver, Wash. Both cities are part of the Portland metro area, as defined by the Census Bureau, and are within easy commuting distance of Portland.'

See the entry on *Sustainable Urbanization* for more discussion.

WHITE FLIGHT

According to the 2001 study, most of the cities in the Midwest score high both on the level of racial segregation in the metro area and on the level of sprawl. It is the decline of the core and its racial problems that contributes to sprawl at the periphery. Many medium-sized cities of the Northeast have a similar problem of a declining and racially segregated core surrounded by a growing suburban region.

'By many measures, the Midwest has both the highest racial segregation and the most concentrated poverty at the cores. That centrifugal push makes it possible for developers to offer ever-more distant alternatives to urban problems.' (El-Nasser and Overberg, 2001)

The same can be said for cities that have declining populations but which are located in sprawling metro regions, such as those in the Northeast.

White flight is a more complex issue in the UK (see entry on *Housing*). In the declining Northern cities this is manifested in the spatial segregation of housing and employment opportunities as the white middle class moves to the rural edge of these cities. In London, the most cosmopolitan place in Europe, the patchwork of the spatial distribution of ethnicity does not preclude white flight, but segregation is less complete as urban professsionals occupy gentrifying areas that still are characterized by a mixture of classes. However, as Malcolm Cross notes:

> '"Race" is therefore integral to the crisis of London . . . it is coming increasingly to define the urban underclass marooned in crumbling estates and weighed down by poverty joblessness and despair.' (Cross, 1992: 116)

As proof, by 2002, Operation Trident had been launched by the Metropolitan Police to combat black on black crime. In areas where this was rife, it had been accompanied by professional and white flight, leaving behind poorer families who suffer the socio-economic and cultural consequences of remaining in these areas.

LOSS OF FARMLAND

Historically the best farmland was located near cities. When suburbanization occurred, it consumed these farms. From 1982–92, the US lost, to urban and suburban development, an average of 400,000 acres per year of 'prime' farmland, the land with the best soil and climate for growing crops. During that same period an additional 26,600 acres per year of 'unique' farmland was lost, used for growing rare and specialty crops.

The lands most suitable for growing crops also tend to be most suitable for growing houses. This is because inland urban settlements in the US have tended to be situated in river valleys and other fertile areas that are also highly productive for farming.

LANDSCAPES LOST

Critiques of sprawl argue that natural landscapes which are beneficial to humans are being replaced by a terrain of sprawl and strip zoning that is 'ugly'. But this argument against suburban development patterns has been made since the 1950s by critics. Aesthetics aside, an overwhelming majority of Americans like the convenience of strip zoning and commercial sprawl, as would the average Brit as the dreams of capitalist modernity are realized through air-conditioned malls, air-conditioned automobiles and the clean lines of new private housing estates in the suburbs and commuter belts.

ECONOMIC LOSS

Over 130 million Americans enjoy observing, photographing and catching wildlife and fish, thus supporting a nature-oriented tourist industry in excess of $14 billion annually. This industry is threatened by the disappearance of open space. Similarly Europeans are having to travel further and further distances to escape the embrace of an increasingly suburban sprawl. In the South-East of England, the most densely populated part of Europe, the sound of the motor vehicle is never far from earshot.

UNHEALTHY AIR

Current development patterns also bring substantial air pollution, largely because of the increased automobile dependence that is associated with sprawl. Motor vehicle use in the US doubled from one to two trillion miles per year between 1970–90. In the 1980s, vehicle miles traveled grew more than four times faster than the driving-age population and many times faster than the population at large. This translates directly into growing emissions of greenhouse gases and the continued inability of our metropolitan areas to cleanse themselves naturally of unhealthy air. According to a US government report:

'Despite considerable progress, the overall goal of clean and healthy air continues to elude much of the country. Unhealthy air pollution levels still plague virtually every major city in the US.' (El-Nasser and Overberg, 2001)

A similar situation reigns in most UK urbanized regions. Recently, an asthma epidemic, particularly amongst the young, has emerged. According to the Department of Health, there is a 1 in 2 chance of children in the UK developing asthma symptoms. The causes are related to modern lifestyles and in metropolitan regions, increased car ownership and usage.

151

RUNOFF

'Haphazard sprawl development also brings runoff water pollution to more and more watersheds, degrading streams, lakes and estuaries. It is now thoroughly documented that, as the amount of impervious pavement and rooftops increases in a watershed, the velocity and volume of surface runoff increases; flooding, erosion and pollutant loads in receiving waters increase; groundwater recharge and water tables decline; stream beds and flows are altered; and aquatic habitat is impaired.' (Benfield, F. et al., 1999)

Typical suburban sprawl completely destroys water habitats for all species. In many areas of the country, pollution from suburban runoff now exceeds that produced by industry. Floods that were once only decades apart now occur regularly.

Runoff pollution is now the nation's leading threat to water quality, affecting about 40% of the US's surveyed rivers, lakes and estuaries.

THE STRUGGLE FOR SOLUTIONS

Most areas of Northeast and Midwest America are comprised of many political jurisdictions which makes the metro region so fragmented that it is difficult to establish a regional planning or governance program. Also, while some localities may restrict growth, others may welcome it thereby perpetuating regional sprawl. Everyone is pushing for 'smart growth' but no one can agree on what 'dumb' growth is (see entry on *Sustainable Urbanization*).

Some planners call for more roads as a way to ease traffic congestion. Others say building or widening roads creates a bigger traffic mess and encourages even more development. Some advocate single family houses on big lots. Others insist the solution is more apartments and small homes to accommodate more people on less land. In the UK, the traffic generation effect of new road space has long been established, yet national, regional and local authorities do not look at comprehensive solutions to the growing demand for more roads.

Some say housing should be built close to mass transit and within walking distance of stores, schools and other services to get cars off the road. Others argue that Americans don't want to live in a more crowded urban setting or give up their cars. Some want strict growth boundaries. Others say that limiting development pushes up housing prices and reduces the stock of affordable housing.

According to the 2001 study, people all agree on one thing: municipalities must plan better. 'Faced with mounting pressure from

152

residents, environmentalists and other interest groups and local officials, eight states have approved comprehensive, growth management plans that require local governments to prevent development where roads and sewers don't exist. But most other states that have been dragged into a problem that's usually left to local government are sticking to laws that get little resistance. They are setting aside funds to buy open space, farmland or forests. Some are creating tax incentives for landowners to donate development rights to the state or conservationists' (El-Nasser and Overberg, 2001).

Among the most vocal professionals attacking sprawl are the New Urbanists (see the entry on page 96). They advocate development schemes that explicitly and directly counteract low density, sprawling growth by claiming that growth should be of high density and planned on the pedestrian, as opposed to the automobile scale. They call for a reinvigoration of cities by bringing new development that is compact, walkable, and transit-oriented. They point to transportation research which indicates that each doubling of average neighborhood density is associated with a decrease in per-household vehicle use of 20–40%, with a corresponding decline in emissions.

As discussed in the entry on *New Urbanism*, there are many limitations to this planning philosophy as well. Above all else, it is critical to note that, since the 1950s, the metropolitan areas of the US have been inexorably developing towards a new form of settlement space, one that mixes low density residential areas with increasingly specialized, functional centers. This new form of space is discussed in the entry on the *Multi-centered Metropolitan Region*. It is quite possible, therefore, that what many see as an aberration of growth that is irrational, may, in fact, be a mode of settlement space that has its own powerful and functional logic while transcending the older model of city-centered urban life. Both processes of de-centralization and re-centralization are at work bringing a kind of order to the alleged chaos of sprawl. Now, the internet and cell phone technology make low density living arrangements even more feasible than in the past. In short, the current push to consider sprawl as a critical social problem may not be misguided, because there are very serious public policy issues that must be addressed, but that same effort must also take the time to truly understand the new form of space – the multi-centered metro region and all its implications.

Benfield, F. et al., 1999. *Once there were Greenfields: How Urban Sprawl is Undermining America's Environment, Economy and Social Fabric*. NY: National Resources Defense Council.

Cheshire, P. and S. Shepperd 1989. 'British Planning Policy and Access to Housing: Some Empirical Evidence' *Urban Studies*, 6: 469–85.

Cross. M. 1992. 'Race and Ethnicity' in A.Thornlet (ed.) *The Crisis of London*. London: Routledge. pp. 103–18.

Duany, A., E. Playter-Zyberk and J. Speck. 2000, *Suburban Nation: The Rise of Sprawl and the Decline of the American Dream*. NY: North Point Press.

Edwards, M. 2000. 'Sacred Cow or Sacrificial Lamb? Will London's Green Belt have to go?' *City* 4 (1) (April) pp. 106–12.

Gottdiener, M. 1977. *Planned Sprawl*. Newbury Park, CA: Sage Publications.

Kunstler, J. 1996. *Home from Nowhere: Remaking Our Everyday World for the 21st Century*. NY: Simon and Schuster.

Leo, C. et al., 1998. 'Is Urban Sprawl Back on the Political Agenda?' *Urban Affairs Review*, 34: 179–211.

Lopez, R. and H. Hynes 2003. 'Sprawl in the 1990s: Measurement, Distribution and Trends' *Urban Affairs Review*, 38(3) (January) pp. 325–55.

Marcuse, P. and R. van Kepen 2000. *Globalizing Cities*. Oxford: Blackwell.

El-Nasser, H. and P. Overberg, 2001. 'A comprehensive look at sprawl in America.' *USA Today*, 22 February, www.usatoday.com, accessed October, 2003.

Suburb and Suburbanization

154

Suburbs represent a physical form of settlement, neither urban nor rural, but something in-between. The field of urban studies has always had a problem defining what is meant by 'urban'. These days the concept of 'suburb' is even more problematic. In fact, the US Bureau of Census does not officially use the term 'suburb' at all. Instead, areas lying outside large cities are defined together with those cities as 'metropolitan statistical areas' or MSAs. It is commonly understood that a suburb is a residential area outside the large central city with less population density but higher than the adjacent rural area. Early conceptions considered these places as dependent on the city and now that is a fallacy, as is the belief that these areas are dominated by residences alone. Historically, for instance, some suburbs started out as cities but were then absorbed by urban growth.

Harlem and Brooklyn in New York, Old Irving Park in Chicago, and Country Club Plaza in Kansas City, are some examples (Gilfoyle, 1998).

Now, if we understand that the form of settlement space is the multi-centered metropolitan region, we can see that areas usually called suburbs are, in fact, quite diverse, multi-functional and connected to cities in different ways. Many white collar and high-tech companies prefer to locate in areas adjacent to but outside the central city. Manufacturing takes place in suburbs. Most of the retailing in metro regions also occurs there. Across the US, sports stadiums and recreational complexes are often also situated in suburban locations. When a diverse and large population is added to this mix, it becomes clearer that these areas are merely a lower density variant of the multi-functional array of activities that comprises developed cities themselves. By the 1980s, in fact, there were already over 20 counties in the US with a large work force and population and a diverse functional profile that could characterize them as 'fully urbanized' even though none possessed a single large city (Gottdiener and Kephart, 1991).

Because of the free market in land and abundant space, early in US history people already exhibited a strong preference for living outside the city in single family buildings with large lots and for tolerating a long journey to work. US suburbs have also been distinctive because of their political independence. In comparison to Europe, incorporated suburbs thwarted movements toward metropolitan governance. Suburbs from Brookline, MA, and Evanston, IL, to Beverly Hills, CA fought annexation and evolved as municipalities (Gilfoyle, 1998). This political power contributed to the emergence of the fragmented, multi-centered metropolis that we possess today.

According to Fichman and Fowler (2003), one way that suburbanization differed markedly from the process of city formation was its racially exclusive nature. For decades in the US, the mass residential developments outside the city were dominated by whites. Even though there is considerably more diversity today, suburban regions remain comparatively more white and more affluent than inner city areas. They also hold the bulk of the US population. In 1998, 51% of the total population was suburban as compared to 29% of the population that resided in the inner cities of the nation, according to the US Census. Across the US, as suburbanization proceeded, inner cities lost as much as 50% of their populations. Places, such as Baltimore, Philadelphia, Chicago, Boston, Detroit, St. Louis, Buffalo and Cleveland have less people than their surrounding regions. Among the few cities that have grown since the period of mass suburbanization beginning with the 1950s are Dallas,

Houston, Phoenix and San Diego, but they have done so largely because they possessed the ability to annex outlying territory. Without such powers in the rest of the country, traditional cities were overwhelmed by the shift of population to adjacent areas in the regional array.

In addition to racial and class exclusion, the vast areas of suburban growth in our society are the result of government programs that favored this pattern of development by promoting family desires for single home ownership. Two programs, in particular, are critical for an understanding of how suburbanization became so popular and so vast a land-use transformation in the US – the homeowner tax subsidy, passed in the 1930s to revive a depression era housing industry, and, the 1950s' National Defense System of Highways Act, which established the means by which the intricate web of interstate highways were constructed across the country. Both policies operated openly to produce massive suburban development outside our central cities and they are responsible for the emergence of regional growth. See entry on the *Multi-centered Metropolitan Region* for a more extended discussion of these forces.

In other entries – *New Urbanism, Sprawl, Sustainable Urbanization* – critiques of suburban living have been discussed. Among the first to lament this pattern of growth was Lewis Mumford. As he most often did, Mumford emphasized the superior benefits of clustered development in the manner of Ebenezer Howard. This critique, however, was directed less against suburbanization, per se, than at the sprawl pattern it assumed. Since Mumford's time, suburban life has often been vilified by critics with a city base. But, their constant attacks have neither prevented the pace of suburbanization from proceeding nor convinced government leaders that the suburban alternative was wrong. Instead, our society has been split between a relatively small group of architects, planners and urbanists who continued to attack the development of suburbs and a large majority that went to live there.

To be sure, the pattern of sprawl presents many problems that have to be faced by our society. Yet, critiques of sprawl often miss their mark because they are mixed together with attacks against the suburban way of life itself. See the entry on *New Urbanism* as an example. From the European perspective however, some writers have questioned this critique by pointing to the fact that the high-tech, information economy, which provides the US with its global comparative advantage, is located more consistently in suburban rather than inner city places.

According to *The Economist* (2000), for example:

'The film *American Beauty* recycles a view of the suburbs, that they are vortexes of tedium and alienation – which has been a staple of artistic contempt at least since John Cheever. This view has probably never been very accurate. But it is getting less accurate by the day, as the suburbs mutate in all sorts of extraordinary ways. If the complaints about the suburbs are doomed to remain forever the same, the suburbs themselves are changing beyond all recognition.

The most obvious change is that the suburbs are the smithies of almost everything that is new and innovative in the American economy. Microsoft sits in a suburb of Seattle. Silicon Valley is an unappetizing sprawl of modest (though costly) bungalows and strip malls. The new economy and the new suburbs are really the same thing.'

This article went on to say that, in agreement with the socio-spatial approach, the current information and high-tech-oriented economy is helping to sustain multi-centered regional development in much the same way that the 18th Century manufacturing system of capitalism produced the factory town. Also noted in the article is the increasing diversity of the areas outside the inner city with regard to both class and race:

'The suburbs are also becoming ever less monolithic and bourgeois. Suburbs can be blue-collar or ultra-liberal. Increasingly though, some are a social jumble within themselves. Nor are the suburbs the all-white enclaves that metropolitan sophisticates imagine. Atlanta, Chicago and Washington, DC, all have thriving black suburbs. In Southern California the new Chinatowns and little Saigons are in the suburbs rather than downtown. Many of the most ethnically diverse places in the US are now suburbs.'

The key issue raised by the dominance of suburbanization seems to be not to do away with the suburb, as New Urbanists argue, but to do something about its negative aspects, especially sprawl. For this reason, political movements such as 'sustainable urbanism' and other holistic approaches are important (see entry on page 158). In fact, both urban and suburban areas are the sites for important social movements that attempt to address key issues of daily living in our society. For an extended discussion, see the entries on *Urban and Suburban Social Movements; Sprawl.*

Lastly, it is a mistake to view the vast suburban areas of countries like the US as devoid of social problems. The issue of sprawl and its negative consequences has already been noted. Suburban regions lack public space and rely too exclusively on the automobile. They lose out to the advantages that higher density, clustered development might provide (see entry on *Sprawl*).

Fichman, M. and E.P. Fowler 2003. 'The Science and Politics of Sprawl: From Suburbia to Creative Citybuilding' Unpublished paper, York University.

Gilfoyle, T. 1998, 'White Cities, Linguistic Turns and Disneylands: The New Paradigms of Urban History' *Reviews in American History*, 26: 175–204.

Gottdiener, M. and G. Kephart 1990. 'The Multi-Nucleated Metropolitan Region: A Comparative Analysis' In R. Kling, S. Olin and M. Poster (eds) *Post Suburban California*. Berkeley, CA: University of California Press.

The Economist, 24 March 2000.

Sustainable Urbanization

According to this concept, social and economic urban development is to be pursued in conjunction with the protection and preservation of the earth's resources for current and future generations; natural resources and the capacity of natural systems to respond and adjust to human-made changes is limited and must be acknowledged in growth plans.

Another term for this is 'livable cities'. One of the key issues from the sustainability perspective when applied to cities is to reduce the environmental impact of all urban activities to a minimum. This means that waste disposal and resource needs be minimized to the local area. This is called the *ecological footprint*. Other aspects of sustainability refer to social costs and economic choices within a given area, but the movement began with intense concern for the way our present pattern of urban development was threatening the environmental vitality of the globe everywhere.

In the UK, sustainable cities are central to urban policy. However, it is not clear what constitutes a sustainable city for British policy-makers. Economic, social and environmental contexts are given in the report, *Towards an Urban Renaissance*, but not how they integrate to create and nourish sustainable cities. There is a stress on excellence in urban design, with the unsustainable form of Houston being compared to sustainable and more compact UK cities, as though the two places were compatible. The Sustainable Cities Research Institute at Northumbria University in

key concepts

158

the UK, is long on single projects on sustainability, but short on definitions of sustainable cities. (http://www.sustainable-cities.org.uk/home.html).

Elsewhere in Europe, the European Commission adopted Communication COM(2004)60 *Towards a Thematic Strategy on the Urban Environment*, in January 2004, which sets out the Commission's ideas for the Thematic Strategy on the Urban Environment due in summer 2005. There are four themes: environmental management; urban transport; sustainable construction; and urban design. The themes are cross-cutting in nature and have strong links with many environmental issues see http://europa.eu.int/comm/environment/urban/thematic_strategy.htm).

Globally, the idea of 'sustainable development' emerged in the 1970s and is the guiding principle in the formulation of policies addressing the relationships among population, environment and industrial development (Marquette, n.d.). With the aim of institutionalizing sustainable development among member states, the UN in 1987 established the World Commission on Environment and Development. The Commission report, *Our Common Future*, is also known as the Brundtlandt Report, after the Swedish minister that chaired the commission. It defined five clear principles of sustainable development for policy-makers:

(1) Changing current patterns of economic growth, technology, production and management which may have negative impacts on the environment and population.
(2) Ensuring employment, food, energy, safe water, and sanitary services for all populations.
(3) Controlling global population growth.
(4) Protecting natural resources for future generations.
(5) Integrating economic, environmental and population considerations in policy decision-making and planning.

Areas of the world that might be beneficially affected by this ideology of growth are not confined to the third world alone. The countries of the former Soviet Union that have transition economies are uniquely positioned to enact sustainable development policies that would improve the quality of the environment. The same can be said of older cities in the developed countries that have been hard hit by de-industrialization and now must redevelop in new ways.

Implementing sustainable development means that government plays a key role as a manager of growth. This is not something that every country, especially ones like the US, will embrace. One prime area of

159

management involves the regulation of the environment through the monitoring of industry, agriculture, energy and transport systems, population health, waste management, and natural resource exploitation.

Those countries that pursue sustainable growth have available the following policy measures: formulating and enforcing laws, undertaking industrial reform, regulation of growth and economic activity, establishing environmental protection funds and incentives, extending environmental education, establishing toxic waste clean up funds, and supporting research (Marquette, n.d.).

Arguments for capitalist market societies to allow increased government intervention include the need to cut the health and environmental damage costs to the society, the result of greater efficiency if this ideology is pursued, reduction in the rate of rising industrial costs in the future due to stewardship of resources.

The sustainable ideology incorporates a strong belief that, in addition to government and private sector intervention, local community groups of all kinds must be actively involved in promoting sound or smart growth. This includes conservation of resources at the level of the household, recycling, and support for public-supplied resources like transportation.

There is also a more sanguine and skeptical view of technology as the savior of resources even with growth. But, at the same time, there is a call to develop new modes of technology that will aid sustainability and help preserve the carrying capacity of the earth.

The Brundtlandt Report also noted that the lifestyle enjoyed by the citizens of the North, and that includes the way in which the cities are built, is not environmentally sustainable. This was the central message which inspired the Rio 'Earth Summit' and resulted in the signing of the massive AGENDA 21 as the basis for turning around the development process towards sustainability. It was recognized by most of the countries of the world that the process of development today is based on *non-renewable* resources and has a damaging environmental impact. This has to be turned around. Now the emphasis is on deploying *renewable resources* in as many ways as possible in both the construction and maintenance of the built environment in order to *sustain* the earth for future generations.

A study by Portney (2003), noted that, in the US, 25 cities recently signed a pledge and committed resources to pursue sustainable growth. These included Portland, Seattle, San José, SF, Boulder, Tucson, Phoenix, Chattanooga, Jacksonville, Tampa, Milwaukee, and Boston, among others. The focus of sustainability however, was different for each city. The core idea of all the efforts was to match growth and resource utilization with the carrying capacity of the local region's natural systems. For example, fishing should match the take for human consumption against the natural ability of fish to reproduce themselves and limit the take to the level that will not upset that balance. Thus sustainability is not anti-growth, per se, but it does emphasize government intervention to manage development. In practice, each of these cities adopted a variety of policies that were all placed under the label of sustainability. For example, Santa Barbara, California focused on the environment; in Cambridge, Massachusetts the aim was much broader and included health and well being, economic security and a community role in planning decisions. Portney's study is the first to measure exactly what cities were doing and how. Although many areas have said, following the Rio Summit in particular, that they were interested in sustainable growth, Portney researched exactly what cities did, if anything, to pursue that goal.

The most difficult task was to develop measures of resource utilization and measures of sustainability. 'Any close reading of the conceptual literature leads to the conclusion that sustainability itself is a multi-dimensional concept, and any effort to measure how seriously a city seems to take sustainability would necessarily also have to account for its many dimensions' (Portney, 2003: 31). The key indicator became whether a city had actually developed a clearly recognizable sustainability plan. Then, the key attribute was whether a city had included 'indicators of sustainability' in the plan. Thus, sustainability is really a way of doing *strategic planning* where the goals of growth are made explicit and where there are well-defined indicators that show whether or not goals are being attained.

Some of the factors that were used in the local vision of sustainability by the 25 cities studied were: existence of a comprehensive area wide plan; environmental goals; health goals; energy efficiency; goals for local economic development; quality of life indicators; issues of environmental and social equity; issues of governance and mandated community participation in decision-making; what administrative arrangements have been made to implement the plan?; is the plan connected to a regional plan?

According to Portney:

'The primary interest here in these sustainability indicators is not to use them to assess whether cities have achieved their goals and become more sustainable. Since so little time has elapsed since cities began their pursuit of sustainability, such an effort would be premature. Rather it is to examine them to see what they consider the important standards and criteria for working toward sustainability, and to see whether they provide an appropriate outcome of what kinds of issues cities need to address if they wish to take sustainability seriously.' (2003: 37)

Another benefit of the comparative study was to uncover the way cities articulated social indicators for use in sustainability planning. The indicators did vary from city to city. However, Portney's study helped to disseminate this information so that locations could determine whether alternative indicators were better suited to local needs. One result was the launching of 'indicators projects' which were designed to find and tailor appropriate measures of sustainability for use in strategic plans.

'These indicators have been developed for the purpose of providing reasonably clear measures and benchmarks for assessing whether progress is being made toward becoming more sustainable . . . Indicators' projects essentially scour existing sources of information available for their cities, and consider which pieces of information potentially provide some insight into progress toward sustainability. Rarely does an indicators project seek to develop new measures of characteristics that are important.' (Portney, 2003: 40)

The following is a summary of the indicators used by some of the cities:

Measures of: air quality, biodiversity, energy, climate change, ozone depletion, food, hazardous materials, human health, parks and open spaces, economic development, population growth, environmental justice, public information and the dissemination through education, solid waste, transportation, water quality, municipal expenditures, and conservation.

Portney's study revealed that, in implementing a plan, the following are all important considerations:

162

- Enabling a community to identify what it values and then prioritizing the values.
- Holding individuals and larger groups accountable for achieving results.
- Building democratic mechanisms of decision-making and participation.
- Allowing community residents to measure what is important and get that to planning process.

Clearly the key issue in the pursuit of sustainability is implementation and the ability of the government to hold groups and individuals in the city accountable.

Portney observed that each of the set of indicators used by a local area was an indicator itself of what the local residents considered most important. Sustainable indicators focusing on ethical, social and cultural issues include: the number of homeless residents, the number of violent crimes, the overall crime rate, and the frequency of child abuse. Political issues include: level of participation, voter turnout, frequency with which residents contact officials, and level of volunteerism.

Finally, Portney was able to develop some summary indicators of pursuing sustainability seriously: Whether there is – cluster residential development, brownfield redevelopment, eco-industrial parks, smart growth zoning and planning, public transit, car pool lanes, limiting of downtown parking, bicycle ridership program, household waste recycling, industrial recycling, air pollution reductions, hazardous waste programs, recycling at all government offices, lead and asbestos abatement programs, renewable energy use, energy conservation, alternative energy programs, water conservation, and involvement of local residents in planning.

Using this index, he ranked 24 cities that say they are pursuing sustainability: Seattle, Scottsdale, San José, Boulder, Santa Monica, Portland, ST, Tampa, Chattanooga, Tucson were all in the top 10. The bottom 10 from 15th to 24th were Cleveland, Brookline, Boston, Orlando, Santa Barbara, Indianapolis, Olympia, New Haven, Brownsville (TX), Milwaukee. The middle 4 therefore were: Austin, Phoenix, Jacksonville and Cambridge (MA).

In summary, Portney found that of all the 24 cities that said they were pursuing some aspect of sustainable development, only eight cities had taken that goal seriously.

GROWTH VS SMART GROWTH

The concept of 'smart growth' is related to sustainability. Sometimes the former is used in political movements that pursue better planning for local areas.

What 'smart growth' does is advocate how growth itself should be tied to the quality of life and how when it isn't, it should not be pursued. Among all the problems, the pattern of sprawl is most hated. Thus, 'smart growth' is a judgment that stands in opposition to contemporary sprawl patterns of development which are considered 'dumb' and damaging to regional prosperity. The villain is always poor planning and poor public management of the environment that has allowed unregulated low density sprawl with traffic congestion and increasing costs for basic social services.

163

According to Portney (2003: 40), 'Smart growth recognizes the connections between development and quality of life. It leverages new growth to improve the community. The features that distinguish smart growth in a community vary from place to place. New smart growth is more town-centered, is transit and pedestrian-oriented, and has a great mix of housing, commercial and retail uses. It also preserves open space and other environmental amenities'.

Many areas of the country have responded to the problems produced by growth simply by enacted state laws that mandate planning before growth can be approved. That is, a master plan must be drawn up and in place. But we know, of course, how all these plans get subverted to growth needs (see entries on *Planning; Real Estate; Sprawl*).

Some examples of successful 'smart growth' are Portland and Seattle. In Portland, zoning regulations were used to protect environmentally sensitive or valuable areas. These so-called *Environmental Zones* were built into the master plan. The entry on *Sprawl* discussed a new study that shows how some of this Portland plan was subverted by developers. The city of Seattle adopted the concept of *urban villages* as the organizing principle behind its master plan which would provide regulations and incentives to create desirable development or smart growth in sections of the city. The major Seattle project was called 'Uptown District', and it is was a redevelopment of a closed Sears store and parking area. This project attempted a mix use urban village complete with residences. See the entry on *New Urbanism* for a discussion of this project and the reasons why it proved not to be a success. In the main, people resisted the idea of abandoning their cars to become pedestrians, despite the best efforts of smart growth advocates to make them behave that way. Both examples, Portland and Seattle, are much quoted in the literature on smart growth and new urbanism, but both have enjoyed only limited success. For this reason it is important to study the way the powerful forces of growth in our society undermine attempts at better planning. Previous entries have provided this information.

164

REFERENCES

Marquette, Catherine, n.d. 'Population and Environment in Industrialized Regions'. International Union for the Scientific Study of Population, Policy and Research, *Paper #8*.

Portney, K. 2003. *Taking Sustainable Cities Seriously*. Cambridge, MA: MIT Press.

Uneven Development/ Boom and Bust Cycles

Uneven development is caused under capitalism by the differential way investment chases the highest rate of return under conditions of a free market in land which leads to the spatial effect of poverty adjacent to wealth.

Urban and suburban settlement spaces flow and develop because of capital investment. The ebb and flow of money determines community well being. Not only are jobs created, but economic activity also generates tax revenue. The latter is used partly by local government to fund public projects that improve the quality of community life. But spending, both public and private, is not uniformly distributed across metropolitan space. Some places receive much more investment than others. Even within cities there are great differences between those sections that are beehives of economic activity and those that seem scarcely touched by commerce and industry.

Within any given business, there are also great disparities between workers who are well paid and those who get the minimum salary. Wages are carried home to neighborhoods, and a significant portion is present in the local area. Hence the well being of a place depends not only on the amount of investment it can attract but also on the wealth of its residents.

Uneven development is not just characteristic of capitalist societies. Socialist cities also display a pattern of inequality in housing, although it is not as distinct as under capitalism.

As capital has become more mobile, its ability to invest and then disinvest in places has become easier. As a consequence, the *boom and bust cycle* that typically plays itself out in places has speeded up. Once prosperous areas, like high-tech Silicon Valley or the inner districts of 'rust belt' cities, lose their manufacturing to locations outside the country as investment shifts globally in search of the cheapest production costs and highest profits. Then these regions decline. Boom and bust cycles, and their spatial consequences, were first observed as extreme examples of the business cycle structurally inherent in capitalism, but they took decades to work out. Shifting periods of prosperity, decline, recession and recovery used to be quite common in US society and are still evident in cycles even though the extremes have been ironed out by fiscal policies since the experience of the great depression. Now we understand that this same cycle can be applied to space. Locations are so dependent on the constant flow of capital investment today that significant fluctuations in that stream of money produce immediate spatial effects. Global capitalism has speeded up the ability of investment to switch from place to place and with this movement comes changes in community well being at a more rapid pace than we have ever before experienced.

Uneven development often leads to more uneven development due to the logic of capitalism. As a result of the inherent desire, under capitalism, not to invest in places that are already depressed and offer little incentive for profit, uneven development usually becomes more acute over time. This pattern increases the polarization between those places that are poor and those that are thriving. But places are made of people, so the spatial disparities result in different life chances for metro residents. As Engels (1973) observed in Manchester, inequities create a problem of social justice as the less affluent members of the working class find it difficult to raise families. Hence the phenomenon of the *Gold Coast and the Slum* was observed almost 100 years before Harvey Zorbaugh wrote it in 1928.

The concept of uneven development can also be applied to entire societies not just their spatial patterns. This more general way of viewing the concept is characteristic of the Marxist analysis of capitalism. According to Marx, 'a major contradiction of capitalism is the simultaneous emergence of concentrations of wealth and capital, on the one hand, and poverty and oppression, on the other. This "general law of capitalist accumulation" as Marx termed it, highlights the capital-labor conflict' (Bond, 1999).

For Henri Lefebvre, this unevenness in accumulation and ownership is expressed spatially in terms of inequalities in the residential pattern and in the provision of urban services. Lefebvre's interpretation is responsible for the perspective of the 'socio-spatial' approach to urban studies (see entry on page 140).

For political economists, like Oskar Lange, uneven development is very clearly a consequence of the differential ownership relations in society and the social relations of reproduction. This leads to social and economic inequality and then to spatial inequality because the uneven development manifests itself as modes of segregation in a free real estate market. Thus, class conflict is stressed more than socio-spatial differences.

Most people analyzing the phenomenon are mainly concerned with its political implications because of what Marx observed – that it is the basis for capitalist-worker conflict.

Another strain of Marxist thinking comes from his writings in the *Grundrisse* (1973) where he states that uneven development is a consequence of the articulation of different modes of production. This would be the structural and most macro conception of the term. As the old mode declines and the new mode ascends, uneven development is produced. But this too has its spatial component. Regions that have been de-industialized but were once prosperous, now must languish, while regions that are home to the new mode of production in high-technology and computer-related business, are now successful.

'In spatial terms, unevenness has been associated with theories of unequal exchange and forms of core-periphery dominance. This is in part because of their grounding in progressive third world nationalism. Such debates have had the effect of over-emphasizing interstate relations and under-emphasizing the flows of capital and social struggles that have more decisively shaped local "underdevelopment".' (Bond, 1999)

David Harvey (1996) argued that historical-geographical materialism entails a consideration of the process of unevenness in more general ways. The key focus of geographical unevenness is the differentiated return on investment that creation and/or destruction of entire built environments – and the social structures that accompany them – offer to different kinds of investors with different time horizons. Meanwhile, different places compete endlessly with one another to attract investment. In the process they tend to amplify unevenness, allowing capital to play one local regional or national class configuration off against another.

While political economists have focused most explicitly on class effects of uneven development, US urban areas also experience uneven development with regard to race. The issue of urban inequality is a somewhat different topic. But, with regard to uneven development, it can be argued that racial discrimination confronts victims with a biased and limited opportunity structure. This is then reflected in differences with regard to educational attainment, medical care, longevity, and the like. Studies on US cities, especially Detroit and Atlanta, have repeatedly shown how, despite considerable effort, space remains segregated with regard to race, *even when* economic conditions improve over time (Dareden et al., 1990).

Two related forces converged in Detroit. On the one hand, local government was controlled by business, more specifically automobile corporate interests and were most responsive to the needs of capital. Pleas for equality from the populous were not addressed. On the other hand, racial segregation in housing progressed as elsewhere in the US through the filtering mechanisms of the real estate industry and bank loan policies. Clarence Stone's study of Atlanta, shows how the second operates as well, as it does elsewhere, but also documented how the first did not apply because Atlanta's government was controlled by blacks. What kept development uneven in this special case were the effects of class among and within the black community. Those that prospered got out. Those that didn't remained segregated downtown and were not as successful as the middle-class in having their needs addressed by local government. In sum, uneven racial settlement is a major problem in US cities, whether they possess progressive governments or not (see entry on *Inequality and Poverty*).

Another important case study is Chicago, Illinois (Nyden and Nyden, 1999: 1). There, as Harvey Zorbaugh noted (1928), the problem of uneven income distribution was already manifested in space 70 years ago. According to Nyden and Nyden, 'The contrast between the Gold Coast mansions just north of the Magnificent Mile (along North Michigan Ave) and the low-income neighborhood just six blocks to the west was still present. In 1980, nine of the 15 poorest neighborhoods in the US were in Chicago. Last year, (1998), Chicago was listed as the third most segregated city in the US, after Gary, In. and Detroit, MI'.

As elsewhere, Nyden and Nyden discovered that this extreme case of racial segregation in Chicago was caused by housing segregation, local race-based politics, and discriminatory lending practices:

> 'The symbolism of uneven development even carries through into professional sports. With its distinct uptown character, Wrigley Field, home to the Cubs, is affectionately described as the "friendly confines".' The historic field in gentrified "Wrigleyville", full of popular bars and trendy restaurants, is a sharp contrast to the cement coliseum built on the Southside for the White Sox. Comisky Park . . . is across a 12-lane interstate from Taylor Homes and Stateway Gardens, two of the greatest concentrations of public housing in the US.' (1999: 2)

Historically, Chicago's lakefront park system was constructed to service better the wealthier and whiter neighborhoods of the Northside. This structural fact continues to produce public inequities in spending. 'In addition to having double the acreage of the southern lakefront, the northern section has more food concession stands, playgrounds, marinas and other amenities' (Nyden and Nyden, 1999).

Chicago also shows a pattern observed elsewhere of uneven investment after the period of de-industrialization in business that is presently oriented towards centers in wealthier districts to the exclusion of other areas. An immense amount of private investment flowed into the traditional 'Gold Coast' on Michigan Avenue bringing with it public sector spending on upgrades to such things as mass transit. Housing and retailing for upscale workers followed. 'At the same time, the city is experiencing an affordable housing shortage, partially produced by the dismantling of concentrated low-income high-rise public housing built in the 1950s and 60s. While the policy of concentrating the poor in high rise housing has been recognized as a policy failure by liberals and conservatives alike, the absence of any clear strategy to build and preserve affordable housing in Chicago has been a major battle line in city and community politic' (Nyden and Nyden, 1999: 2). The pattern of loss for affordable housing continues.

In short, because of the power of the free market in the US, there are clear examples in this country of both uneven development in both class and racial terms as well as disruptive boom and bust cycles in the well being of place.

REFERENCES

Bond, Patrick, 1999. 'What is Uneven Development?' in P. O'Hara (ed.) *The Encyclopedia of Political Economy*. London: Routledge.

Darden, J. et al. 1990. *Detroit: Race and Uneven Development*. Philadelphia: Temple University Press.

Engels, F. 1973. *The Condition of the Working Class in England*. Moscow: Progress Publishers.

Gottdiener, M. and R. Hutchison 2000. *The New Urban Sociology*, 2nd Edition. NY: McGraw-Hill.

Harvey, D. 1996. *Justice, Nature and the Geography of Difference*. Oxford: Blackwell.

Marx, Karl 1973. *The Grundrisse*. NY: Vintage.

Nyden, Phil and Gwen Nyden 1999. 'Battling Uneven Development in Chicago' from *Footnotes*, July/August.

Zorbaugh, Harvey 1928. *The Gold Coast and the Slum*. Chicago: University of Chicago Press.

Urban and Suburban Social Movements

A social movement is an organized political campaign directed at government and demanding structural changes in social organization.

Urban and suburban social movements target local governments. Individuals and communities often organize in efforts to influence their political leaders. When participants aggregate in significant numbers a social movement is born. In the past, such movements have mobilized around issues of renter's rights, community control of school boards, welfare rights, neighborhood policing and community redevelopment. More recently, the campaigns for smart growth and sustainable development could be considered social movements.

Residents of a city often deal with inconveniences on a daily basis. Sometimes these irritants, such as inadequate garbage collection or dangerous traffic intersections, persist as problems. When people perceive that these situations require political attention, they may organize to influence city hall. Often these protests are resolved through direct intervention by the mayor or her/his staff. There is also a class effect operating in these outcomes. When wealthier neighborhoods complain, their concerns are more promptly addressed than less affluent districts. When nothing adequate is done however, a social movement might result. Most often, local neighborhoods try to maintain their contacts with city hall through their elected representatives so that a full-blown mobilization can be avoided. This give and take between urban administrators and local residents comprises most of the daily business of city politics.

City governments are concerned with maintaining the quality of life. As revenues have dropped over the decades as a consequence of urban economic declines, many city regimes have experienced a 'fiscal crisis' (see entry on page 29). That is, they can no longer support public services at the level of quality or price that they have in the past due to lack of funds. In response, the cost of public transportation might rise. Cutbacks in services might occur. Firehouses or municipal hospitals may be shut down. All urban residents are affected. This same phenomenon may impact suburban areas as well. The fiscal crisis of local government has hemmed in the horizon of politics for some time. Most often relief has been sought through programs initiated at the State or Federal level. The quality of city life has been sustained for the most part, despite decades of decline, precisely because of national programs.

Often sheer spending is not enough. In such cases, social movements can arise to affect the quality of life for the better. However, the danger is that many social movements become professionalized and formalized. In East Germany up to the 1980s, there were very few opposition groups to the former communist regime. As pressure grew for liberalization, following Gorbachev's *glasnost* program in the Soviet Union, citizen groups sprung up in East Berlin, Leipzig, Dresden and other East German cities. After unification, all these movements became subsidized or underwritten by local authorities, thereby losing their independence and legitimacy (Rink, 2000). In the UK, the squatters, cooperative and self-build movements of the 1970s have found themselves incorporated into social housing, which is now a multi-million pound business drawing on loans from international banking interests. In short, urban social movements are often coopted precisely because they address issues that local governments must eventually face. However, in order to continue to fight for their particular interests, they need to remain independent. Hence, the situation of many urban social movements is a contradictory one.

Suburbs also have social movements. These can differ from those of the city on the basis of the concerns expressed and housing tenure status, that is, on whether people are home owners or renters. One common suburban concern involves traffic controls. As suburban areas develop, the mature pattern of automobile commuting may emerge over time. Intersections that were once quiet and safe become treacherous. When this occurs, residents must organize in order to get their elected representatives to intervene with new traffic controls. Often this is not easy, because of the low density of suburban living. People in the most affected subdivision must organize residents not significantly affected by the increased traffic in order to acquire the numbers that might influence government. Because of the greater need for organizing, a social movement can develop.

One area of concern held in common by almost all suburban residents involves the ownership of housing. Single family home owners have interests that require protection no matter where they live in suburbia. A frequent issue involves the affects of rapid growth when these areas are developing. Residents that were the first to move into a place often resent the consequences of having progressively more people living there, such as increased traffic, taxes, drains on community resources or problems with overburdened educational systems. When these problems are of sufficient magnitude, it is quite common for suburban residents to organize in order to control future growth. These 'growth control' movements comprise a significant part of suburban politics because it is generally believed that local government should preserve the quality of life and this is commonly threatened by rapid development.

Growth control initiatives that pass often result in the re-zoning of remaining land that is undeveloped into larger parcels, thereby limiting the future population by restricting the number of new homes constructed. These same measures also have the effect of raising the dollar price of new houses. Less affluent households then find it increasingly difficult to move into communities that have enacted growth controls. This places such areas at odds with state or county legislators concerned about equal housing opportunities. For this reason, local suburban politics can become quite contentious.

Another common political movement in the suburbs is the tax revolt. Suburban services are supported by property tax as the principal fiscal instrument of revenue. Often residents perceive this form of taxation as excessive. For example, increases in property taxes in order to pay for expanding educational facilities for newer residents can be opposed by older ones that have already seen their children grow up and move on. Conflict ensues between those that still need tax supported services and those that feel they do not. In the 1970s and 80s, as suburban development reached its height, tax revolts broke out in many parts of the country when residents organized to block new increases. Measures, such as Proposition 13 in California, that rewrite the tax codes in order to obtain relief for older residents have a lasting effect on the public support for social services.

REFERENCES

Gottdiener, M. and Ray Hutchison 2000, *The New Urban Sociology*, 2nd Edition, NY: McGraw-Hill.

Rink, D. 2000. 'Local Citizen's Initiatives During the (East) German Transformation' in P. Hamel, H. Lustiger-Thaler and M. Mayer (eds), *Urban Movements in a Globalising World*. London: Routledge.

172

—— Urban Politics and —— Suburban Politics ——

Before the 1960s, city governments were powerful. In addition to people making money from control over the resources of capital and land, control of the bureaucracies and decision-making power of government was a separate means of acquiring wealth. The power to tax or regulate both land use and public services gave local government officials significant leverage over other people's money. Because of public sector services, cities are also major employers. For all these reasons organized interests have always competed with each other for influence over and control of local government. This struggle provides the drama of politics whether it takes place in cities or suburbs.

Prior to the 1980s, typical urban regimes reflected the participation of traditional ethnic groups, such as the Irish, the Poles, Italians and Jews. More recently, this composition has changed because of the growing influence of minorities within central cities. Over 300 US cities have minority mayors, most commonly, African-Americans, but now there is a growing power of the Hispanic community reflected in urban leadership. In the suburbs, which are overwhelmingly white, powerful interests are best characterized in terms of middle-class concerns rather than ethnic influences. Suburban governments are invariably controlled by real estate developers and active representatives of middle-class homeowners interested in maintaining the quality of family-oriented services and the value of homes.

The issue of who controls local government has been an important one in the urban literature. Three perspectives were argued – the elitist, the pluralist and the state managerialist. Floyd Hunter's studies of Atlanta in the 1960s established the *elitist* perspective. He argued that cities are controlled by some powerful elite. Influential leadership groups are most often composed of financial and select business interests, including real estate developers, as well as career politicians that operate from a community power base. Other analysts, such as Robert Dahl, countered this view by arguing that *pluralist* interests were reflected in local politics. According to Dahl, despite the presence of a select group of influential people, many community interests were recognized in local politics. Today we understand that local governments are most often a combination of elite and community interests. Powerful people do not need to control every decision. They only intervene when their immediate concerns are at stake. Even advocates of pluralism, like Dahl, came to acknowledge this truth of how elite power operates. Community interests are usually recognized by local government, except when these clash with the concerns of the business elite. Consequently, this mix of interests characterizes local politics best. In addition, however, another perspective qualified this view. Now we also know that government employees and administrators may have their own independent interests. This *state managerialism* perspective is also important in understanding local politics.

In the UK, Prime Minister Margaret Thatcher attempted to destroy any vestige of urban politics, as the 'urban population' represented the site of opposition to her imposition of market ordering in the 1980s. New Labour, under Tony Blair, has attempted to revive cities and partially committed the party to regional government. However, its technocratic approach, borrowing examples from the US and trying to impose them in a British context, attempts to avoid a revitalization of urban politics. Current urban policy in the UK revolves around the *Core Cities* which seeks to re-vitalize the urban downtowns using technocratic and managerial means to improve competitiveness of these cities. Citizen participation and enabling communities in these cities to improve their lives, is notably absent from this scheme (www.odpm.gov.uk).

While elites are invariably entrenched, their composition does change over time as a result of different groups competing for power. There is considerable evidence, for example, that many cities today are dominated by banks and financial interests because this faction of the business community still has investments downtown, such as banking centers. Suburbs and some of the newer cities of the Sunbelt, in contrast, possess dominating elites with interests in real estate and local corporations. But, the succession of economic elites is just one way to look at changes in local government. Politics is a dramatic enterprise. It involves struggle, coalition building, competition and compromise.

In the 1800s, when US cities were developing rapidly, city regimes were powerful because they commanded considerable wealth. Most often a select group of politicians took control of local government and ran it in order to make money. This arrangement was called a 'political machine'. The machine used graft and corruption to amass cash that helped generate votes which kept it in power. The principal characteristic of a machine was that it functioned solely as a means of administering the city, including the patronage positions to its supporters that were financed by graft and corruption. This particular form of elite control did not possess any ideology of governance. The goal was the mobilization of votes in order to remain in power where favors could then be performed for business interests in return for cash. By the late 1800s, community leaders had tired of the corruption associated with this style of administration. Progressive reforms were passed at the turn of the 20th Century that made local government more professional, more middle-class, and more honest. Under the old machines, cities were carved up into 'wards' where local leaders provided favors to residents in return for votes. Candidates merely had to win their wards in order to advance to the seats of city government. Progressive reforms did away with this arrangement.

They aggregated sections of the city into larger districts that were mixed and less dependent on favors to particular groups or individuals. In the extreme case, progressives made election to office dependent on majority voting from the city population as a whole. In short, reformers of machine politics changed the structure of local government by combining districts and cutting down on the way local interests could be represented. The result was a greater need for consensus building and, therefore, a more *political* local politics.

The experience of the UK and other European countries has been similar. The municipal socialism of 1950s was a byword for corruption, particularly around building contracts. But the associated politics was about delivering local services and infrastructure for local residents and not the imagined politics of the post-80s generation which seeks to use local office for global advancement.

At present the situation is quite reverse. Neither city nor suburban governments are powerful. Sprawl patterns of population deconcentration have fragmented the metropolitan region and representative voting has lost its clout on the local scene (see entries on *Sprawl; Multi-centered Metropolitan Region*). For this reason, political regimes must do the best they can to supply necessary services while dealing, at the same time, with their dwindling resources. In 1966, for example, the city of Atlanta outspent its suburban counties by two to one. Twenty years later, in 1987, however, Atlanta accounted for only 10% of spending on services within the expanding multi-centered region. The suburban counties in that area became more powerful.

A second reason for the decline in power is that participation in local elections and in political affairs is limited. Voter turnout is low and the best and brightest people are no longer attracted to run for office. In both cities and suburbs there is a crisis in the quality of public services (see entry on *Education and the Reproduction of Labor*, for example). This state of affairs is not helped by either the decline in manufacturing and industry within central cities or the reluctance of suburban residents to pay local taxes. As the quality of public services declines and as people feel the pressure from inadequate schools, roads, economic development and tax relief, these concerns are expressed as the content of local metropolitan politics. Occasionally, discontent spills over into an organized effort seeking change. When this happens we experience a social movement. This topic is covered in the entry on *Urban and Suburban Social Movements*.

Key concepts

Often the goals of politicians are pursued through the use of planning programs that claim to benefit the whole, but really mask special interests. One example is the effort led by local politicians using federal money to revitalize downtowns called 'urban renewal'. Most of these interventions were aimed at slum clearance and so they removed thousands of low-income residents from the center of US cities. Little was done to encourage investment in affordable housing. Instead, revitalization really meant that corporate interests supporting politicians now had a way of channeling money into downtown real estate. In the end, two decades of urban renewal programs beginning with the 1960s left large amounts of city land vacant and most downtown department stores struggling despite the construction of pedestrian malls and the clearance of slum housing.

In the 1960s, another kind of politically-lead planning appeared, one that was more reformist in nature. In response to the ghetto riots that ripped across the nation, US cities elected reformist mayors who used planning tools to affect more equitable resource allocations. One such case was the administration of Mayor Carl Stokes, the first African American elected to lead a large city – Cleveland, Ohio. Stokes announced a new regime called *equity planning* with a goal to 'providing more choices to those who have few, if any, choices'. An ideology emerged from this experience that challenged the traditional view of the urban planner as simply a technician who managed land use. Instead, Cleveland's planners, under Mayor Stokes, tried to acquire both power and resources to support the improvement of public space, of housing, and of public transportation. This change in the profile of city planners is also called *advocacy planning*, when work is carried out with and for the benefit of local communities (see entry on *Planning*).

Not everyone supports this more activist role of planners in the US and it is very much of a political issue, meaning that powerful interests in the private sector oppose a principal focus on equity planning in place of the more traditional one of pursuing economic growth. Yet, the Cleveland administration of Carl Stokes had one notable victory: with the city in a weakened state, a powerful private utility company sought to purchase Cleveland's publicly-owned electrical company which could only run with the benefit of continual public subsidies. The equity planners knew that, once the utility would be privatized, affordable electricity would be forfeited and the poor would suffer. With an effective political campaign, this privatization effort was finally blocked. However, the case points out the very close connection between urban planning in the US and local

176

politics. It is usually the latter that uses the former for its own ends, often with negative results as profit-making is subsidized while cities continue to decline.

SUBURBAN POLITICS

Suburban politics is much more straightforward than the city variety. There is one overriding interest in suburbia – single family home ownership. Suburban politics is home owner politics and elected officials in suburban areas tend to be non-partisan managers of property taxes. The aim of their administrations is to preserve the quality of suburban life. Most often this involves appropriate road maintenance for automobile traffic, adequate crime control and the raising of money for amenities, such as parks, recreational centers and civic events. If the mayors of US cities have lost their stature over the years as political players because their populations have declined, suburban leaders have even less stature because they never did have much clout in the first place. Metropolitan regions are notoriously fragmented, meaning that town officials cannot command many votes outside their own area. Yet, suburbanites are quite satisfied with these arrangements. What their governments lack in overall political power they make up for in approachability and attention to local concerns. Suburban politics serves the people in a direct, although limited way. One issue that has mobilized suburban residents in all areas of the country is the control of growth. This topic is addressed in the entry on *Urban and Suburban Social Movements*.

THE NATURE OF LOCAL POLITICS

Is urban politics an independent force in society or is it so dependent on economics that it is totally derivative? Of course, local politics is important precisely because it is the only way that cities and suburbs have real power. They exist as political units even if the form of space has transcended their boundaries. For this reason, cities and suburbs remain relevant as aggregate actors in the regional urban array. What of the issue of power elites? Yes, they exist. But elites also change over time depending on the confluence of the most powerful interests operating in the local area at particular phases of development. It is not always real estate elites that are the most influential. In the past, industrialists and railroad interests comprised the urban elites. Today banking and professional service interests are the ones with clout downtown. When suburbs are young, growth interests seem to control politics. Yet, as they mature, residents become more concerned about controlling growth and avoiding its problems, such as heavy traffic. Variations in influence and the contentious nature of urban interests makes local politics an excellent way of illustrating and distinguishing the real differences that action and local activities play in relation to structural factors of change in our society.

CITIZEN PARTICIPATION

Active participation by local residents of a municipality is said to be a hallmark of democracy. Some new perspectives on revitalizing the city, such as the New Urbanism, hold increased participation as a core goal (see entry on *New Urbanism*). Yet, this concept, like others we have examined, has a confusing array of connotations. Sherry Arnstein (2003) did a study that attempted to sort out these meanings and identify the role that participation plays in local politics. She states that, 'citizen participation is a categorical term for citizen power. It is the redistribution of power that enables the have-not citizens, presently excluded from the political and economic processes, to be deliberately included in the future. It is the strategy by which the have-nots join in determining how information is shared, goals and policies are set, tax resources are allocated, programs are operated, and benefits like contracts and patronage are parceled out' (2003: 236).

Arnstein argues that there is a typology of participation from the lowest level where people are simply manipulated which she calls 'non-participation', to a second level called 'tokenism' where citizens are consulted and allowed to attend information meetings, to a growing involvement that she terms 'citizen power' and which includes forms of partnership and even control.

Arnstein also shows that the desire for citizen participation has been inflected by federal policy guidelines that have often shifted as a consequence of the political ideologies of the existing presidential administrations at the time. In the 1960s, following the graphic social unrest in cities, federal legislation asked for 'maximum feasible participation' of local residents. This imperative was implemented in the Model Cities programs run by the Department of Housing and Urban Development (HUD). Later, in the 1970s, when it was decided by bureaucrats that the communities were acquiring too much control over federal funds, new legislation was passed requiring all poverty program monies to be run through city hall. Cities were required to create a new bureaucratic arm, the City Demonstration Agency (CDA) in order to manage the funds. The CDAs reduced the participation of local citizens back down to a level of consultation and access but not direct decision-making or partnership. The result was that local community boards in cities became simply advisory to the planning and execution of development strategies.

Not all of this history resulted in declines of citizen power. In a number of cities, such as Dayton and Columbus, Ohio; Minneapolis, Minnesota; St. Louis, MO; Hartford and New Haven, Conn; and Oakland, CA, Arnstein writes that local residents were able to maintain majorities on local Model Cities boards and enact plans that they favored. Consequently, the issue of participation involves many levels of agency and collective action that results in variable outcomes dependent on the balance of political power between bureaucrats and residents, with the federal government looking over everyone's shoulder and special interests passing national legislation in accordance with their ideologies.

Now the concept of *citizen participation* has been revitalized by the sustainable growth social movement. Critical perspectives on planning, such as the New Urbanism, also try to reinvigorate the active involvement of local residents in town planning through their discussion mechanism of 'charettes'. (See entries on *Sustainable Urbanism; New Urbanism.*)

REFERENCES

Arnstein, S. 2003. 'A Ladder of Citizen Participation.' in R. LeGates and F. Stout (eds) *The City Reader*, 3rd Edition. London, UK: Routledge. pp. 244–254.

Urban Violence and Crime

179

When people speak of crime, they usually mean violent crime and occurrences of violence, especially random street crime, that are very troublesome in cities. From the 1960s through the early 1990s urban areas in the US were plagued by frequent acts of violence associated with robberies, street muggings and gang-related shootings. A significant amount of property crime also occurs in both cities and suburbs, but these acts are perceived to be less problematic than the violent variety which is also associated more with the downtown areas of large cities.

In 1990, New York, Los Angeles, Chicago, Houston, Philadelphia and Detroit all had more than 500 murders, that is a rate considerably exceeding one a day. New York City, for example, had 2,245 murders, Los Angeles 983, Chicago 851 and Houston 568. Per capita, however, cities like Dallas, Seattle, Detroit and San Antonio have the highest rates. Property crime is also a problem in urban areas although it exists in suburban regions as well. In 1990, NYC had over 500,000 incidents of property crime, Los Angeles and Chicago over 200,000, and Houston over 160,000. These statistics suggest that cities are dangerous places. However, in any urban area, crimes are not spread out evenly; they are committed in certain distinct locations, usually in the poorer sections of town. There are, therefore, high and low crime areas in any city and visitors should know about this difference. For any US city, despite the troubling rates of crime, there are areas that are quite safe.

Sophie Body-Gendrot (2003: 84) tries hard to say something profound when she argues that our vocabulary for urban violence and crime lumps different offending acts together. She notes: 'What link is there between the Oklahoma bombing, a mugging on Main Street, the Los Angeles riots, the Columbine massacre, or ethnic confrontations in Crown Heights? The link is provided by journalists and politicians who use the same terms – urban violence, urban crime, riots, disorders, disturbances, unrest, urban danger, rebellion, confrontation, lawlessness, delinquency, and many more – to characterize such events. The use of similar terms makes all things look alike.'

But, these are not the same terms at all and Body-Gendrot seems not only hopelessly confused, but also quite mistaken regarding the nature of the subject that she purports to write about. Violence has indeed been a characteristic of cities historically, but the acts and causes vary greatly. It seems only Body-Gendrot, from her vantage point in Paris, France, believes that these events are all run together by the same vocabulary, despite the obvious evidence to the contrary. This is certainly true of the London situation which Body-Gendrot appears to believe conforms to some global norm. Crime figures in the UK's capital cause much huffing and puffing each time they are released. The difficulty for the authorities is whether any increase in the crime figures is a function of increased reporting or actual crimes. Furthermore, despite the rise in the number of female rapes and indecent assaults, young men are predominantly the victims of crime in London. Burglary still remains the most frequent offence. The rise in gun crime may cause headlines as the number of murders rise. Yet, for most citizens of London, the danger of gun crime is marginal to their existence, as it occurs most frequently among some communities and is strongly correlated to territorial fights over the drugs trade. London is a complex city, but it is a relatively safe place, as is the case with other cities in Europe, compared to urban areas in the US. Having made these points, it must also be noted that, for many European cities, like Paris, London, Milan, Rome and Frankfurt, recent immigration from less developed countries has led to an unprecedented level of city crime with all the social consequences that this correlation implies.

High crime rates are troubling because they affect the ability of people to use city space. Public spaces such as parks, piazzas, and streets are some of the most attractive features of urban life. When these spaces cannot be used because of crime, then that negatively affects the attractiveness of living there and those people that can, will move out to the suburbs. Today the use of much public space in urban areas is limited. In the 1990s a young woman who worked on Wall Street went to Central Park in the evening to jog, as did many other people who use this public space daily for that purpose. On that particular day a group of adolescents entered the park and brutally attacked her. She was raped and then beaten within an inch of her life. Miraculously she survived, but this urban professional became a symbol of the toll crime takes on keeping public space attractive and useful.

Crime pushes up the security budgets of companies and households and results in billions of dollars in unnecessary medical expenses for the victims of violent actions. It can also devastate property values. In areas of the city with high crime rates, the value of property is depressed. Thus, innocent households suffer doubly in crime-infested areas because they are both victims of crime, in many cases, and also because the value of their property declines.

During the latter part of the last century, urban crime remarkably declined. In New York City between 1990–95, all crimes declined by over 40%, in Los Angeles and Houston the decline was over 20%, while other cities, such as Philadelphia, Detroit, and Dallas, all saw their rates drop. One theory for the decline is that the population of young adult and disadvantaged males had declined and this group historically contains the highest percentage of perpetrators. Another possible reason for the decline is the reduction in the use of drugs. Robberies and burglaries are often committed in association with drug trafficking. Drive by shootings and random street assaults are also related to the drug trade. In fact, statistics show a disturbing relationship between violent crime and drug use.

181

During the late 1980s and early 1990s, crack cocaine was a major problem on the streets of US cities. With the decline in the use of this drug and the arrests of many perpetrators involved in the drug trade, violent city crime also declined.

At present both cities and suburbs are safer places to be than they were in the 1990s. Violent crime has declined. However, the level of property crime still remains comparatively high. It is much more troubling a problem in the US than in Europe, for example. Suburbs as well as cities are afflicted with auto theft, credit card theft, identity theft, robberies and other acts that involve the theft of property. There is little hope that these numbers will decline in the immediate future. But, it is also certain that most inhabitants of metropolitan regions are concerned about violent and not property crime and for the former, at least over the last several years, the rates have been going down.

URBAN, SUBURBAN AND RURAL VICTIMIZATION RATES, 1993–98

According to the National Crime Victimization Survey (2000):

'Violent and property crime victimization disproportionately affected urban residents during 1998. Urbanites accounted for 29% of the US population and sustained 38% of all violent and property crime.' In 1998–51% of the US population were suburban residents. They experienced 47% of all violent and property crimes. The average annual 1993–98 violent crime rate in urban areas was about 74% *higher than* the rural rate and 37% higher than the suburban rate.

Urban crime victims were more likely than suburban and rural residents to be victimized by a stranger – 53% compared with 47% and 34%.

In short, the argument that victimization is partly a function of place of residence is validated. Also, when people move from the city to the suburbs in order to escape crime, they are acting on accurate data.

From 1976–98 the number of homicides in large US cities, defined as those with a population of 100,000 or more, was 50% of all homicides.

Firearm usage in the commission of a violent crime was 12% for cities, 9% for suburban areas and 8% for rural areas.

Urban males experienced violent victimization rates 64% higher than average combined suburban and rural male rates and 47% higher than urban females.

RACIAL VIOLENCE

Finally, US cities, in particular, have been the scenes of racial riots, often in response to racial segregation and discrimination. Despite advances in tolerance and inclusion, major disturbances have increased since the 1900s. According to Berger (1978: 267), among the major occurrences between 1908–68 were:

1908 – Springfield, IL; 1917 – East St. Louis; 1919–Chicago; 1921 – Tulsa; 1935 – Harlem; 1943 – Harlem, Detroit, LA; 1960 – Greensboro, NC; 1963 – Birmingham, Savannah, Cambridge, Chicago, Philadelphia; 1964 – Jacksonville, Cleveland, St. Augustine, Jersey City, Elizabeth, Paterson, Harlem, Bed-Stuyvesant, Philadelphia, Rochester, Chicago; 1965 – Selma, Watts, Chicago; 1966 – Watts, Chicago, Cleveland and 15 other cities; 1967 – Detroit and 175 other cities; 1968 – Newark and 157 other cities.

REFERENCES

Berger, A. 1978. *The City: Urban Communities and their Problems*. Dubuque, Iowa: Wm. C. Brown and Co.

Body-Gendrot, S. 2002. 'The Dangerous Others: Changing Views on Urban Risks and Violence in France and the United States' in J. Eade and C. Mele (eds) *Understanding the City*. Oxford, UK: Blackwell. pp. 82–106.

National Crime Victimization Study. 'Urban, Suburban, and Rural Victimization, 1933–98.' US Department of Justice, Federal Bureau of Investigation, 2000. Wash. DC: Government Printing Office, October, NCJ #182031.

Urbanization and Urbanism

Both these terms are old and have been used for some time to describe city-based processes. Now they present a question of whether they can be extended to the concept of fully urbanized regions. We think they can and, in loose usage, they already have. The global city argument, for example, often conflates the region with the large city (see entry on *Globalization*). Postmodern approaches often tie subcultures that are region-wide together, and so on (see entry on *Postmodern and Modern Urbanism*).

URBANIZATION

This concept has been traditionally defined as the process of city formation and city growth. Urbanization involves the way social activities locate themselves in space and according to interdependent processes of societal development and change. Its analysis is often historical and comparative. Urbanization charts and tries to understand the rise and fall of great cities.

Historical studies are most concerned with urbanization. They try to answer such questions as: How did cities first form? What were the conditions that produced them? What were early cities like? Is there a necessary social organization without which urbanization cannot proceed?

Contemporary studies are divided among those addressing developed and those addressing relatively underdeveloped or developing regions of the world. In the advanced countries, especially those in Western Europe and the US, issues of urbanization often involve the question of de-industrialization and its consequences. Shifts to new, high-technology and financial services industries are important, as are their social consequences for structural changes in the labor force. Gentrification of older and formerly under-valued housing are also issues that are addressed (see entries on *Globalization*; *Housing*). In the less developed or developing areas of the world, urbanization studies involve the implosive growth of large cities and the rural to urban migration as it affects both the city and the countryside. These topics are actually more traditionally associated with the process of urbanization.

In the 1940s, the historian V. Gordon Childe presented a theory of city growth (see Gottdiener and Hutchison, 2000: 26). His argument, called the *urban revolution*, remains relevant today for the study of urbanization in the third world, although there have been some critiques in recent research.

THE URBAN REVOLUTION

Ten traits of early cities are as follows:

(1) Urban settlements were densely populated and large in territory.
(2) Cities supported crafts people full-time and in specialized jobs.
(3) Farmers produced an agricultural surplus controlled by rulers.
(4) There was the presence of monumental public buildings.
(5) The agricultural surplus was controlled by ruling elite and priests within the city.

(6) Cities were centers for developing ideas and recording them.
(7) Cities were centers for the arts.
(8) Cities were centers for the 'predictive' sciences.
(9) City organization was based on residence not kinship.
(10) Cities imported and exported, i.e., the urban dwellers engaged in trade.

This theory had the virtue of defining precisely how the economies of early civilizations were able to support entire groups of people who did not produce agricultural goods. The extraction and control by a ruling elite of the agricultural surplus was the basis for the type of hierarchical social organization that supported city life. The problem with V. Gordon Childe's view is that it is an *evolutionary* model. Recent evidence suggests that city growth was discontinuous and that multiple stages existed together, such as the development of an agriculturally-based economy alongside the development of science and crafts. Also there is some evidence that in ancient cities, like Catal Hyuk in Turkey, commerce and trade were the key factors in providing a basis for the urban economy, rather than an agricultural surplus. In fact, throughout history, cities were the sites of an active market serving a much larger region. It is impossible to separate the market in some form with the settlement known as a city in the ancient world, if not also today.

CONTEMPORARY URBANIZATION

At the turn of the 21st Century, 2.8 billion people lived in cities, representing 47% of the world's population. Much of this concentration actually exists within urbanized regions, because there is often no distinction between the 'city' as a compact urban form and an expansive region of urbanization associated with a central place. In any case, by contrast, in 1950 fewer than 750 million people or 29% of the world's population were city dwellers, according to United Nation statistics (UNCHS, 1987, 2001). By the year 2006, more than half of the world's population is projected to live in cities (UNCHS, 1999). Such rapid urbanization, on a massive scale, and over a short period of time, has been propelled to a great extent by the developing countries and almost all population growth in the near future will take place in the cities of the developing world. The number of urban residents in the developing countries has exploded from fewer than 300 million (17%) in 1950 to over 1.9 billion (40%) in the year 2000, a figure that is expected to double in the three decades to come. The share of the world's population living in urban areas of developing countries continues to soar from 12% in 1950 to 68% in 2000. By the year 2015, this figure will have reached 75% of the world's population and the number of urban dwellers in developing countries will be about the same size of the current world's population, 2.8 billion. In short, urbanization in the developing world is an explosive phenomenon replete with many social problems that will only grow worse in the future.

The process of urbanization in developing countries can be captured by increases in the number and size of cities. The number of large cities with more than one million urban population increased during the second half of the 20th Century. The number of large cities has increased from 80 in 1950 to 365 in the year 2000. This rise in large cities has been more dramatic in the developing countries, from 31 in 1950 to 242 in 2000 (UNCHS, 1999). Over the last two decades, the number of large cities more than doubled. In addition, the size of cities is also rapidly increasing. In 1950, New York was the only megacity with 10 million or more residents in the world; out of five megacities in 1975, three were in developing countries; at the outset of the 20th Century, 15 out of 19 are now in developing countries (United Nations Population Fund [UNFPA], 2000: 6). These megacities in developing countries are expected to grow faster than those in developed countries. In most cases, however, the concept of 'megacity' actually refers to the new form of space, called the Multi-centered Metropolitan Region, despite the persisting importance of a large and built up central business district (see entry on page 87).

In contrast to the characteristics of the traditional bounded city, the new form of settlement space can be typified by two features: It extends over a large region and it contains many separate centers, each with its own abilities to draw workers, shoppers, and residents. Not every country of the world is experiencing the new form of multi-centered metropolitan growth (MMR), but all countries seem to be subjected to a process of urban development that produced gigantic cities and urbanization on a regional scale. This explosive growth implies an immense social crisis for the developing countries.

URBANISM

Urbanism is a way of life characterized by density, diversity and complex social organization. Most often the term today means the culture of cities. However, here too, analysts conflate the culture of cities with that of suburbia, although the latter is usually described in stereotypical terms.

Both areas are typified by high consumption life styles and the participation in an advanced, information-based economy. Urbanism has traditionally been associated with a greater sophistication in understanding and consuming the arts, expensive dining, sophisticated entertainment and fashion. Suburbia is typified as family and private home centered with a reliance on the automobile as the dominant mode of transportation and a daily life exemplifying the value of privatism. It is not clear whether such sharp distinctions can be made today, although it is certainly true that city and suburban living differ because of the respective modes of housing and transportation – the one characterized by high rises and public transportation; the other by the single family home and the automobile (see entry on *Pedestrian and Automobile*).

Discussions of urbanism often emphasize that city life is more tolerant of strangers and so-called 'deviants' than the suburbs. There are special districts in the city that come alive only at night where people engage in partying activities (see entry on *The City* for more discussion). Cities are supposed to be more diverse ethnically, racially and with regard to class than suburbs. There is still an implicit understanding that city people are more interested in hustling for advantages in economic and social relations, while those people living in the more suburbanized areas of metro regions assume a steadier view of employment and share intimacy only with their select circle of friends.

Today it is not clear whether these sharp social distinctions can be made between urbanism and suburbanism. All areas of the multi-centered metropolitan region have become increasingly diverse in recent years. Immigrants no longer select the inner city as their place of initial residence. Subcultures abound throughout the region. The emphasis on a high consumption lifestyle seems to characterize all areas.

Historically, there is a theory that sought to characterize life within the big city as relatively unique. It was articulated by Lewis Wirth of the 1930s Chicago School (see entries on *The Chicago School; The City*). There is also recent evidence that inner cities have nurtured entertainment districts which cannot be found in the suburbs on such an extended scale and which produce a street life at night that is definitely a city phenomenon (see entry on *Nightlife and Urban Nightscapes*). Finally, it must be observed that, when dealing with the truly global cities of the developed countries, their repositories of art, music, dance, fashion, design, architecture, and all other aspects of what was once called 'high culture' are unprecedented in quality, quantity and accessibility with no comparable experience offered by any other spatial form.

187

Urbanization and Urbanism

REFERENCES

Gottdiener, M. and R. Hutchison 2000. *The New Urban Sociology*, 2nd Edition. NY: McGraw-Hill.

United Nations Center for Human Settlements (UNCHS) 1987. *Global Reports on Human Settlements*. Oxford, UK: Oxford University Press.

United Nations Center for Human Settlements (UNCHS) 1996. *An Urbanizing World*. Oxford, UK: Oxford University Press.

United Nations Center for Human Settlements (UNCHS) 1999. *Basic Facts on Urbanization*. Nairobi, Kenya: UNCHS Habitat.

United Nations Center for Human Settlements (UNCHS) 2001. *Cities in a Globalizing World*. London: UK: Earthscan.

United Nations Population Fund (UNFPA) 2000. *The State of World Population*. NY: UNFPA.

key concepts

188